The Great Game

The Great Game

A Tale of Two Footballs and America's
Quest to Conquer Global Sport

Andrés Martinez

BLOOMSBURY ACADEMIC
NEW YORK • LONDON • OXFORD • NEW DELHI • SYDNEY

BLOOMSBURY ACADEMIC
Bloomsbury Publishing Inc, 1359 Broadway, New York, NY 10018, USA
Bloomsbury Publishing Plc, 50 Bedford Square, London, WC1B 3DP, UK
Bloomsbury Publishing Ireland, 29 Earlsfort Terrace, Dublin 2, D02 AY28, Ireland

BLOOMSBURY, BLOOMSBURY ACADEMIC and the Diana logo are trademarks of Bloomsbury Publishing Plc

First published in the United States of America 2026

Copyright © Andrés Martinez, 2026

Cover design: Devin Watson
Cover images: © istock/ilbusca, © istock/artisteer

All rights reserved. No part of this publication may be: i) reproduced or transmitted in any form, electronic or mechanical, including photocopying, recording or by means of any information storage or retrieval system without prior permission in writing from the publishers; or ii) used or reproduced in any way for the training, development or operation of artificial intelligence (AI) technologies, including generative AI technologies. The rights holders expressly reserve this publication from the text and data mining exception as per Article 4(3) of the Digital Single Market Directive (EU) 2019/790.

Bloomsbury Publishing Inc does not have any control over, or responsibility for, any third-party websites referred to or in this book. All internet addresses given in this book were correct at the time of going to press. The author and publisher regret any inconvenience caused if addresses have changed or sites have ceased to exist, but can accept no responsibility for any such changes.

A catalog record for this book is available from the Library of Congress.

ISBN: HB: 979-8-8818-0182-3
ePDF: 979-8-2162-0158-8
eBook: 979-8-2162-0157-1

Typeset by Deanta Global Publishing Services, Chennai, India
Printed and bound in the United States of America

For product safety related questions contact productsafety@bloomsbury.com.

To find out more about our authors and books visit www.bloomsbury.com and sign up for our newsletters.

To Seabass and Victoria, Hall of Famers

Contents

Acknowledgments viii
On the Terminology Conundrum xiii

Prologue 1
1 America's Conundrum: Only One vs. #1 13
2 Socialism in One Footballing Country 37
3 Away Games 59
4 Mother England's Conundrum: Homegrown vs. #1 81
5 Who Says No to Morgan Freeman? 107
6 Big Media's Conundrum 137
7 How Women Americanized the World's Game 161
8 But What About the Men? 185
9 Send the Word, That the Yanks Are Coming 203
10 The Great Game in Kansas City 231

Notes 259
Index 278
About the Author 287

Acknowledgments

I have been fortunate throughout my life to be surrounded by people who take sports seriously. I don't necessarily mean surrounded by world-class athletes (though I somehow married one of those), but rather by people who value sports both as a physical activity that is integral to a healthy, well-rounded life and, equally important, as a worthy pursuit of the spirit and of the mind. None of the serious, impressive people in my life (starting with my parents and my older brother) ever discouraged me from being an avid sports fan or a student of sports' power as a cultural, business, and political force. It was only well into adulthood that I discovered that there are plenty of serious people out there who *don't* take sports seriously, and I worry they might have "obstructed view" seats when trying to discern how the world works and how America fits into it.

The concentric circles of wonderful people who encouraged me to take sport seriously beyond my three initial nuclear family teammates included my two *padrinos*, Purdy Jordan and Gastone Guglielmina, my former wife Kathy and our son Sebastian, and my friends and schoolmates I grew up playing and watching football with; among them Joaquín Sotelo, Rubén Camacho, Federico Terrazas, Alfonso Márquez, Ramón Carrasco, Gustavo Nevarez, Ted Chung, Brett Lawrence, Uwe Brandes, Chris Yates, Duc Trang, Mark Williams, and Greg Wiercioch.

Gail Ross is an agent of infinite patience and *near* infinite (being a Tottenham fan) wisdom, and I am eternally grateful for her belief in me and in this book. I am equally a fan of all she's done for so many other writers. Likewise, I am indebted to Christen Karniski, my editor at Bloomsbury, for her enthusiastic support of the project, her smart edits, and her steady guidance throughout.

At Arizona State University, I am inspired every day by President Michael Crow and his Chief of Staff Jim O'Brien, my *jefes* here, and grateful that I have been able to contribute in a small way to their quest to redesign the future of higher education, to better serve the needs of our twenty-first-century democracy. This book wouldn't be possible if they didn't believe in the power of sport as an important vehicle to advance our students' (and the broader public's) understanding of what makes our society and world tick. We are building out a Great Game Lab at ASU and developing courses that focus on the subject of how America connects to the world through sport, and on the increasing convergence of global sport, media, and geopolitics. Isabel Migoya, our managing editor, has been an indispensable partner in making the Great Game Lab a reality, much as she has been on numerous other projects. We are grateful to León Krauze, Andy Markovits, Afshin Molavi, Amira Rose Davis, Julie Duhaut-Bedos, Narayanappa Janardhan, Russell Jones, Ubiratan Leal, Des Linden, Ana Paola López Yrigoyen, Ed Malyon, Sarah Spain, and Suzanne Hogan for agreeing to be our inaugural Great Game Lab Fellows.

This brings me to my Great Game Lab co-director, and co-director in life generally, my wife Victoria Jackson, who is a sports historian on our faculty, as well as a former professional and NCAA champion runner. She has taught me much of the history reflected in this book (except the Stalin bits, which we can't blame on her) and has guided me in connecting some of the less obvious dots in the Great Game. Victoria is also a tireless role model as someone who looks critically at unfolding trends and developments in sport without ever becoming jaded, always maintaining her underlying faith and optimism in sport's potential to do wonders in our individual lives and in our societies. As he fast approaches that pivotal sixth grade, her maps-and-flags-obsessed son Carter shows every sign of becoming a Great Game ambassador himself.

I owe a big thank you to many other colleagues at ASU for encouraging me in this journey and for being generous colleagues and team players: our "Sparky's Cup" mastermind Julia Rosen; Brazil guru Glen Goodman, my Team Mexico colleagues Paola Garcia, Miguel Sigala, and Jennifer Madrid; ASU Media Enterprise's fearless leader Mi-Ai Parrish; as well as Günes Murat Tezcür, Ron Broglio, Moira Shourie, Erin Yunt, Kristi Kappes, Pam Hintze,

Chris Fiscus, Nancy Gonzales, Chris Howard, and Andrea Cayley. I am particularly thankful to Scott Brooks and Ken Shropshire for the Global Sport Institute's backing of my early research on foreign ownership in the English Premier League, and to Patrick Hruby for working with me on some posts for the *Global Sport Matters* blog.

I have learned a great deal about writing, editing, and collaborative teamwork from my colleagues on our Future Tense Fiction/Center for Science and Imagination project. I won the lottery when I got to work closely with Torie Bosch for more than a decade, and then with Ed Finn, Joey Eschrich, and the one-and-only Mia Armstrong-López. Mia first entered my life as a bright student researcher, and upon graduation she helped lead ASU's efforts in Mexico while becoming one of the most talented editors you'll ever meet (check out her *Doing Well* newsletter). We've co-taught writing classes where I end up learning as much from her as our students do.

I am also grateful to the leadership of our Cronkite School of Journalism and Mass Communication—Battinto Batts, Rebecca Blatt, Brett Kurland, Jessica Pucci, and before them Kristin Gilger and Chris Callahan—for allowing me to develop my interest in The Great Game by developing courses with a sports, media, and globalization framing. Cronkite is one place where the importance of sports in society is fully acknowledged.

I also benefited from the research assistance of some fabulous ASU students through the years as I wrote this book, designed courses on this subject, and conceptualized the Lab with Victoria. Thank you, Arvik Shah, Tyler Johnson, Mia Osmonbekov, Ainsley Pfeiffer, and Venkateshwaran Anirudh for all your help in getting me to the finish line.

At New America, my think tank home for almost two decades, I learned a great deal from Steve Coll and Anne-Marie Slaughter, and have benefited enormously from their support and friendship, as I did also from such talented and team-first colleagues as Rachel White, Fuzz Hogan, Faith Smith, Peter Bergen, Paul Butler, Lilian Coral, Caroline Esser, Kirsten Berg, Becky Shafer, Marie Lawrence, Elizabeth Weingarten, Adam Sneed, Jamie Holmes, Anthony Nguyen, Emily Fritcke, Jacob Brogan, Jane Carr, Joe Wilkes, Angela Spidalette, Jodi Narde, and Awista Ayub. It's also been such a great privilege to collaborate throughout the years with such remarkable New America Fellows as Amanda

Ripley, Tim Wu, Charles Kenny, Christine Rosen, Katherine Mangu-Ward, Louisa Thomas, Bina Venkataraman, Shane Harris, Romesh Ratnesar, Chris Leonard, Louie Palu, Konstantin Kakaes, Christina Larson, Nick Schmidle, Nick Thompson, Daniel Kurtz-Phelan, Jorge Castañeda, Joel Garreau, Steve LeVine, Dayo Olapade, and Frank Foer (a pioneer in explaining the world through sport and international football).

As a journalist, I was blessed to work with, and learn from, some tremendously talented and generous newspaper colleagues and editors, without whose encouragement and nudges forward I wouldn't have ended up writing a book like this. They include Mike McGough (the Ballon d'Or winner for mentoring), John Craig, Michael Newman, John Allison, Phil Taubman, Howell Raines, Bob Semple, Gail Collins, Terry Tang, Matt Welsh, Susan Brenneman, Eryn Brown, Sarah Rothbard, Nick Goldberg, and Michael Kinsley.

You will find many sources throughout *The Great Game* who shared their stories and expertise with me, and I am extremely grateful to them all for doing so, and equally grateful to a number of people in and out of the sports industry who helped enlighten me along the way but preferred not to be quoted. I am glad this project allowed me to reconnect and spend time with my cousin Frank Barnhouse, a Texan who has lived outside London for three decades, and his lovely family. Frank has been my patient guide to all things British, much as my friend Chris Leonard has been for all things Kansas City (except when he's had important Zoom calls to rush off to). I also appreciate the support and wisdom through the years of José Antonio Fernández Carbajal in Monterrey, who has established at FEMSA such an impressive benchmark of how to run an organization.

Then there are all the talented people, some of whom I know and many of whom I don't, doing amazing work to increase our collective understanding of these subjects. Connecting sporting dots across borders has become a less lonely endeavor in recent years with the arrival of voices like the Man in Blazer himself, Roger Bennett, and the fantastic work routinely done on the business and culture of global sport by *The Wall Street Journal*, *The Financial Times*, *Sportico*, *Puck*, Kent Malmros of *Founding Futbol*, and the astonishing collection of writers and podcasters assembled by *The Athletic-New York Times* colossus. I won't compare the acquisition of the former by the latter to

Roman Abramovich's acquisition of Chelsea, but it might have been equally consequential. Also, although I have never met them, I consider Max Rushden & Co. over at *The Guardian's Football Weekly* podcast part of my extended brain trust and support group trying to make out how and why sport proves as powerful as it does in binding us.

I have great memories of playing sports through the years, but at the risk of sounding like a couch potato, I will confess that if I have two foundational memories at the heart of this inquiry, one is of my ten-year-old self watching the Steelers in their 1970s glory years with my dad in our family room in Chihuahua, Mexico. The other, four decades later, is of watching Arsenal on TV with my ten-year-old son in our DC area home. And in both cases, those conversations we had! An intergenerational tale of two footballs.

Seabass grew up playing soccer (the IRL version and the on-screen FIFA one) and basketball, then ultimately fell for track and field. I admire the discipline, competitive fire, and empathetic goodwill and sportsmanship he brings to every training session and meet as a collegiate runner. I am also excited by what the future holds for him; his was the first generation of Americans to be fully connected to the rest of the world through sport. I can't wait to watch him watching sports on TV with his ten-year-old kid (or kids, but no pressure) and to hear the conversations they'll be having about what it all means.

Hopefully, I will be eavesdropping.

On the Terminology Conundrum

Soccer or football? Anyone delving into the subject of global sport and the century-and-a-half-old schism in the footballing world has long been bedeviled by this terminology conundrum. Which term to use for the game in which ten humans face off against another ten humans, each side endeavoring to kick a ball into nets on either end of the field defended by an additional human who typically wears longer sleeves, gloves, and still has possession of his hands and is allowed to use them in defense of his net?

This is a fraught stylistic choice with the potential to irritate millions of readers (OK, an author can dream) on either side of the schism.

Throughout *The Great Game*, I use the terms somewhat interchangeably, aiming for both contextual coherence and clarity, so you will see I generally talk about "football" when overseas and "soccer" when in America. At other times, I use the term "international football" when the f-word feels right but still want to avoid any confusion with American football..

I generally don't get too caught up in the semantic battle between the competing terms applied to the world's default sport but understand the cultural sensitivities underlying why many people feel very passionately about this question of terminology.

Without them, after all, there'd be no *Great Game*.

Prologue

Opening Day

Rebirth. Redemption. Renewal. The promise of warmer days, longer evenings, greener grass, crackling wood, national anthem sing-alongs, A-10 Air Force flyovers, seventh-inning stretches, and plenty of hot dogs. Could there be anything more soothingly American or reassuringly timeless than our springtime harvest festival of Opening Day? I don't think so.

And could there be anything more mischievous than showing up for a ballgame at two o'clock on a Thursday afternoon? It's seventy-five degrees and sunny at Kansas City's Kauffman Stadium, and we 39,393 fans in attendance—kids and adults alike—are all giddy, adolescent Ferris Buellers for the day.

Well, 39,392 of us are, everyone except my date for the game, my friend and proud Kansas Citian Chris Leonard. He is the author of very serious books and couldn't rearrange an important Zoom call later in the afternoon, which should coincide with the sixth, seventh, or possibly the eighth inning, depending on how things go—one of this sport's pastoral charms being the lack of a clock.

Chris laughs off his predicament and resolves to enjoy the festivities and early innings, which is what the day is all about: fresh starts and new beginnings. No games behind, boundless promise, and better futures for all. Chris tells me about coming to watch the Royals as a kid. The Haygoods, a Branson sensation, sing the national anthem a capella, Whiteman Air Force Base provides the soaring planes and troops to hold onto the jumbo flag stretched out across the field. The entire Royals roster is introduced for the season, and then it's "Play ball!"

The older gentleman seated to my left introduces himself and is then disappointed to learn that we are not fellow season ticket holders, setting forth with him on an 81-game odyssey. His wife gave him season tickets for his birthday, he shares, to which I tell him he must have done something right. The spirited woman on Chris' other side is here as part of an office outing. She is in sales, something to do with cybersecurity. She is feeling the Ferris Bueller vibes. Playing hooky with your whole office is still playing hooky.

A few hours later, the beginning is over, and the Royals are a game behind. Lost 7-4. One down, 161 to go. It did take ten innings, but the Royals should have put the game away in the eighth. Instead, two baserunning errors resulted in what baseball experts call a real pickle: two outs, and a chorus of groans at the derailment of what should have been the decisive game-winning rally. Fortunately, by then, Chris had slipped out to head back home for his meeting, so he was spared the agony.

I have loved sports, especially the two footballs and a number of the rackuet ones, for as long as I can remember. My dad wanted me to grow up to play tennis on Mexico's Davis Cup team, alongside my brother Roberto. My first Jack Kramer Wilson racket was nearly as tall as I was. Ro and I let dad down; neither of us came anywhere close, though I still think of dad every time I do go out and play the game, which I have reconnected with in middle age.

Mostly, though, my childhood was shaped by the two footballs—playing them, following them, and navigating between them as a kid and then as an adult with a foot in each of their two worlds. Dad might have wanted me to play tennis, but he was also eager for me to watch American football with him. If memories had a temperature, among the warmest of them all would be those Sunday afternoons spent in our family room in Chihuahua (there was even a parrot involved) watching the fabled Steelers of Terry Bradshaw and the Steel Curtain together. Dad would get extra excited when we'd watch them beat up on Cleveland, where he'd gone to college as an international student, and he'd try to explain how cold it was in those stands with the wind coming off Lake Erie and tell me about nights he'd spent listening to Notre Dame games on the radio. He was an ambassador for American soft power, a walking advertisement for the value proposition of welcoming students from abroad as a means of spreading our ways and influence. Dad was one of the people responsible for the fact that we could even watch these NFL games on Mexican TV; a few years earlier, he'd worked for a Mexican broadcaster that had gone knocking on the NFL's door to ask if it could air some games in Mexico, long before the league harbored any such international ambitions. Dad was eager to share this amazing American product with viewers; surely something Clevelanders froze their asses off to watch live was a spectacle worth watching on your TV set in Mexico. The league's response was some variant of "Sure, I guess, why not," and a nominal fee was agreed upon.

My years growing up were delineated by the two football seasons, the longer *fútbol* one that tracked the school year, and the achingly short NFL one. I chose well with the Steelers, but once the NFL went dormant, things got rough. My Atlético Español team in the Mexican league was pretty awful—lovingly awful to me, stupidly so to my classmates—and in middle school we mercilessly treated each other as if we managed the teams we supported. Monday mornings following an Atlético loss were like brutal post-match press conferences where I had to answer for all the team's shortcomings and assume responsibility, once more, for a poor result. All while the gaggle of kids who slavishly followed Club América (yes, they were the same kids who rooted for the Dallas Cowboys) glided through their Mondays.

If our football seasons paced us through our years, the ultimate global sporting event, FIFA's glorious World Cups that only came once every four years, demarcated different epochs, providing the punctuation and periodization to our lives. Argentina '78 came in the final weeks of sixth grade, and I can recall huddling over a small black-and-white TV with classmates during recess to catch some of the grainy action; I'd turned sixteen by the time the Third World War was unleashed by the Germans and French in their crazy semifinal in Sevilla in Spain '82, a tournament we recreated by playing pickup games at Parque Leos, which we'd renamed for the kid who lived across the street from it. Then came Mexico '86, or was it Maradona '86? Italia '90 I watched with Kathy in Buenos Aires while on a law school fellowship; we watched Argentina lose the final to Germany in a movie theater and pretended to be as mournful as everyone else. In '94 our friend Mark Williams invited us to the opening game in Chicago; France '98 I shared with my beloved godfather Gastone in the twilight of his years, and with Dennis Bergkamp of course. Japan/Korea

2002 was an ingenious FIFA innovation to ensure I could keep my day job and watch all the games played throughout the night, and I am grateful my friend Kyle Pope would cross Manhattan at 3 a.m. to make it a party. Skip ahead to Brazil '14 and I took my ten-year-old son Sebastian to Europe to experience how the world lives the world's game. "Don't you know it's in Brazil?" friends would ask when I'd tell them we were going to Europe to watch the World Cup that summer. Yes, but it's also everywhere. We had a blast watching games with throngs of fans in an Amsterdam park, a crowded square in Leuven, and at a fanzone in the shadows of Berlin's Brandenburg Gate. With any luck, when I am old and broke, Seabass will take me to Brazil to watch a World Cup being played in Europe.

I happened to be back in Berlin for the 2022 World Cup final, this time with my wife Victoria, and this time in a cozy bar rather than an outdoor fanzone (given the novelty of a winter World Cup). Victoria is a colleague at Arizona State University, a sport historian who has helped educate me on the origins of the curious relationship between the United States and global sport, and my co-conspirator in establishing a Great Game Lab to delve deeper into these subjects. We normally see eye to eye on things (such as our shared love of Arsenal), but on this occasion we were on opposite sides of the thrilling Messi-Mbappé showdown that went into overtime.

Whatever our sport, we all have these memories of it connecting us to a time, a place, and to each other—immediate loved ones and a more universal community also sharing in the experience. There are people I have yet to meet with whom I will still be bonding over the memory of that Sevilla semifinal or Bergkamp's goal against Argentina.

My interest in sport is undiminished from when I was a kid, but increasingly I've come to realize that what interests me most is what sport does for us off the field or court. What it means to those of us watching, how it binds us together in a way that transcends all the forces pulling us apart in society. This shift became clear to me a few years ago when I went to the National Football Museum in Manchester, England. Beyond the impressive permanent collection and displays, I was most drawn to a visiting exhibit of photographer Stuart Roy Clarke's work that captured spectators across England, at every level of the game. Photos that captured the power of fandom and of the experience of experiencing sport. Next time you're able to attend a live sporting event, turn around and look behind you. Take in all those people and their unspoken stories.

Sport has become the world's most powerful form of entertainment, the last remaining form of media consistently able to deliver mass audiences sharing an experience simultaneously. Given the depth and power of the emotional connection so many of us have with sport, it isn't surprising that so many forces and interests in our society want to latch onto that connection and be associated with it. Imagine if someone could bottle the feelings evoked by my memory of watching those Steeler games with my dad—or more recent memories of watching Arsenal together with Seabass and Victoria—and manage to have me redirect them towards any cause or product. That would be priceless.

In a sense, that's what beer brewers, pizza joints, automakers, and a seemingly endless parade of insurance companies try to do every weekend as they invest heavily to sponsor the sports we follow and are passionate about. And so it shouldn't come as a surprise that nation-states and cities do this, too, eager to be associated with big-time sports and bolster their "soft power" and "brand" through them.

Having grown up outside the United States, I have an appreciation for both the power and limits of American culture and soft power. And as both a Mexican and an American, I have long been fascinated by the fact that sport, this tremendously powerful form of global pop culture, isn't dominated by the United States. It's a bit of a head-scratcher, really, when you consider that the United States is the world's most dominant pop culture superpower in almost every other respect *and* that we consider ourselves a sports-mad country.

Indeed, if you brought teenagers together from Argentina, Nigeria, Korea, and Germany (or picked any other four countries at random), US culture would provide most of their common references—American music, the latest Hollywood blockbusters or TV shows, consumer brands, and social media platforms (except TikTok). If they could communicate at all, it would be in English. But sports would likely be the one exception to American culture providing their lingua franca. Chances are, these teenagers would be more interested in discussing the last World Cup or arguing about whether Messi, Maradona, or Pelé is the best player ever, than they would be interested in discussing US sports figures or teams.

Another way to think about this is to consider how limited the reach of American sports are compared to other American cultural products. Hollywood blockbusters make more money overseas than in the United States, Taylor Swift held more than two-thirds of her Eras Tour concerts abroad. Most successful consumer brands make more money outside the United States too, because that's where three-quarters of the world's purchasing power resides. Successful American tech and social media platforms also have far more users outside their "home" country. Meanwhile, the Super Bowl, our most successful and iconic sporting production, is still watched by more people every year within the United States than outside of it. And the stars in that most popular of our professional sports don't get to do something that the most popular professional athletes get to do everywhere else: represent their countries in international competition. There's no one to play against.

When I first moved to the United States at the age of fifteen, I didn't expect to suffer from any culture shock or difficult adjustments, as ours was a pretty *gringo* household in Mexico. That proved partially true, but when it came to sports, I most definitely felt like a foreigner; I might as well have been plopped down behind some sports Iron Curtain. We had followed the NFL in Mexico, so I did have that going for me. But in terms of the sport that I had grown up obsessing over, watching, and playing around the clock, the sport that connected me to kids in my neighborhood and around the world, I had gone off the grid. In the United States of the early 1980s, it was very difficult to find any pickup games, or any soccer on TV, let alone a classmate to talk to about the last World Cup, or about whether Barcelona or Munich would rule Europe that year.

My sense of alienation back then made a lasting impression and led to insights that have informed my professional work ever since, and that animate this book. The most important of these is the power of sport, and of sport fandom, to help define our identity, situate ourselves in the world, and connect us to each other and to place.

For years I thought of writing a book that chronicled the epic showdown for global supremacy between America's top three domestic sports and international football, the world's default sport. It struck me as the highest-stakes Great Game of all, a clash between egotistical billionaires, some of the world's most powerful corporations, and a key set of nation-states, to win the hearts and minds of avid fans the world over, and the riches their attention represents.

But an unexpected plot twist has superseded that contest: the rise of soccer within America and the rise of America within the world of international football. All US sports leagues will continue trying to grow their market share abroad, but America's ongoing conquest of the world's leading sport is the new, rapidly accelerating development. Much like Hollywood before it, America's sporting interests now understand they cannot afford to disregard three-quarters of the global market, especially not at a time when sport has become so indispensable to media. It is no longer viable for the United States to be the world's media superpower and sit on the game's sidelines.

The sporting Iron Curtain is no more. Playing their own Great Game, women, immigrants, and computer geeks conspired over the years to pull off the Americanization of the once foreign football into American society. Since I came to the United States, a generation of kids has grown up playing youth soccer, mimicking the world's greats on their Xboxes and PlayStations, and cheering on our inspiring women's national team at the Olympic Games and World Cups. And you can now watch leagues from everywhere in the world on American TV.

Meanwhile, our dynastic professional sports franchise-owning families and Wall Street investment firms, driven by their emerging leaders who grew up in this new, more cosmopolitan sporting environment, are globalizing a business once deemed inherently local, rushing across the Atlantic to buy up prestigious European soccer clubs. We have long had multinational companies peddling beer, autos, and most other consumer goods, but not until now have we seen the rise of multinational entities operating the sports teams that fans everywhere have long considered their own.

There is another protagonist or antagonist in the Great Game, as America's push into international football coincides with an equally determined push into the sport (and other sports) by Persian Gulf States and other regimes that pursue a different, state-sponsored model of sport. Together, America's sporting capitalists and these nation-state sporting projects are co-conspiring to accelerate the globalization of sport at a time when that process has stalled in most other arenas.

The Great Game is not the showdown I'd originally envisioned between our homegrown sports and the world's default sport; it's more a contest to conquer and control all global sport. And at the heart of that Great Game is the century-and-a-half-old schism between the world's two footballs, which explains much about the universal power of sport and about America's place in the world, and is in the process of being healed.

This contest is entering a crucial stage as governments and markets have realized that there is nothing comparable to the media power of sport, and both footballs are ascendant in their respective competing cultures. Against this backdrop, as it aspires to become the world's new global sporting hub, the United States is set to host the world for a FIFA men's World Cup in 2026 and a Summer Olympic Games in 2028.

The last FIFA men's World Cup held in the United States, in 1994, amounted to an outside effort to jumpstart interest in the world's game among Americans (and launch a new domestic league). The upcoming 2026 World Cup shared with our two North American neighbors, by contrast, is largely an NFL-hosted extravaganza. Much of what I wrestle with in the chapters that follow is what happened to America's sporting relationship with the world in the generation's span bookmarked by the country's two FIFA men's World Cups.

After the Royals' game ended, I walked across the parking lot of the Truman Sports Complex, toward Arrowhead Stadium, just a few hundred yards away. Kauffman and Arrowhead stand side by side, twin temples of American sport, in this revolutionary half-century-old complex. Both Royals and Chiefs are now in the process of plotting moves to their next homes, but when the two stadiums opened in the early 1970s, they were considered futuristic marvels for their aesthetics and for breaking with the trend of cookie-cutter multipurpose venues. They were also a statement that, occupying the pinnacle of American life as they did, baseball and football each deserved their own houses of worship, built to their own specifications and needs.

The two stadiums share parking, and originally the plan was for them to also share a rolling roof, but that was dropped as impractical. But the main significance of this ambitious complex is that the two spectacles had been severed and would hover over all their surroundings just off I-70. You can also read some historical and cultural import in their respective scales. Kauffman seats just under 38,000, Arrowhead more than 76,000, and they were inaugurated shortly after baseball had passed the baton to the NFL as the nation's top sport and entertainment.

I walk up to the statue of Lamar Hunt outside the stadium's entrance. "Man of Vision," the inscription reads, though as his son Clark, the current CEO of the Kansas City Chiefs, reminded me in an email exchange, his nickname was always "Games."

Hunt, who passed away in 2006, is as good a candidate as any to be the Great Game's patron saint. No one is more responsible for the NFL's commanding presence in American life today than the founder of the American Football League that would force the NFL to expand beyond its comfort zone and into a merger that created our other national sporting holiday, the Super Bowl. And the Hunts, father and son, have been the leading voices among NFL owners to take America's game overseas, leading the charge for more and more league games to be played abroad.

Yet Lamar Hunt isn't just in the NFL's Hall of Fame. He is also in the National Soccer Hall of Fame, because no one did more to introduce Americans to the world's game and to drag America into the global sporting community. If archaeologists stumble across the Truman Sports Complex centuries from now, they will discern that the civilization that built this sacramental space had two supreme forms of worship. But at various times, Hunt's beloved Arrowhead—his "favorite place on earth," Clark told me—had to accommodate a third form of worship derived from the Hunts' ecumenical embrace of all footballs. In the early MLS days, the family's Wizards team shared the stadium with the Chiefs.

And now, this interloper football is coming back: Even as the Chiefs plan to move on to a more modern home, Lamar's beloved Arrowhead is about to have its biggest moment in the global spotlight, hosting six World Cup matches in the summer of 2026. As Joe Reardon, the head of KC's Chamber of

Commerce, put it to me in an interview: "No one could have possibly imagined when Arrowhead was opened in 1972 that it would be home to a World Cup someday, even if they knew what that was. Except Lamar, of course, he was probably already planning on it."

When asked what attracted him to the other varietal of football after watching the 1966 World Cup final on TV, Lamar Hunt replied: "I was especially impressed by the internationalism of the game. The *nation* of England against the *nation* of [West] Germany—not the type of thing I was accustomed to seeing in American sports."[1]

Clark Hunt also remembers his dad talking about the first big soccer match he watched live, before Clark was born:

> When he was dating my mother, they went on a trip to Ireland, and part of the agenda was to check out various Irish sports. They went to a hurling match at Croke Park, a Gaelic Rules Football game between Dublin and Galway, and a soccer match featuring Ireland's most successful team at the time, the Shamrock Rovers. That Shamrock Rovers match was actually the first professional match my dad ever attended, and it was probably the first time he began to envision bringing the sport to America in a major way.

Clark's childhood was also punctuated by FIFA World Cups and his dad's enthusiasm for them. The first one he attended, at the age of nine, was Germany '74, and he recalls dumbfounding German onlookers by being able to score a goal in a tight hoop in a game set up in a public square. No one over there thought Americans knew what *fußball* was. The Hunts skipped Argentina '78 because of security concerns (so did the world's best player then, Johan Cruyff), but Clark Hunt has attended every men's World Cup since, cheering on Brazil when the United States wasn't in the mix.

"The thing that has always struck me about the World Cup," Hunt shared,

> and the thing that makes this tournament so different, is that you get people from all over the world coming together to celebrate the sport of football. People from all corners of the world, from different cultures, different religions, different political persuasions—during the World Cup,

they're all celebrating. Yes, they are cheering on their team, but they are also celebrating this amazing cultural gathering.

Hunt grew up playing youth soccer in one of the game's early hot spots in America, the Dallas metro region, and he went on to play right back on SMU's soccer team, a position his son Knobel played on the same team before graduating in 2025. His streak of attending World Cups since Argentina will be extended, as he managed to bring the 2026 World Cup to him, having served as co-chair of the Kansas City bid. The bid succeeded because of KC's demonstrated enthusiasm and organization, but also as a tribute to Lamar Hunt's legacy.

Prior to the World Cup, Clark Hunt will travel with his Chiefs down to Brazil to play in the NFL's second game in that country, to kick off their 2025 season, in yet another testament to the cross-border convergence of the footballs. Hunt told me his dad would have been proud the Chiefs were going to play in South America.

I am sure he would have been proud of his team, yes, and of his son. But based on everything I have learned about "Games," I bet he would have been a bit envious too.

The Great Game is an exciting competition to behold.

1
America's Conundrum
Only One vs. #1

One of the greatest TV ads ever made brought together two of my childhood passions: Coca-Cola and the Pittsburgh Steelers. Specifically, Coca-Cola and Mean Joe Greene. It first aired during a Monday Night Football telecast in October of 1979, though it wouldn't become a cultural phenomenon until a few months later when it aired during Super Bowl XIV, which just so happened to feature the Steelers and its formidable Steel Curtain defense anchored by Greene, winning their fourth title in six years.

In the ad, Greene is hobbling alone down a gloomy stadium tunnel toward the locker room, injured and dejected, his jersey draped over his shoulder. You can hear the game still going on and see fans at the end of the tunnel focused on what's happening on the field. Except for one: a young boy who's followed Greene a few steps, to haltingly tell him he's still the best, and to offer him his bottle of Coke. The defensive tackle hesitates, declines once, but then takes it when the boy persists with an earnest, "Really, you can have it." The result is a rejuvenated Mean Joe and the peppy "Have a Coke and a Smile" jingle. The boy turns to walk away, wistfully saying, "See you around" to his hero who seems more interested in gulping down the beverage than in talking to him. But as the boy starts shuffling off, Greene calls out after him, "Hey kid, catch," as he tosses him his weathered jersey.

The ad was produced by Coke's longtime ad agency, McCann-Erickson. Marcio Moreira, the Brazilian creative director on the Coca-Cola USA account, told *The New York Times* in the summer of 1982 that shortly after the ad had started making waves in the United States, he "showed it around" to international clients, including overseas Coke bottlers.[1]

"And they all loved the idea," he told *The Times*, "But they had no idea who Mean Joe Greene was. So we proposed using their national sports heroes."

Hence the creation of what Moreira and his team described as the "Mean Joe Maradona" and the "Mean Joe Zico" commercials, in time for the 1982 FIFA World Cup in Spain. I can recall watching the Diego Maradona one on Mexican TV—the same lonely hobble down a sad tunnel with a similarly earnest wide-eyed boy reaching out with his Coke and subsequently receiving a jersey in return—in this case the soccer superstar's Argentina team jersey instead of a Steelers one. My friends and I cracked up at the heavy Argentine accent and expressions, such as Maradona's use of the term *pibe* for kid.

Different game, different language, but the same commercial in all the ways that mattered. The same emotion. The same vulnerability of a child's hero worship of flawed athletes. The same power of small gestures. The same secret formula for the uplifting fizzy drink. The same catchy tune.

I would have had a hard time explaining why back then, but I remember being impressed watching Coke leverage sports fandom speaking different languages—and different footballs—to different national audiences. It was a powerful illustration of cultural dexterity on the part of a company (or at least its ad agency) that had mastered the art of being both a global player and a local presence. Indeed, few things manage to be as simultaneously global and ubiquitously local as Coca-Cola.[2] (The world's most popular sport is another.)

The fact that this Atlanta-based company was international football's first global sponsor speaks to its paradoxically dual identity. It makes little sense, at one level, for an iconically American brand (rooted in the Deep South, no less) to have signed up to be FIFA's pioneering corporate partner in 1974, back when Americans didn't care much for the game and wouldn't have even been aware there was a World Cup happening in Germany. Little sense, that is, until you also acknowledge that Coca-Cola wasn't just an American icon: it was also the most widely distributed product on earth.[3]

In 1976, after its '74 World Cup sponsorship, Coca-Cola agreed to underwrite FIFA's World Football Development Program, which was heralded at the time as the first truly global sports sponsorship by a company. The $10 million from Coke provided FIFA, and its new boss João Havelange, with resources to share with national federations around the world, to invest in developing their game. This became the template for FIFA leadership's lucrative success over the next half-century in redistributing corporate revenues to its members to pursue both idealistic aims (such as expanding access to sport in economically disadvantaged communities) and leverage political patronage (securing the support and loyalty of national federations who'd receive payments from Zurich with few strings attached).

Coke's partnership with FIFA, which continues to this day, also became the template for many other blue-chip US brands that needed to attach themselves to the world's sport to reach overseas consumers, even as consumers in their home country (and often these companies' own top executives) knew or cared little about the sport they were investing in. Companies like McDonald's, Budweiser, and VISA also became prominent FIFA global sponsors, all the while continuing to market themselves within the United States through those other sports that Americans preferred to play on their own.

Electronic Arts is another example of a US company developing a dual sporting identity to fulfill its global aspirations, though not always as part of its leadership's master plan. In the late 1980s, EA Sports had launched the successful Madden NFL video game franchise, which was a phenomenon in the US market and enjoyed decent overseas sales. But a few designers at the company, and executives in its London office tasked with growing international business, were convinced the company also needed a soccer game.

Mark Lewis, who set up the London office, told *The Guardian* in 2016 that "Almost the entire U.S. organization was opposed to our idea, they felt that soccer was too complicated a sport."[4] The same newspaper account contains plenty of confirmation to that effect from Trip Hawkins, EA's founder ("There was great skepticism in the U.S. about the future of soccer, nobody cared") and Neil Thewarapperuma, then EA Sports' marketing manager ("EA didn't give a shit about FIFA").[5]

Of course, it wasn't initially clear that the soccer video game, if it got made, would bear the name of the game's international governing body; that would only become possible after one of the most profitable licensing deals in media history (the EA-FIFA relationship would lapse after three decades in 2023, when EA's FIFA game changed its name to FC). And before that could happen, Lewis first had to save the game from efforts by US-based colleagues to name it "Team USA Soccer," which would have seriously hampered its street cred overseas.[6]

Launched in 1993, Electronic Arts' FIFA game went on to become the biggest-selling sports video game of all time. By 2018, EA Sports reported that its FIFA game had outsold Madden globally by a 2-to-1 ratio over their respective lifetimes: 260 million to 130 million copies, respectively.[7] And while FIFA and EA parted ways in 2023, the game remains an IP behemoth, with licensing deals with thousands of players, hundreds of clubs, and dozens of leagues around the world, to maintain unflinching authenticity. Its dual sporting identity fully established, Electronic Arts no longer refers to the game as soccer; in discussing financial results, the company and its CEO, Andrew Wilson (an Aussie), tend to talk about their "American football" and "Global football" titles.[8]

What is fascinating about EA Sports' role in America's sporting exceptionalism—or in helping to erode it—is the fact that its FIFA property wasn't just a hit overseas, a global analog to Madden, equivalent to Coke's Mean Joe Maradona commercials meant solely for an overseas audience. The FIFA game was hugely successful within the United States too. Indeed, over the past generation, the game has been one of the primary forces altering America's relationship with the global game. Normally you think of people migrating from IRL sports to their video game version, but in the case of EA Sports' FIFA, this was a two-way street. Plenty of American kids went outdoors to kick a ball thanks to the video game. Back in 2014, an ESPN poll found that 34 percent of Americans became soccer fans by playing the video game.[9]

Growing up in Mexico in a pre-EA Sports age, my friends and I inhabited the small intersection of competing sporting spheres in the Great Game's Venn diagram. We belonged to the world's footballing community, passionately following our own Mexican and European leagues and international tournaments. But because of our geographic and cultural proximity to the United States, we also followed its sports leagues as if they too were ours.

I proudly hung a Pittsburgh Steelers pennant in my bedroom in sixth grade that proclaimed my team—that awesome edition of Greene's "Steel curtain" defense, Terry Bradshaw, Franco Harris, and Lynn Swann years—"World Champions." The Steelers had won two Super Bowls in recent years and would soon win two more before that stellar group passed from the scene.

That pennant was a source of both pride and bemused confusion. Pride that my Steelers, that scrappy industrial-town bunch who could only seem to afford a logo on one side of their helmets and had no use for cheerleaders, had eclipsed the formidable (and awfully popular) Dallas Cowboys, making me feel like there was karmic justice in the universe. In the same way that knowing Luke Skywalker had prevailed in the end, against another glitzier side. The Steelers bolstered my confidence and social standing in the brutal milieu of middle school boyhood and offset my disastrous choice of Mexican soccer team, the hapless Atlético Español, whose penchant for losing provided my classmates with endless material with which to mock me. Sadly, their season was far longer than the NFL's, so after January I was on my own.

My pennant confusion, meanwhile, had to do with its declaration that ours was a "world" title. I was eleven, sure, an age when fandom lends itself to hyperbolic exaggeration, but even I suspected this might be a bit of a reach. Seemed a bit cheeky that a nation could opt out of the world's football, invent an alternative variant no one else played that was more hands than feet, and then proclaim the winner of that domestic league "world champions." And didn't my fellow gringos across the border do the same with baseball and its "World" Series?

There is a significant difference between Coke's classic Mean Joe Greene commercial and its global variants that I didn't give much thought to as a kid. It wasn't just that they featured stars from different varietals of football; it was that the United States ad featured a player representing his domestic league club, the Steelers, while the Argentinian and Brazilian versions of the ad featured stars representing their countries.

Mean Joe meant a lot to me and to the rest of us Steeler fans, but the ad might have had an even bigger emotional payoff for Coke in this country if it had tapped into its audience's patriotism, as it had in Argentina and Brazil. The only problem, of course, is that Mean Joe Greene never donned a Team USA jersey. Nor have Tom Brady or Patrick Mahomes, for that matter. And that's because the United States is the only major country on earth whose biggest stars in the most popular professional sports league never get to play for their country. Hardly anyone else plays the game.

There is no shortage of academic tomes that set out to describe and explain America's historic exceptionalism and isolationism (closely interrelated, at times interchangeable, concepts), but perhaps the single best work ever on the subject was a four-and-a-half-minute *Saturday Night Live* sketch that aired on October 28, 2023. It featured that episode's host, the comedian Nate Bargatze, playing George Washington commanding the Continental Army in 1777. Bargatze's Washington exhorts a trio of his men resting before a campfire to remember what they fight for—"a new nation where we choose our own laws, choose our own leaders . . . and choose our own systems of weights and measures."[10]

"Yes, I dream that one day our proud nation will measure weights in pounds and that two thousand pounds shall be called a ton," Bargatze went on, to stirring music and his troops' growing confusion. "And what will one thousand pounds be called, sir?" [Comedic pause] "Nothing."

Washington then boasts that in this new country, people will be free to measure distances in inches, feet, yards, and miles, with 12 inches to a foot, and three feet to a yard. "And how many yards to a mile?" asks one confused soldier. The general's answer: "Nobody knows." But of course, it's 5,280 feet to a mile, "a simple number that everyone will remember."

Meters and kilometers, Bargatze's Washington adds, will only be used in "certain unpopular sports like track and swimming; for popular sports like football, we will use yards."

"Football, sir?" asks an exasperated soldier.

"Yes, it's a sport where you throw a ball with your hands"

"So, in football there is no kicking?"

"There's a little kicking," he admits. "You kick the ball to get points."

"How many points, sir?"

"Sometimes one, and sometimes three."[11]

For years I had been comparing America's historic rejection of the world's football to our rejection of the metric system, so you can imagine my delight at seeing these themes so brilliantly and hilariously teased out in an *SNL* skit.

The question of how much of football is to be played with our feet, as opposed to our hands, dates back to the early 1870s disagreements between Harvard, Yale, and Princeton over the rules of the game.[12] At a more profound level, however, the ensuing footballing schism between the United States and the rest of the world is a manifestation of the larger American conundrum that presidents setting foreign policy or companies like Coca-Cola and EA Sports pursuing profits have all had to navigate: whether to stand apart from the rest of the world or be a global player.

This foundational American identity conundrum can make our nation's interactions with the rest of the world confusing at the best of times and seem almost schizophrenic at others—especially to people elsewhere, caught between America's conflicting impulses to avoid dealing with the outside world versus wanting to remake it in our own image.

The concept of American exceptionalism has always contained within it a belief that ours is a country with a special, providential destiny. But much of our history, certainly the history of US foreign policy, can be seen as a debate about what exactly that providential destiny is. Even the Puritan leader John Winthrop's seventeenth-century call for the new Massachusetts colony to be a "city upon a hill" (upgraded by subsequent embellishment to "a *shining* city upon a hill") was ambiguous. A virtuous city upon a hill that will please God by standing apart from the corruption of the Old World it left behind? Or a city upon a hill that will please God by serving as a beacon to the rest of the world that spreads its virtuosity for the benefit of people elsewhere, so as to not leave them behind in the blight?

Most other countries don't have this luxury of debating whether, and how, they want to engage the rest of the world. Most tend to have a constant worldview and international role; with reality dictating their place. Elites in Poland, Colombia, Tunisia, and most other places are in no position to consider opting out of world affairs and setting their own course, free of any compromising entanglements, as George Washington (the real one, not Nate Bargatze) exhorted his countrymen to do in his famous Farewell Address. Presumably, our first president would have been onboard with Americans becoming obsessed with a game no one else played, and which therefore would entail no international drama.

But even in Washington's day, there were plenty who disagreed with him, including his top lieutenants who bickered over whether we should ally with Britain or revolutionary France, and over which values our young country should embrace and propagate.

The competition between America's conflicting isolationist and messianic impulses has been a constant ever since. Both impulses always coexist, alternating in their ascendance, giving people elsewhere whiplash when trying to keep up (or simply being impacted) by shifting US answers toward its identity conundrum. Consider, for instance, how quickly the United States went from a consensus to stay out of the First World War to backing President Woodrow Wilson's call to win the war that would "make the world safe for democracy," and design a new system of collective international security that would ensure an end to all such wars. Only to then quickly shrug off the effort at war's end, pivot back to a more comfortable isolationism, and refuse to even join the League of Nations that was born out of America's own messianic impulse.

The Second World War and its nuclear aftermath appeared to forever alter the balance of power between our conflicting impulses. Retreating to our shining city on the hill and minding our own business on our own bountiful continent no longer seemed as viable an option in an age of intercontinental missiles—not to mention an age when American economic power and interests (and our cultural "soft power") reached every corner of the world. And so, the postwar era, the so-called American Century and Pax Americana, did bring more constancy to how Americans viewed their global duty and responsibility. We created alliances and multilateral organizations to secure the peace and facilitate international trade, went to admirable lengths to alleviate suffering and improve people's lives elsewhere (the Marshall Plan is but one example), but also blundered horribly on occasion due to the blinding hubris of our messianic impulse (Vietnam, to name the costliest quagmire).

John F. Kennedy was fond of citing Winthrop's "city upon a hill" sermon, and he interpreted it in a Wilsonian manner. His Inaugural Address pledge to "pay any price, bear any burden, meet any hardship, support any friend" in defense of liberty was the antithesis of Washington's Farewell Address. But even within the internationalist postwar consensus, America's attitudinal pendulum continued to swing between bouts of idealism and realpolitik, sometimes within the same administration. Ronald Reagan became president as a hardline anti-communist determined to stand up to the Soviet Union but ended up pursuing (unsuccessfully in the end) starry-eyed deals that would have rid the planet of nuclear weapons. George W. Bush ran for president vowing to conduct a "humble" foreign policy and forego ambitious "nation-building" exercises elsewhere but ended up launching an invasion of Iraq predicated on a naïve Wilsonian belief that once we overthrew the tyrant in Baghdad, we could easily bestow democracy on an appreciative Iraqi population.

Then along came Donald Trump to question that internationalist postwar constancy in his own inimical way, and so America's foundational identity conundrum about our place in the world lives on.

Our sporting ties with the outside world have been affected by this history and by America's protracted cultural and economic dominance in the postwar era. Our domestic sporting ecosystem may have been designed to reinforce our separateness and distinctiveness, but as American culture became the world's lingua franca, it's only natural that our homegrown sports would acquire new adherents beyond our borders. As already stated, I grew up in an NFL-crazy Mexico. The NBA has fans sprinkled all over the world, and baseball's footprint—an arc sweeping from the Caribbean basin across North America and across the Pacific to incorporate Korea and Japan—resembles a map of American colonial influence as closely as a map of the British Empire resembles a map of cricket's reach. Foreign business conglomerates and foreign occupying armies tend to leave their foreign games behind, and within a generation these games are no longer deemed foreign. It's a delicious irony that some of Latin America's foremost leftist icons in modern history—Fidel Castro, Che Guevara, Hugo Chávez, and to a lesser extent Mexico's Andrés

López Obrador—who made a career of railing against US imperialism were obsessed with *el imperio's* national pastime, *el béisbol.*

Americans have always liked to prove their exceptionalism and Manifest Destiny through sport. Athleticism has long been central to the American creed. We are a hearty, vigorous frontierspeople, or would like to think so at least, and others have often seen us as that. Ours is a society in which physical activity has often been equated with civic virtue, as if fitness were an attribute of good citizenship. That's one reason sport, especially highly competitive sport, is more ingrained in our schools than it is in schools elsewhere in the world.

It is difficult, however, for a nation to reconcile its desire to play its own games with a desire to prove that it's the top athletic power in the world. Fans want to chant "We're number one," not "We're the only one," but when it comes to baseball, basketball, and especially American football, it has been hard for us to develop international rivalries. As basketball became more global, we have seen some rivals emerge, and baseball has launched its World Baseball Classic, but it's been a gradual, at times contrived process.

American football—our top domestic passion, fanwise—remains a game of solitaire at the international level. If the rest of the world had dropped soccer for our football, the NFL's all-star team could go face off against France and Brazil. But, as it is, NFL players have never been able to represent their country on the field. The game's fans, for their part, have been deprived of the opportunity to experience that heady mix of sport fandom and nationalistic fervor so familiar to aficionados of the other football around the world who get to watch their nations face off against each other in their favorite sport. Perhaps it is to compensate for this absence that NFL games embrace all the patriotic trappings, from the anthem to the field-sized flags unfurled by servicemen and the jet fighter flyovers. It's as if we're saying, it might be Jacksonville against Carolina today, but who knows who we might need to take on tomorrow.

American football, baseball, and basketball all trace their origins to the nineteenth century, and each of these sports was mobilized not just to reinforce a new American identity but also to address a newly urbanized, industrialized society's concern about an increasingly sedentary workforce losing its physical vigor. Dudley Sargent, appointed director of Harvard University's gymnasium in 1880 and later known as the father of physical education in this country, voiced a widespread concern of that era when he bemoaned in his *Physical Education* treatise that because "steam, gunpowder, and electricity are now doing the work and fighting the battles of the world . . . we have almost ceased to regard the physical vigor as one of the factors in human progress."[13] Sargent's concerns were echoed in the "Muscular Christianity" movement that led to the founding of the YMCA and YWCA, elite colleges' embrace of serious sport as a calling, and President Teddy Roosevelt's endorsement of the "strenuous life" (an expression identified with both his calls to play sport and to go off on foreign military adventures). Proponents of American football and baseball sought to outdo each other in scrubbing any foreign taint from their games' genealogy. Colleges adapted our football away from its "football association" roots, and a "Special Baseball Commission" convened in 1905 by Albert Spalding and A.G. Mills endorsed a fanciful origin tale for baseball far removed from the English game of rounders.[14] It was the Y and its muscular Christianity that begat basketball, the most Wilsonian of American sports, and were eager to ship it overseas from inception to help spread our way of life.[15]

It's no accident that Teddy Roosevelt's presidency coincided with the pouring of the foundation on which the future of American sport would be built. That first decade of the twentieth century saw the birth of the World Series, the National Collegiate Athletic Association, and the hosting of the first Olympic Games on US soil.[16]

Over time, the Olympics would prove the venue in which America could compete head-to-head with other nations and attempt to prove its superior athleticism. That symbiotic relationship between nationalism and sport made the Olympics the outsized media event it would become in the second half of the American Century. Supremacy in our most beloved but insular sports was never at stake, but across-the-board athletic bragging rights over our geopolitical rivals—whether it was the British Empire, the German Reich, or most compellingly during the golden era of broadcast TV, the Soviet-led Communist bloc—were up for grabs.

The Summer Olympic Games and FIFA World Cups have shared the pinnacle of international sport in the postwar era, with each global mega-event alternating every two years, and each serving a very distinct, complementary purpose and audience. World Cups pit soccer powers against each other and are fueled by fans' existing passion for the game; the Olympics pit actual superpowers desperate to prove the superiority of their way of life against each other. The contested sports themselves at the Olympics were almost secondary; at its height, the Cold War rivalry was heated enough that a coin-toss match between Soviets and Americans would have drawn a crowd. All that mattered was the medal count.

Sport was a proxy battlefield in a nuclear age when actual warfare had become obsolete. As historians Robert Edelman and Christopher Young argue in their introduction to *The Whole World Was Watching: Sport in the Cold War*, sport provides geopolitics with "the hardest form of soft power and the softest form of hard power."[17]

The "Miracle on Ice" upset win over the Soviet hockey team at the 1980 Winter Olympics in Lake Placid was one such classic moment of geopolitically charged sporting glory, imbued with extra meaning by the Soviet invasion of Afghanistan and the takeover of our embassy in Tehran. A beleaguered President Jimmy Carter, then in the middle of fending off a humiliating primary challenge from Senator Ted Kennedy, phoned the locker room to tell coach Herb Brooks that his team's victory showed that "our way of life is the way to continue."[18]

From its earliest days, the modern Olympic Games became a contest for prestige among nations and a useful barometer of national vitality. "The United States," as Matthew Llewellyn and John Gleaves wrote in *The Rise and Fall of Olympic Amateurism*, "more than any other nation, embraced the Olympic stage as a medium for constructing, propagating, and maintaining images of national prowess," in opposition to the British Empire.[19] Great Britain won the most medals overall at the 1908 London Games, but the Americans won thirteen gold medals to Britain's five in track and field events. The US athletes returned to a New York ticker-tape parade and a visit with the country's "strenuous life" commander-in-chief Theodore Roosevelt.[20]

In the interwar years, the fascist regimes of Italy and Germany became the athletic antagonists of western democracies, only to give way after the Second World War to the Soviet-led Communist bloc, which saw in sport a viable means of proving itself against the West. By 1949, presaging the decades-long showdown that was to come, a popular Russian journal noted: "The increasing number of successes achieved by Soviet athletes in sport has particular significance today. Each fresh victory is a victory for the Soviet form of society and the socialist sports system; it provides irrefutable proof of the superiority of socialist culture over the decaying culture of the capitalist states."[21]

The Cold War revived Teddy Roosevelt-era concerns about the physical fitness of the population and its readiness to compete with our adversaries in sport and possibly beyond. In December of 1960, President-elect John F. Kennedy (who had run for president denouncing a fictitious "missile gap" with the Soviets) penned an article entitled "The Soft American" in *Sports Illustrated*, in which he lamented how the physical fitness of America's youth was falling behind that of kids in other countries, which he considered a dire issue because "the physical vigor of our citizens is one of America's most precious resources. If we waste and neglect this resource, if we allow it to dwindle and grow soft then we will destroy much of our ability to meet the great and vital challenges which confront our people."[22]

Linking kids' fitness to national security, Kennedy upgraded a youth fitness office President Eisenhower had established into a far more active Presidential Council on Physical Fitness, overseen by the accomplished University of Oklahoma football coach Charles "Bud" Wilkinson, which constantly exhorted Americans of all ages to get off their couches and meet certain fitness goals and standards.[23]

The modern Olympic movement, for its part, wasn't launched to provide a battleground for clashing nationalisms or conflicting ideologies. Pierre de Coubertin, the entrepreneurial founder of the modern Games, and his internationalist Olympic Charter spelled out that the Games were contested by individuals, not nations, and the Olympian founding father and his acolytes (none more fervent than Avery Brundage, the American who would head up the IOC from 1952 to 1972) would denounce the spread of "patriotic professionalism" in sport.[24] At times the IOC even sought to discourage publication of nations' medal tables and to refute the idea that any one nation could "win" an Olympics.[25] This effort to downplay the adversarial geopolitics of the Olympics—and their coverage as score-settling confrontations between great powers that might otherwise occur on battlefields—was doomed to failure; it's what fueled the popularity of the Games.

There was, additionally, one distinctive article of Coubertin's—and later Brundage's—Olympic creed that suited the US-Soviet rivalry and further helped distinguish the Olympics from that other quadrennial giant of global sporting events, the FIFA World Cup. Whereas FIFA decided from the outset that its tournament would be played by professionals, the Olympic movement clung to elitist nineteenth-century British notions of gentlemanly amateurism well into the twentieth century. And Soviets and Americans proved willing co-conspirators in indulging the Olympic mythology around pure amateurism.

In the United States, colleges had developed into sporting-industrial complexes whose professionally developed and trained athletes were students, often on scholarship. The National Collegiate Athletic Association shared the International Olympic Committee's belief in the redemptive, chivalrous ideal of amateurism and the need to keep enforcing the ideal long after it was practical to do so. When the Soviets, for their part, decided to rejoin the international sporting order after the Second World War, they realized that instead of continuing to attack the elitism of Anglo-American amateurism, they could simply game the system and hoodwink the world by insisting that their state-sponsored athletes also met the vague Olympic definition of amateurs.[26]

Cold War Olympics thus became a confrontation between state-backed "amateurism" and collegiate-backed "amateurism," with the IOC turning a blind eye to the excesses of both, which often accused the other of fielding "shamateurs." The Soviets complained about the "extravagant" scholarships US athletes were given, which they likened to salaries for training, but there was little comparison between the support and aid available to Olympians in the two systems. The Soviets and their allies in East Germany mobilized their entire state apparatus to create a system for discovering, nurturing, and harnessing sports talent, often with the aid of coercive sports science and unethical medical interventions.

The Olympic movement's insistence on maintaining the amateur ideal was always controversial and always subject to uneven enforcement and inconsistent rules and standards across different sport federations. To preserve the illusion that Olympic athletes were true amateurs, the IOC (especially, and ironically, under the American Brundage's leadership) subscribed to the fanciful fiction that Soviet sport was less of a state project than the Soviet military. That fiction soon tilted the medal count in the Communists' favor, while adding to the romance of cheering on our underdog amateurs going up against the foot soldiers of totalitarianism. In the decade prior to the "Miracle on Ice" 1980 hockey upset, Americans were unnerved that the false equivalence between our college athletics and the Soviets' militarized sporting complex was costing us global supremacy. Jack Kelly, the president of the Amateur Athletic Union (and brother to Princess Grace), mocked the arrangement between amateurism-obsessed Olympic officials and Communist bloc athletics as "the same unholy alliance you find when the bootleggers and the clergy combine their votes to maintain Prohibition."[27]

In 1975, faced with America's declining prospects in the Cold War Olympic era, Gerald Ford established the President's Commission on Olympic Sport to "determine what factors impede or tend to impede the US from finding its best amateur athletes for participation."[28] The previous year, in his last full month as vice president prior to Richard Nixon's resignation, Ford, who'd played football at Michigan, wrote his own Kennedyesque *Sports Illustrated* article riffing on his relationship with sports.

He didn't quite come out and call Americans "soft," but he did express his concern that as a nation we were losing sight of why winning matters:

"The reason I make reference to those winning seasons at Michigan is that we have been asked to swallow a lot of home-cooked psychology in recent years that winning isn't all that important anymore, whether on the athletic field or in any other field, national and international. I don't buy that for a minute. It is not enough to just compete. Winning is very important. Maybe more important than ever.

Broadly speaking, outside of a national character and an educated society, there are few things more important to a country's growth and well-being than competitive athletics. If it is a cliché to say athletics build character as well as muscle, then I subscribe to the cliché. It has been said, too, that we are losing our competitive spirit in this country, the thing that made us great, the guts of the free-enterprise system. . . . For one, do we realize how important it is to compete successfully with other nations? Not just the Russians, but many nations that are growing and challenging. Being a leader, the U.S. has an obligation to set high standards."[29]

Throughout the subsequent decade of the 1980s, amateurism's hold on the Olympic movement began to weaken. Sports such as tennis, skiing, ice hockey, and soccer began chiseling out exceptions to absolute bans on professionals at the Games. Then in April 1989, FIBA, basketball's global governing body, passed a resolution by a vote of 56–13 that opened the door to NBA players' participation at the next scheduled Games.[30] It's worth noting that both the Soviet Union and the United States voted against the measure that would enable the participation of the "Dream Team" at Barcelona '92.

Winning is always sweet, but it turns out that winning as a scrappy underdog with college kids representing the Stars and Stripes might be sweeter than any win, no matter how resounding, by world-renowned pros wearing those same Stars and Stripes. The 1980 Winter Olympics "Miracle on Ice" ("Do you believe in miracles?" was Al Michaels' iconic call as the game's final seconds ticked away) semifinal hockey triumph over the Soviets at Lake Placid arguably remains the high point of international sporting euphoria in American cultural history. Not because of how much most Americans cared about ice hockey (indeed, despite how little most cared), but because of the narrative behind the win—of a ragtag group of college kids prevailing against the well-oiled Soviet machine of robotic "shamateur" Communist ringers. Because of what their win said about us . . . and them.

The Soviets had their own version of this tale, played out eight years earlier on the basketball court, when they upset the Americans in the men's gold medal match at Munich. Upset in every which way, as the Americans, who were 63–0 in basketball Olympic matches dating back to the 1936 Berlin Games, considered themselves victims of corrupt officiating in the last three seconds of the game. Down by a point, the Soviets were given three attempts to desperately inbound the ball after an American free throw. The third attempt, after the Soviet team had been allowed a substitution when rules normally would preclude it and game officials had mysteriously ordered American players to back off and give the Soviets space to go deep, led to the most improbable score that had Russians asking themselves if they believed in miracles. The Americans unsuccessfully protested the result to a five-judge panel that included three members from Soviet bloc nations; to this day, those American team's silver medals remain the only unclaimed medals in Olympic history.[31]

The Russian narrative around their 1972 basketball triumph glosses over any controversy, mirroring instead the American "Miracle on Ice" tale. In my classes, I project the trailer for Disney's 2004 *Miracle* movie ("Discover the story behind the greatest moment in sports history"), followed by one for the 2017 *Going Vertical* Russian movie about the 1972 basketball showdown ("Everything is possible while you're alive"). My point isn't subtle: it's basically the same movie. A plucky group of misfits is pushed by an obsessively determined coach whose belief in the possibility of victory is not shared by the sporting apparatchiks around him, or even the players themselves at the outset of their quest. But then, against all odds—spoiler alert!—these teams coalesce around their coach when it matters and prevail against the humorless (and dirty-playing!) superpower rival. *Going Vertical* is one of the highest-grossing Russian films of all time.[32]

Twenty years after the Munich debacle for Team USA and four years after settling for bronze in Seoul 1988, the famous "Dream Team" composed of NBA stars and one token college player represented the United States at the Barcelona Summer Games, thanks to FIBA's 1989 vote to open the Olympics to full-fledged professionals.

American Olympic officials weren't thrilled by the "Dream Team" phenomenon, which threatened to overshadow the rest of the delegation and their pursuits, but fans couldn't get enough of the epic coming together of the game's titans. Spanning two storied generations of NBA glory, the team included Larry Bird, Magic Johnson, Michael Jordan, Charles Barkley, and Patrick Ewing under the US banner. For the first time, Americans could savor what people across the global footballing world had experienced for decades—that intoxicating patriotic rush of seeing their famous professional all-stars in a sport they avidly follow, rivals from different domestic league clubs, take on all-stars from other countries. And not for a paycheck, but out of national pride.

For all its cosmopolitanism, basketball wasn't as deeply entrenched elsewhere to provide the type of competitive parity seen in international football among that sport's superpowers. The Dream Team won all its games in Barcelona by an average of 43.8 points.[33] The highlights of the Dream Team's summer included the spectacle of millionaire superstar Olympians preparing for the tournament in swanky Monte Carlo and staying apart from the rest of the US Olympic delegation in Barcelona, at the luxurious Ambassador Hotel. And then there was Charles Barkley, ever the outrageous entertainer, creating a stir with his nocturnal wanderings down Las Ramblas, and with an unnecessarily ferocious elbow to the face of 174-pound Angolan forward Herlander Coimbra, who happened to worship Barkley (opposing teams asking the Americans for their autographs was an odd staple of this Olympic tournament). At the pre-match press conference, Barkley had done nothing to counter the stereotype of the self-involved American athlete with little interest in the rest of the world when he had said: "I don't know nuthin' about Angola. But Angola's in trouble."[34] As it turned out, 116–48 kind of trouble.

Neither Disney nor anyone else could ever claim the Dream Team's cakewalk to gold amounted to "the greatest moment in sports history," or anything close to it, but the incongruity of it all was a compelling spectacle in its own way.

As *The New York Times* noted on the Dream Team's gold victory:

On the gold-medal stand tonight, in their corporate-sponsored suits with logos purposefully hidden, the multimillionaire professionals from the National Basketball Association were flanked by teams from tiny breakaway republics that could barely scrape together the funds necessary to attend.

To their right was the Croatian team it had just defeated for the gold medal, 117-85, in their bland, identification-less uniforms straight out of the 1950's. To their left were the Lithuanians, jubilant bronze medalists after their 82-78 victory over the Unified Team, in their tie-dyed shirts and shorts that were paid for by a rock band, the Grateful Dead.[35]

The biggest drama on the night, alluded to in the story's lede, was the clash between Team USA's Olympic sponsor, Reebok, and the sponsors of individual stars, especially Michael Jordan's beloved Nike. Hence the artful idea of draping flags over the inconvenient Reebok logo. "Everyone agreed that we would not deface the logo," Jordan told *The Times*, as if reliving the game's crucial play, "The flag can't deface anything." Jordan also told the newspaper that the greatest basketball he'd ever been involved with was in Monte Carlo, referring to the Dream Team's intra-squad scrimmages.

Undoubtedly, the most memorable matchup at Barcelona did not involve the Dream Team. The most poignant and exciting game was the bronze medal match that saw newly independent Lithuania triumph over its former Soviet/Russian masters (who competed under a "Unified" banner of the Commonwealth of Independent States that included most of the former Soviet republics).

Larry Bird conceded to *The Times* that the lopsided nature of the team's wins got in the way of a compelling story: "I've cried at home when I've seen Americans win close races," he said. "I think you would've seen a lot more emotion up there if we hadn't won every game by 50 points."[36]

There were doubts originally as to whether the millionaire NBAers would show up to play for their country, and plenty of suspense around the question of whether stars of competing NBA clubs could get along on the same team, but there was never any doubt as to how they'd do against international competition. Indeed, for the foreseeable future, any basketball, baseball, and (if we ever get there) American football game between a US national team and another country, regardless of where it takes place, is essentially a "home" game for Team USA. We enjoy home-field advantage in the sports we invented.

The rise of international football within the United States, by contrast, has offered American fans a rare opportunity to embrace a true underdog identity, at least on the men's side. The dominance of American women at FIFA World Cups and Olympic Games, as we shall see in a later chapter, has helped expand soccer's popularity in the United States. But the sheer averageness of the men's team in international competition has provided American fans with the novelty of cheering on their nation *against all odds*. In what other walks of life do Americans cower with dread at the thought of going up against the likes of Uruguay, Belgium, or the Netherlands, as we have at recent men's FIFA World Cups?

The United States has only qualified to play in eleven of twenty-one men's World Cups. The United States has not advanced to a semifinal since the very first one, contested between only thirteen teams in Uruguay in 1930, and has only made it to the quarterfinal stage one other time, in 2002. The recent trend (setting aside the 2018 tournament in Russia, for which the United States didn't qualify) has been toward making the round of 16. Solid, in other words, with no assurances we will ultimately prevail, but with enough potential to imagine the possibility of a "Miracle on Ice" moment in this sport we increasingly care about but did not invent and can't claim home-field advantage in, even when the games are played here.

Playing global football forces (or allows?) Americans to acknowledge (or pretend?) that we are just another country, one of many, as the generation of kids who grew up playing EA Sports' FIFA game on their TVs knows all too well from the game's player and team ratings.

The tension between claiming an underdog identity and expecting the spoils that come from being top dog is an American conundrum that transcends sport. Think of your classic Second World War movie, depicting wily American GIs as regular guys oozing street smarts but little interest in wearing uniforms, which they do sloppily when compared to the nattily attired Nazi soldiers. The scrappy American troops in these movies always appear outgunned but manage to overcome the enemy in the end, thanks to their tenacity, smarts, and initiative. What fun would it be to cheer on the GIs in a movie that dwells on the fact that they're backed by once unimaginable material resources and an industrial output and societal wealth that dwarfs anything any of the other warring powers could ever possibly mobilize?

We cling instead to an image of ourselves as an underdog whom no one believes in. An underdog since our ancestors came together as a motley crew of colonial militias without proper uniforms to vanquish the King's redcoats to declare our independence and establish a republic that many considered foolishly unsustainable. Underdog because we're a country of individualists who cherish our freedoms and don't empower a collectivist, oppressive state apparatus like some other societies against whom we must then compete. Throughout the Cold War, we considered ourselves the underdog at the Olympics, confronting a totalitarian empire that leveraged all its resources to win at all costs. Such are the narratives we tell ourselves about who we are, even as people elsewhere might see the United States as anything but an underdog.

Most Americans want to embrace this underdog identity without accepting a perennial underdog's results. In Hollywood tales and on TV broadcasts of recent Olympic Games, the United States is always the underdog and always wins. In the real world, however, you can't have it both ways: win constantly, and you don't get to retain your underdog status.

The alternative, though, of an America as a true perennial underdog with the checkered results to prove it, is hard to fathom. It's hard to imagine twenty-first-century Americans being content as one of the top twenty or thirty nations in the world in a sport we deeply care about, let alone in terms of economic or military might. Imagine how things would go for a president who said they were honored to lead a country that strives to get out of the proverbial group stage, a country that might win some, lose some ... be they athletic tournaments, economic competitions, or wars. That probably wouldn't go well, which is why US leaders are continuously going on about this being the greatest country on earth. Even Barack Obama, who was chided at times for appearing uncomfortable with such rote boasting and embrace of American exceptionalism, called the United States the world's only "indispensable power in world affairs" in his 2012 State of the Union address.[37]

The tension lives on in sport. We want to be #1 in the sports we care about, but not by being the only one who plays them, as is currently our American football conundrum. We do crave the international competition, but maybe not too much of it, so we can reliably win, as we do in basketball.

The question thus remains: How successful must the United States become at soccer before the world's most popular sport establishes itself as part of what the renowned political scientist, sport sociologist, and longtime University of Michigan Professor Andrei Markovits calls a nation's "hegemonic sports culture?"

In *Offside*, an absorbing book he coauthored in 2001 on soccer and American exceptionalism, Markovits posited one scenario for the future of America's engagement with the world's game being predicated on leveraging the success of the women's game:

Interest in MLS and the U.S. men's national team might piggyback on the popularity of the women's game and engender a wide proliferation of interest in soccer for many American sports fans, male and female alike. This would be sacrilege and/or farce to most of the millions of (male) soccer aficionados in Europe, Latin America, and elsewhere, but well in tune with the American exceptionalism in sport.[38]

I reached out to Markovits twenty-three years after his book first came out (and twenty-three years after I had talked to him about it when I worked at *The New York Times*) to see if he now felt the United States had become a little less exceptional, and whether the global game had now established itself as a hegemonic sports culture.

We're getting there, Markovits enthusiastically told me. Or at least all the ingredients are there: a vibrant domestic league, legions of young participants in the sport, improving international competitiveness, the strength of the women's game, and that looming World Cup.

Markovits, who recently retired from teaching, remembers the 1994 US World Cup as a win for the sport, but in a totally different context. "Back then, FIFA rented the USA to bring the circus to town," he said, "and it was a huge success as this great event that people fixate on for a couple of weeks before moving on to the other thing." He views North America's upcoming 2026 men's World Cup, by contrast, as coming at a time when the country has moved from the periphery of the sport to its semi-periphery, on its way to being a core player.

He doesn't see soccer yet as a hegemonic sports culture in the same way as our big three homegrown sports (three-and-a-half, he adds, when you consider his beloved hockey). "It isn't just a question of whether millions of kids play, because soccer has that more than any sport, it's a question of what sports are being discussed, followed, obsessed about in our shared culture. What are the sports that everyone, not just their own fans, are expected to know about?"

Markovits arrived with his family in the United States in 1960, fleeing the virulent antisemitism of his native Romania, and has led what he calls a "bifurcated life" ever since. He has embraced American culture with the zeal of the naturalized citizen. He loves the Yankees, afternoons at the Big House in Ann Arbor, and the Grateful Dead. But for much of his life, he was also part of that fifth column in this nation that would be transfixed by Brazil's Seleçao at World Cups and would try to catch Manchester United, whom he'd followed since their tragic 1958 airplane crash in Munich, on TV.

It was relatively late in his career, initially as a "lark" and subsequently at the behest of colleagues, that Markovits turned his comparative political science expertise to a study of comparative sporting cultures that help define and differentiate societies on either side of the Atlantic—to study, in other words, the gulf in his own bifurcated life.

But now he is hopeful that his worlds are converging. "I was amazed to have a student recently from Michigan's Upper Peninsula who'd wander around campus wearing the jersey of his favorite sports team: Sporting Lisbon," he told me. "That kid didn't exist when I wrote *Offside*."

Still, Markovits believes the US men's team must do well at the upcoming World Cup we are co-hosting to help propel soccer onward to the next level in this country. "Winning it might be too much to ask for, but we need to get to the quarterfinals at least and then lose gloriously to a Brazil or an Argentina," he said.

Even Lamar Hunt, who did more than most to bridge the two footballing worlds, would fret about the limits to soccer's popularity within this country so long as the US men weren't global contenders. "I have no doubt that soccer will be a major sport in the United States," he said, after being involved with promoting the game for some thirty-five years at the time, but "I'm probably not going to live to see that day because Americans are a little afraid of getting interested in something at which they're not very good. . . . But I have no question that we're going to see the sport become a major success in the United States."[39]

But for now, let's take a closer look at how the NFL became America's most popular and successful sporting venture in the absence of any such internationalism.

2
Socialism in One Footballing Country

The Cleveland Bulldogs won the National Football League title with a 7-1-1 record in 1924, the NFL's fifth season. In those days, much like in European soccer leagues today, the team with the best record throughout the season was proclaimed champion; the first NFL playoff was still eight years away.

There is no record of what Joseph Stalin in Moscow made of the Bulldogs' triumph, not even a rushed "Wait, I thought they were the Browns?" diary entry.

It had been a busy year for Stalin. Vladimir Lenin had died in January, and Stalin was hustling to consolidate his status as the revolutionary leader and party founder's successor from his perch as the party's General Secretary. The revolution and its emboldened acolytes in power were experiencing a seven-year ideological itch since their 1917 takeover of the vast Russian empire, which Stalin cleverly capitalized on that fall by articulating his new doctrine of "Socialism in One Country."[1]

Previously, the Bolsheviks had adhered to the orthodox Marxist belief that socialism, and ultimately communism, could only take hold and flourish in places that had already experienced the most advanced phases of capitalist industrialization. That the supposedly worldwide proletarian revolution had first succeeded in a Russia that remained far more agrarian and far less developed than Western European nations was considered a historical fluke, explained by the upheavals of the First World War. Orthodoxy required the Bolshevik rulers to continue prioritizing the "permanent revolution" that would ultimately bring about the main event, the proletariat's takeover in countries like Germany and France, even at the expense of Russia's national interest.

Ever the pragmatist, Stalin put an end to what he considered starry-eyed counterproductive nonsense and proclaimed the new gospel of "Socialism in One Country." Instead of continuing to treat their historical role as subservient to events elsewhere, Stalin insisted that what was good for international communism was the rapid development and strengthening of a Soviet state that spanned a sixth of the world's landmass. The USSR would make a proper hub for global communism for the foreseeable future. Stalin had flipped the hierarchical order: from then on, Communist true believers in the West were in the service of Moscow, not the other way around.

Having dusted off some cobwebbed Soviet history from my school days, I will spare you here the full account of how things transpired from there for Stalin's "Socialism in One Country" in Russia. Suffice it to say that despite some wins along the way, it was a crushing failure in the end. The Cleveland Bulldogs didn't make it either; they were gone by the end of the decade, having first moved to Detroit, where they played briefly as the Wolverines, before being absorbed into the New York Giants. Cleveland's Browns were still a couple of decades away from taking the field as a charter member of the All-America Football Conference, from where it would then join the NFL.

Which brings us to the one place where "Socialism in One Country" has succeeded like nowhere else. Stalin's portrait might not hang in the league's Park Avenue headquarters in Manhattan, but the Soviet *vozhd* would be impressed with the NFL's success and how rooted it is in a radical egalitarianism that is a rare norm in American cultural and economic life.

This league makes no sense, really. How is it that thirty-two billionaires preside over the most socialist enterprise in American life, which is somehow also one of American capitalism's supreme achievements?

The NFL is famously obsessed with parity, abiding by Marxism's central tenet: "from each according to their ability, to each according to their need." Its downtrodden, the team finishing in last place each season, gets to pick first in the college draft and is also given an easier schedule. All teams, regardless of their performance or the size of their local markets, receive the same exact cut of the league's bountiful TV and commercial sponsorship revenues. Moreover, all teams, regardless of their owners' means, are subject to the same teamwide salary cap that is set at a manageable percentage of their slice of the shared revenue. Such ironclad equality is what allows smaller cities like Green Bay and Buffalo to field competitive teams.

I have found the comparison to socialism irresistible for all my adult fandom of the game and even got *The New York Times* to advance the argument in an editorial we published on Dec. 30, 2000, under a "Socialism Triumphs on the Gridiron" headline. Writing on behalf of the editorial board, I credited the former NFL Commissioner Pete Rozelle with pursuing a "Utopian vision of a league founded on parity, one where all teams could compete as equals."[2] I repeatedly came back to the counterintuitive theme of NFL owners as improbable Bolsheviks in signed Editorial Observers I wrote for *The Times'* Opinion pages (my boss Gail Collins would teasingly accuse me of being a frustrated sports reporter) and for other publications later.[3]

It's become far more common in the intervening years to characterize the NFL as socialistic, and with good reason: some analogies or metaphors are just too good to pass up, and the comparison was apparent to some contemporaries even as these measures were being considered.[4] In his engrossing history of the NFL, *America's Game: The Epic Story of How Pro Football Captured a Nation*, Michael MacCambridge traced what would become the most significant of many parity-enforcing aspects of the league's business model (the pooling and equal distribution of all TV revenue) to a proposal first raised, and rejected, at a baseball owners' meeting in Scottsdale, Arizona, in 1952. Leading the charge against the idea, L.A. Dodgers owner Walter O'Malley called his fellow owner who'd raised it "a damned Communist."[5] Baseball to this day suffers from its overreliance on a localized approach to managing media and commercial rights, and the inequities that arise from that approach. In April of 2025, *The Athletic* reported that Major League's spending gap has never been wider, contrasting the Dodgers' league-high payroll and luxury tax of $476.6 million to the Miami Marlins' lowest payroll in the league of $69.1 million, a nearly 7-to-1 ratio.[6]

Bert Bell, Pete Rozelle's predecessor as NFL Commissioner, read with interest about the 1952 debate within baseball, and he tried to get his owners to approve a partial TV revenue-sharing agreement. TV revenue back then was still a small slice of the league's overall revenues, but Bell wasn't confused about where things were headed, and he was already concerned about the disparities, correlating to market size, among his franchises' TV revenues. In 1953, for instance, the Rams would earn nearly $100,000 from TV, while the Packers earned a twentieth of that, some $5,000.[7] In the 1940s, Bell would make famous the oft-repeated adage that "On any given Sunday, any team in our league can beat any other team." He'd already started down the path of weighted schedules featuring weak teams versus weak teams and strong teams versus strong teams that Rozelle would later perfect.[8]

Bell had also been responsible for one of the other notable measures to advance league parity as far back as the 1930s, before he was commissioner, as owner of the Philadelphia Eagles. In 1935, he convinced his fellow owners that at the end of each season, they should pool the names of all eligible college seniors and take turns making selections in reverse order to their previous season's standings. Bell never called this innovation, meant to avoid a stratification of the league into contenders and permanent has-beens (including his Eagles), a "draft," but journalists immediately did, and so the term stuck.[9]

The New York Giants, one of the league's dominant franchises in those days, stood to lose from an embrace of parity, but team owner Tim Mara set an early precedent of NFL owners prioritizing the collective in accepting the draft:

> People come to see a competition. We could give them a competition only if the teams had some sort of equality, if the teams went up and down with the fortunes of life. Of course, that meant that no team would in the future win a championship every third year and people would start saying, "What happened to the Giants? They aren't the team they used to be." That was a hazard we had to accept for the benefit of the league, of professional football and everyone in it.[10]

As commissioner, it would take Bell a bit longer to get NFL owners onboard with his proposed sharing of TV revenues, which were initially seen as a form of local marketing by teams. Throughout the 1950s, though, the NFL perfected a national TV strategy that included local blackouts to protect attendance figures, and the cause of collectivism within the NFL was ultimately aided and consolidated, by three major developments: the fact that the league's most formidable competitor embraced an even more stringent socialism; public policy that enabled a more centralized command-and-control league-wide governance; and the marketing genius of Pete Rozelle, Bell's successor as league commissioner.

Lamar Hunt was the son of one of America's wealthiest tycoons, H. L. Hunt, which makes it all the more paradoxical that he was among the most zealous advocates for parity in football, initially in the American Football League, which he'd founded to compete with the NFL. Late in the 1950s, while still in his twenties, Hunt sought to acquire an existing or an expansion NFL franchise but was rebuffed by the league. So instead, he assembled a group of deep-pocketed investors across the country to establish the competing AFL that would include his Dallas Texans, who'd move after two seasons to Kansas City and change their name to the Chiefs. Even before the new league started playing, its teams were guaranteed more TV money than the NFL's franchises because of a blockbuster contract with the upstart ABC network, which was trying to take on the more established NBC and CBS in the same way the AFL was taking on the NFL. Most previous TV revenue-sharing proposals included complicated formulas with varying percentages allotted to home teams and to the common pool, but Hunt pushed for a far cleaner, more radical approach: one pot of TV money, shared equally by all. Like Bell, he'd been intrigued by the TV revenue-sharing proposals that baseball owners had considered but rejected. The AFL proved such a potent challenge to the NFL, and vice versa, that the two agreed to merge within a few years. The first Super Bowl (a term coined by Hunt) in 1967 was instituted as the championship between the winners of each league, soon to be the enlarged league's respective "conferences" when the merger was fully implemented in 1970.[11]

Hunt launched the AFL and doubled down on a business and governance model optimized for parity in the years when American football was overtaking baseball as the nation's most popular spectator sport. The sport was far nimbler than America's more entrenched "pastime" in organizing itself to suit the needs of the TV medium and its national aspirations. And football also came into its own at a time when the government was willing to encourage and protect the nascent symbiotic embrace between media and sport. In 1961, Congress passed the Sports Broadcasting Act, which granted the NFL and other leagues antitrust immunity to negotiate packaged broadcast contracts for all its teams, whom the law might otherwise view as competitors within one industry acting as a cartel. There are occasional calls to revisit this dispensation, such as in May 2025 when Republican Senator Ted Cruz held hearings to examine sports leagues' plans to migrate more of their games to streaming services (hurting consumers, presumably).[12] In the unlikely event that Congress ever did withdraw the NFL's antitrust immunity, the league's highly centralized, socialist design would be in immediate peril. If the Dallas Cowboys and Jacksonville Jaguars had to go out and sell their own media rights individually, the resulting disparities in their revenue and spending power would look a lot like what we find in baseball.

Pete Rozelle, the public relations-savvy General Manager of the Los Angeles Rams, was named NFL Commissioner at the age of thirty-four in 1960. The league's "child czar" understood the paramount importance of marketing the league above teams, and he took bold, innovative steps to centralize not only control of the game's revenues but also of its image and storytelling. In *America's Game*, MacCambridge describes Rozelle's creation in the early 1960s of NFL Films and NFL Properties (the fabled in-house highlights production company and an entity that would control all league merchandising and sponsorship deals) as a tipping point for "pro football's eclipse of baseball."[13]

From time to time, certain NFL owners have balked at the league's socialist structure and have sought to change things, but an overwhelming majority of them have backed the arrangement. Recent years have seen less dissension and more harmony than ever in the prosperous club, with team owners able to scratch their more capitalistic and competitive itches by upgrading their stadium amenities and local marketing deals—the sources of revenue they do not share with other franchises. For the 2023 season, each NFL franchise received $427 million from league-wide media, sponsorship, licensing, and merchandise deals, plus an additional $25 million from the NFL's shared box office (a third of all stadium ticket proceeds are pooled, then divvied up equally).[14] This collective pot amounted to 67 percent of the NFL's total $20.5 billion in revenue for the year. The other third is made up of those luxury suite sales and local marketing activities, where some teams in bigger markets or newer stadiums can outearn their peers.

How to explain the riddle of our idiosyncratically national game, a violent sport that tests players' virility and trades in metaphors of warfare and conquest, organizing itself as a socialist nirvana governed by principles otherwise alien to American economic life? Imagine asking some NFL owners to extend their NFL practices to their other business interests. Get together with your competitors to form a cartel, share the bulk of your revenues equally with them, and allow your vanquished competitors—those companies you outsmarted, outhustled, and outsold—to pick the most talented executives coming into the business, and give them an easier set of challenges over the coming year.

One possible answer to the riddle is that many of the NFL's founding families didn't fit today's profile of billionaires who buy into sports leagues. They were scrappy devotees of a scrappy game, successful entrepreneurs or gamblers, but no stalwarts of the nation's business elite. Several of them shared Irish Catholic backgrounds. They were trying to keep their game afloat in the shadow of the national passions for baseball and college football, not to mention the ravages of the Great Depression. Survival was never a given and seemed to call for collective solidarity. As the game found itself on more solid footing in the 1950s and early 1960s, the adoption of an equal split of TV money flowed naturally from the league's foundational parity-reinforcing norms already in place and from the fact that few yet grasped the magnitude of the cash waterfall TV income would come to represent. And nowadays, the answer to the persistence of the riddle lies in its proven commercial success. NFL owners preside over the most profitable sports league ever created, whose collectivist "one for all and all for one" philosophy has served them well. The NFL's revolutionary concept that the rest of the sports world is only belatedly trying to replicate is the idea that there is far more brand equity in the league itself than in its franchises, and that each franchise's valuation will be diminished if that brand equity isn't consistently evident across all teams.

A more idealistic answer to the riddle might lie in a cultural speculation about American notions of fair play, equal playing fields, and fans' right to expect, without engaging in groundless delusion, that on "any given Sunday" or in "any given season" their team might win, even if it plays in a far smaller city than New York but is going up against the Giants. When we play Monopoly, we all start with the same $200; why should it be any different in sports?

Has the NFL established an American way of sport, or does it simply reflect preexisting cultural notions of fair play? Or are baseball's structural inequalities equally American?

Given the NFL's outsized influence as the most profitable and seemingly well-run sports league, its ways are more likely to be perceived, certainly outside the country, as setting American mores and standards for sport. This is compounded by the NFL's undoubted influence over the design and development of Major League Soccer and the National Women's Soccer League. Both these leagues incorporate features that promote parity and double down on NFL-style centralized control by organizing themselves as single entities, whose "team owners" are shareholders in the entire league enterprise and franchisees operating one of its teams.[15] In the past ten years, eight MLS teams have won the league's title.

The competing United Soccer League is planning to entice American fans with more of the agony and the ecstasy fans of the game are accustomed to elsewhere, by creating a hierarchy of three divisions across which clubs will be promoted and relegated.[16] Other American sports leagues are concerned, to lesser and varying degrees, with competitive parity, but to fully appreciate how extreme the NFL's socialism is, consider how the world's other football leagues organize themselves. In Europe, which supposedly embraces a less cutthroat version of capitalism than we do, the most popular sport and form of entertainment is governed by an unbridled and inequitable "survival of the fittest" Social Darwinism.

In European football, the rich have a way of getting richer, while the poor struggle to survive. The higher a team ends in the standings, the larger its share of league revenue. The top teams in each league across Europe also qualify for continental competitions that bring in even more TV and matchday revenue, creating a virtuous cycle of success being rewarded and perpetuated. The game's downtrodden, the bottom two or three teams in major European leagues each season, aren't given American-style remedial help for the following season in the form of the best young prospects or an easier schedule. Far from it. They're "relegated" to a lower division, their places taken by "promoted" teams from those lower leagues. Imagine if the teams at the bottom of MLB standings at the end of the season had to drop down to Triple A; or if the Cleveland Browns were relegated to play in the Big Ten (OK, that would be complicated) after finishing 3–14 in 2024. It's all very much a cycle of life. Terribly exciting for fans, in the way horror films are exciting.

I visited Swansea, in Wales, in the spring of 2018, when the local, American-owned club was battling relegation. When I met with Chris Pearlman, the club's American Chief Operating Officer, at his office in the stadium, he told me: "It's one thing to understand the idea of relegation as an intellectual matter and appreciate its drama from afar—it's quite another thing to live through it." The "Swans" went on to lose against Chelsea that following weekend and to be relegated at season's end, after a seven-year run in the Premier League. [17]

Some relegated teams bounce back in a year or two, some never do. Swansea hasn't yet. Some of the fans I spoke to at the Chelsea match were ambivalent about staying up; one called it a "joyless grind" to spend each season just trying to survive against superior, deep-pocketed competition. For the clubs themselves, the prospect of relegation wreaks havoc on business projections and valuations; relegation from the Premier League brings with it the loss of tens of millions in TV revenue (with "parachute payments" softening the blow over a couple of seasons). Conversely, that threat of relegation is one of the factors making European football clubs seem so affordable to American investors unaccustomed to the idea that sporting failure can have dire financial repercussions. Only six English teams—Arsenal, Manchester United, Liverpool, Tottenham, Chelsea, and Everton—have avoided relegation since 1992, when the top division was rebranded and relaunched as the Premier League.

Leicester City was the ultimate sporting Cinderella of this century when it overcame 5,000-to-1 odds to win the English Premier League in the 2015–16 season. Smaller clubs aren't meant to do that. And sure enough, within seven years of this remarkable accomplishment, Leicester was relegated to the Championship (as the second tier of English football is confusingly called). *Sic transit gloria mundi.* It bounced back up the following season and then got relegated back to the Championship in the spring of 2025, having gone from champion to "yo-yo" club.

Contrast the existential drama of late-season matches of teams near the bottom of the table in European football struggling to survive with the chill, bored vibes at late-season NFL games featuring teams with no prospect of making the playoffs, and no sense of jeopardy that their losing ways might have any consequences. On the contrary, lose enough, and the reward might be the top draft pick. On the final weekend of the 2024 season, New York Jets fans were annoyed that their team pulled out an improbable win over the Miami Dolphins, thus dropping down a few notches in their draft pick order. In European leagues, the stakes for underperforming teams in these late-season games couldn't be higher: their continued existence as a top-league team. In *Ted Lasso*, when the naïve American coach is complaining about the perplexing specter of relegation his Richmond FC club is facing, his players ask him whether it is any different in America; that surely there must be some consequences for losing. "Nah," Jason Sudeikis' character responds, "we just call them the New York Jets."

And the Jets, along with other teams that struggled last season, get an easier schedule the following season, with a disproportionate number of their discretionary, non-divisional matchups arranged against other teams that didn't make the playoffs. Such is the parity and mobility within NFL ranks that I hesitate to pick on the Jets and Browns here, because within a relatively short period of time you might be reading this wondering, "What's he talking about? The Browns just made it deep into the playoffs." The Cincinnati Bengals played in the Super Bowl in 2022, having won only two and four games in the prior two seasons.

NFL teams make a great show of always trying to win games, even when they might benefit from a late-season loss to improve their draft picks, though at times they are accused of more show than trying. In the NBA, which also features a draft in which teams select young players coming from college or elsewhere in reverse order of their place in the league, the prospect of teams "tanking" games to improve their chances of selecting a generational talent that will alter the team's trajectory for years to come is more openly acknowledged, if still controversial. The league fined the Dallas Mavericks in the spring of 2023 for owning up to what other teams had done in the past but not talked about—throwing their last two games.[18] Two years later, concerns over tanking had only increased—a story from *The Athletic* near the end of the 2025 regular season read: "Nearly a quarter of the league has a strong incentive to lose right now."[19]

If NFL teams all face the same salary cap dictating how much they can spend each year and are handed more than enough in shared league-wide revenue to cover their bills, the reality in European football is very different—again, far more ruthlessly capitalistic in a manner more usually associated with American business.

Spain's La Liga now features a tightly enforced salary cap that it polices in real time. But unlike the NFL's salary cap, which is optimized for parity, European football's spending limits are concerned with solvency. Burnt by too many speculators and sham businessmen who run their teams into receivership, leagues want to ensure that their clubs live within their means, spending no more than a certain percentage of club revenues. For better or worse, this freezes existing inequalities in place. Prior to the 2024–5 season, for instance, La Liga's accountants set Real Madrid's salary cap (for first team players, coaches, and development youth squads) at €755 million; Barcelona had to make do with €426 million; Atlético Madrid with €310.7 million, and so on. Ten smaller clubs had salary caps below €60 million.[20] That's like playing Monopoly and starting off with $15 when your brother starts off with his $200.

Not surprisingly, the big three clubs in Spain tend to vie for the top places each year, sometimes joined by one unexpected interloper. Only four teams have won La Liga this century, with Barcelona claiming it twelve times and Real Madrid nine. In that same period, fourteen NFL franchises have won a Super Bowl, while six teams have won in each of Germany's Bundesliga, England's Premier League, and Italy's Serie A.

In the past four years, the NFL has seen twenty-eight of thirty-two teams make the playoffs, while in the Premier League, eight teams finished in the top four spots in any of those seasons, and three of those teams only once.

The Premier League's economic imbalances are extreme when compared to the NFL, but not as extreme as elsewhere in Europe. *The Athletic* reported that in the 2022–3 season, Chelsea's £539 million wage bill (including transfer fees) was the league's highest, while Brentford's was the lowest at £109 million. The English league has also become stricter about enforcing its "profit and sustainability rules" (PSR), which set a limit on permissible losses over three years, again with an eye on protecting clubs from their own profligacy. But in the spring of 2024, the league also agreed to embrace spending caps starting in the 2025–6 season set as a multiple (expected to be five times) of revenues for the smallest club in competition.[21]

The idea of anchoring one club's spending to a ratio (even a lopsided one) of another club's fortunes—moving away from the idea that limits should only be about each club's solvency—is a step toward NFL-style sports socialism for European football. It reflects the NFL's influence as a business model and the power of branding a league (which can only be as strong as its weakest members) and not just its more storied clubs. It still isn't quite "on any given Sunday/in any given season" parity, but it's a tentative step in that direction.

The Premier League sits somewhere between the NFL and continental leagues in its level of collectivism. More of its TV revenue is distributed evenly to clubs regardless of size, though big clubs still make additional windfalls from qualifying for European competition, and each club pursues its own commercial sponsorships, which can account for a significant percentage of their overall revenue. For the 2022–3 season, for instance, Manchester City's commercial revenue was £347 million, almost thirty times higher than Bournemouth's. But City's allotment of overall Premier League TV revenues was only 1.8 times higher than that of the team receiving the smallest check that year, Southampton (£167 million vs. £94 million)[22]

Over the past decade, the Premier League has consolidated its leading position among Europe's five top soccer leagues, thanks in large part to those TV checks clubs like Bournemouth and Southampton are receiving. They might be smaller than those received by their biggest rivals in England, but they are substantial enough to make all Premier League teams wealthy by European standards.

Real Madrid tops Deloitte's Annual Football Money League for the 2023–4 season, having broken the billion-euro mark for annual revenues, but six of the sport's ten highest-revenue clubs in the world are in the English Premier

League. And the league's dominance only gets more pronounced and is more novel further down the ranks. Historically smaller and less glamorous English clubs now have the means to woo top talent—both players and coaches—away from more established European clubs, or from elsewhere in the world.[23]

One reason European football leagues are far weaker than the NFL or NBA vis-à-vis their constituent clubs is because these clubs are seen as community assets (as opposed to mere league "franchises") that often predate the leagues themselves. They simultaneously play in several different competitions beyond the control of any one league. In any given season, for instance, Manchester City might be competing in the Premier League as well as the English Football League Cup (overseen by the English Football League), the FA Cup (overseen by the Football Association), and the European Champions League (overseen by Europe's regional federation, UEFA). Even within the league play they do control, the member teams competing in the English Premier League or Spain's La Liga will vary over time because of promotion and relegation.

My Pittsburgh Steelers, by contrast, don't play games beyond the NFL's gridiron; their identity and entire existence revolve around being an NFL *franchise*, a term that isn't applicable to European soccer clubs, much in the same way it wouldn't be applicable for American college teams. The Steelers don't start each season pursuing four trophies in different competitions awarded by different entities; their sole aim is to be handed the Vince Lombardi Trophy by the NFL Commissioner upon winning the next Super Bowl.

Our college football teams don't play in international competitions either; but as institutions that are deeply rooted in their communities, often tracing their origins back to the nineteenth century, they are more analogous to European soccer clubs than to our professional sports teams. No English football club or US college team is going to pick up and move to another city, the way many of our professional franchises have. With the shifting conference realignments and ambiguous overlay between conference titles, national rankings, and the evolving college playoff system, college football programs navigate a complex jurisdictional patchwork that is more akin to European professional football than the NFL's tidy setup.

The influential and brilliant book *Soccernomics* by Simon Kuper and Stefan Szymanski took on the question of relative parity across the two varieties of football on either side of the Atlantic, and they sought to disprove two widely accepted truisms: that the NFL is much more equal than European soccer, and that sports fans like equality.[24]

I always lean in for smart, contrarian takes, and Kuper and Szymanski did a valiant, though ultimately unconvincing, effort on the first point. They argued, convincingly, that the NFL hasn't attained true parity, at least not when it comes to results. They compared the NFL's standard deviation of win-loss records with those of a hypothetical coin-tossing league (where each side has a 50-50 shot of winning) to prove that America's football league isn't a Marxist paradise where equality reigns.[25]

They also argued that the identity of winners and losers is "pretty stable" in both the NFL and the English Premier League over time, noting that the New England Patriots won 79 percent of their regular season games from 2007 through 2016, while the Green Bay Packers and Pittsburgh Steelers won 66 percent and 64 percent, respectively, over the same period—compared to 73 percent for Manchester United, 72 percent for Chelsea, 69 percent for Arsenal, and 67 percent for Manchester City.

Six years after this latest edition of *Soccernomics* was published, those once dominant New England Patriots would finish the 2024 season dead last in their division, for the second year in a row, with a 4–13 record. None of England's top six clubs will plausibly finish at the very bottom of the table, though Tottenham and Manchester United made a valiant rare effort over the 2024–5 season. Leicester's miracle aside, the identity of potential winners and endangered species in England is a lot clearer to fans. The two NFL teams with the best regular season record that same 2024—the Kansas City Chiefs and the Detroit Lions—didn't merit a mention among *Soccernomics*' perennial winners. Conversely, *Soccernomics* lists the Rams as one of the NFL's perennial losers during the decade they highlight, but the team would go on to win a Super Bowl two years after its publication. The book also dismisses relegation in England and the NFL's playoffs (a "randomization device" that prevents the best regular season teams from always winning) as factors that muddle the real picture, when in fact they are highly relevant factors to the inquiry at hand, affecting over time the cast of clubs that can contend and those that can't.

But Kuper and Szymanski's larger point is undeniable. There is a huge gap between the NFL's aspirational parity and its results. The league may be designed to ensure parity, but teams like the Jets, Browns, and Jaguars still manage to defy the system by being consistent losers, despite the algorithmically favorable scheduling, the equality of resources available to all, and all those high draft picks (and here I am opening myself up to being mocked by hindsight if by the time you read this the Browns have celebrated their first Super Bowl win). Conversely, teams like the New England Patriots (despite their recent dip) and the Kansas City Chiefs still manage to be consistent winners over time, despite the lower draft picks, tougher schedules, and salary cap that prevents them from keeping all their coveted stars. The league can distribute revenue equally, and establish rules that nudge all teams to revert to the mean over time, but it cannot ensure that each of them will have equal measures of competence in their ownership and management, and that is where the variance creeps in.

The second truism *Soccernomics* sets out to challenge in its comparative analysis of the two footballs is the idea that fans always prefer equality in their sports, and on this one Kuper and Szymanski offer some compelling arguments.[26] They point out that dynasties offer up more drama and command more passion and interest from fans. They tend to have more followers, so their wins attract more attention and elicit more joy; over time, conversely, they also tend to attract more haters. Think of Manchester United, the New York Yankees, and the Dallas Cowboys—or the Kansas City Chiefs, in more recent years.

Most NFL fans approvingly parrot the "any given Sunday" parity mantra, appreciate that their team can't be wildly outspent by those in bigger markets or owned by wealthier billionaires, but some of these same fans also lament the scarcity of enduring dynasties and the rivalries between them. Then there's what Kuper and Szymanski call "one of the joys of an unbalanced league: the David vs. Goliath match."[27] They argue that the possibility of a David win, which happens more often than you think because David always tries harder, makes these matches inherently more interesting than most even matches.

Sports fans outside the United States are more fatalistic in my experience, so the David vs. Goliath mindset comes more easily to them. NFL fans might appreciate such contests on the day, but we all feel our team has a "right" to be among the Goliaths. During the languid days of mid-summer, every NFL team's fanbase asks itself whether this might be the year they will emerge as Super Bowl champions. Fanbases for European soccer clubs are also asking themselves questions in the dog days of summer, but the question varies by club. A very small number of fanbases will ask themselves if this is the year they will win the league; for others it's whether they can qualify for one of the European places; stay in the top half of the table; or avoid relegation and stay afloat for another season. Fans elsewhere are more accepting of their societies' geographic, social, and class fragmentations spilling over into their sports. Not every team in their *Monopoly* game starts with the same amount of money. Clubs and their fans know their place and compete against expectations.

Soccer itself, as a game, is a more fatalistic pursuit than America's homegrown sports. Soccer's nativist US detractors can be quite tiresome, but they aren't wrong in saying there's something inherently anathema to American culture about a scoreless tie. When soccer clicks, it is "the beautiful game," but on other days it can mirror life's struggles. A 0–0 match reflects an acknowledgment that sometimes things just don't work; that the game can be too hard, and that what you yearn for is not attainable.

American games, by contrast, reflect our culture's can-do optimism, our instant-gratification worldview and society, and our demand that sport provide us with escapist entertainment. If soccer can at times frustrate American sensibilities because scoring is too difficult, basketball is a game that has been mastered to the point where *not scoring* when in possession is more newsworthy than scoring. And football overtook baseball as our true on-the-couch national pastime because it encapsulates the postwar American belief that there is a management solution to any intractable problem. Depending on your favored analogy, American football provides generals or CEOs (the coaches) a vast array of astonishingly powerful, highly disciplined, and specialized resources to deploy against each other, carrying out precise instructions between every movement in the drama. Measures of time and space, as well as the adjudication of any disputes on the field, are meant to leave nothing to chance, or fate, but are undertaken with the rigor and exactness of a high-stakes scientific inquiry. Or a military campaign.

For an article I wrote years ago about the glaring inequality of German soccer, and how paradoxical it seemed given Germans' fondness for tut-tutting about inequality in America, I called up Professor Szymanski at his office in Ann Arbor and first heard his argument questioning the widespread assumption in this country that sport must feature competitive parity to remain interesting. He pointed out that while many of us pay lip service to this ideal, our behavior as fans often belies this belief. Sports fans everywhere appreciate greatness and dominant athletes and teams, whether it's Tiger Woods, the Michael Jordan-era Chicago Bulls, Roger Federer, or the Patriots during the Bill Belichick and Tom Brady years. And even if you're not rooting for the dominant stars in their prime, the question of how far they can extend their dominance becomes a compelling narrative for those rooting both for and against them.

A couple of months after my conversation with Szymanski, in the summer of 2014, I took my ten-year-old son Sebastian on the trip of a lifetime (mine at least), riding trains through Europe and watching World Cup games beamed from Brazil. We caught Dutch games in a park in Amsterdam and a café in Maastricht; a Belgian game in Leuven's medieval central square; and German games at an outdoor dance club along the Rhine in Cologne, at a student café in Munich, and at a massive Fan Zone in the shadows of Berlin's Brandenburg Gate.

Late one afternoon while in Munich's idyllic English Garden, Seabass and I played a pickup game against an engineer named Michael and his 12-year-old son. Chatting afterward, I asked if they were fans of local powerhouse Bayern Munich. Not just fans, it turned out, but members and season ticket holders. I asked how things looked for the following season, and Michael looked stressed, talking about how they needed reinforcements, but he wasn't sure whom the club would sign over the summer.

At first, this struck me as performative concern. Bayern Munich was stacked with talent, always is, and they had won the title for the past two seasons. The club's dominance is so notorious that people joke that all other players in the league are just trying out for a spot on the team.

Rather pointedly—I remember feeling I was being a bit rude even as I blurted out the words—I asked Michael: "Doesn't it get boring, rooting for a team that is expected to win every year and can outspend everyone else to do so?"

He looked at me perplexed, as if I were speaking to him in a foreign language (well OK, I was, but he spoke it perfectly). I then chuckled as if to convey I was just kidding; all good, who doesn't like to win?

But Michael turned somber and talked about the stress and pressure of meeting those expectations week in and week out, year in and year out, on top of the pressure of having to prevail in European competition. I might have even said "must be tough" at this point, without even being sarcastic. It was as if his Bayern fandom were the stoic duty of a loyal resident, but one who secretly yearned to support some unassuming mediocrity like Holstein Kiel or Heidenheim, and be freed of any expectations, free to lose with abandon, or to relish every victory against a big club like a miracle for the ages.

Instead, Michael's burden was written all over his face, knowing his club is allowed no margin of error and little room to celebrate its expected triumphs. He was reminding me of how much sports fandom is an anguishing obsession—for all of us. Although, for the record, Bayern Munich did go on to win the Bundesliga title that following season . . . and for the following eight seasons after that. I hope Michael is doing all right.

We have no way of knowing whether the NFL's supremacy in America's sporting culture would be as pronounced if its teams competed on a playing field as uneven as the Bundesliga's, or even Major League Baseball's, with some of its franchises spending multiples of what others do, and some fan bases perennially hoping for little more than respectable mediocrity. Is the league's relentless egalitarianism core, or incidental, to its success? Would the NFL still be the NFL, the country's most popular spectator sport by a mile, if the New York Giants' payroll were six or ten times greater than the upstate Bills' payroll, or if bottom-ranked teams went last in the college draft? Or is the stoic fatalism of fans who keep supporting teams that only have the means to aspire to mediocrity an inherently "foreign" attitude?

What we do know is that under its socialist orientation, the NFL has become one of our capitalist society's most admired and most successful enterprises, in any industry. It is in a league of its own when it comes to monetizing sport, and it reigns supreme as a TV product. The first Apollo moon landing is the only broadcast that isn't a Super Bowl on the list of the ten most-watched TV programs in US history.[28] In 2024, the NFL accounted for seventy-two of the one-hundred most-watched programs on US television.[29] The previous year, absent the competition of a heated presidential election which propelled 16 programs onto the list, the NFL accounted for an astonishing 93 of the top 100. For its 2025 broadcast of Super Bowl LIX in New Orleans, Fox was able to charge a record $8 million for thirty-second commercials. The game boasted its highest ratings ever, with a domestic audience of 126 million viewers.[30]

Back in 2021, the NFL was able to cash in on linear television's desperate dependence on the spectacle it has to offer. Its primary rights holders—the four traditional TV broadcast networks, plus Amazon—agreed to fork over a total of $110 billion for NFL games from 2023 to 2033.[31] That nearly doubled the value of the previous TV deals, but the league is already expected to trigger an early option to exit and renegotiate these agreements at the end of the 2028 season, because it feels it can do better, especially with other potential bidders, including deep-pocketed tech streamers like Netflix, Apple, and YouTube TV, potentially wanting in. Since the 2021 agreements, the NFL added YouTube TV as its partner for the Sunday Ticket package that provides diehard fans access to all games and its 2025 Brazil game. It also created a separate Christmas Day package for Netflix to dip its toe in the game. Sport, and particularly the NFL, is deemed indispensable by both traditional linear TV and by the disruptive streamers hoping to displace it.

The NFL's TV riches, divvied up into thirty-two equal payments by the league office, have inflated the valuations of its franchises to an average of $6.5 billion.[32]

The league's success as a commercial and cultural juggernaut in the world's largest market has made it the envy of the sports industry worldwide. The NFL is the gold standard as a business model, studied and marveled at by other sports. Inspired by it, European football leagues, starting with the English Premier League, have made belated moves toward creating a slightly more even playing field, and toward branding themselves as a collective that transcends their individual clubs.

The very existence of a "Premier League," as England's top division rebranded itself in 1992, owes a lot to the influence of the NFL, down to the introduction of "Monday Night Football" and extended pre-game televised hype. David Dein, Vice Chair of London's Arsenal at the time, was one of the Young Turks who wanted to modernize, commercialize, and clean up the top flight of English football under a new Premier League branding and a rich new TV contract signed with Rupert Murdoch's Sky TV. He told me in an interview that his "wake up moment" came a couple of decades before the Premier League's launch, when, in his American wife's hometown of Miami, he was taken—here's a bit of Hollywood-esque foreshadowing—to watch Don Shula's "invincibles." Dein recalls sitting at the Dolphins game trying to focus on the game's complex rules as they were being explained to him but being utterly distracted by the sheer spectacle and entertainment of it all—the hot dogs, in-stadium promotions, the cheerleaders, the pyrotechnics, "the whole way the NFL projects and markets itself." Well before he was in a position to do anything about it, Dein was struck by how much "English football was in the Dark Ages" by comparison, a ritual of people grimly attending frill-free matches in grim stadiums with extremely grim restrooms (don't get Dein started on the facilities . . .), absent any pre- or post-match entertainment. "That for me was the starting point to say we need to move on," he told me, and then beamed when I said today's Premier League is the NFL of international football.

"Well, that's very kind of you to say."[33]

Of course, certain NFL attributes are hard to replicate, and this brings us to the second half of Stalin's ideological formulation that so aptly describes the league. It isn't just socialism; it's socialism *in one country*. We so take for granted the isolationism American sporting exceptionalism affords our variety of football that we don't often think about how much it shaped and nurtured the NFL's idiosyncratic development.

The league operates within a uniquely closed sporting ecosystem, which grants it a level of control no other league exercises over its sport. It's a bit like Apple ruling over all aspects of its operating system and app store, with the other football (and our other big US sports, to a lesser degree) operating in the more untidy, interconnected PC universe (or Android, if you prefer the mobile analogy).

NFL teams do not need to build out academies to develop younger talent. They benefit instead from the massive investment in the nation's intercollegiate athletic industrial complex. For the better part of the century, the NFL has been able to rely exclusively on college football to develop and source its talent, and college stars have fixated solely on the NFL as their desired next step in life. It's been an entirely closed, vertically integrated labor market, without any of the untidiness introduced by competing sources of talent and alternative destinations for that talent. The more global nature of the labor markets for soccer, baseball, and basketball enrich those sports but weaken any one organization's ability to control all aspects of it.

The NFL's control over its sport, by contrast, is evidenced by its salary cap and other aspects of its collective bargaining agreement and its masterful management of its TV contracts. The league has been able to funnel all incoming talent through the development filter of the college game and maintain its near-airtight system of allocating this talent through the parity-reinforcing draft first instituted by Bert Bell back in the 1930s, and it has been able to do all this for the same reason that Tom Brady and Patrick Mahomes have never suited up in a Team USA uniform: because no one else plays this game.

International football leagues like the English Premier League and Spain's La Liga operate in a dizzyingly chaotic interconnected world of overlapping competitions and jurisdictions. Those leagues have responsibilities to the lower divisions of the game and the grassroots "football pyramid," in addition to figuring out how to scout and develop their next generation of players globally. They also contend with pesky governing bodies and federations regulating and making constant demands of them. Roger Goodell, by contrast—and sticking to our Russian metaphors—is the tsar of all professional American football, though of course he does need to placate his thirty-two team owners.

If Goodell went to London to take over the Premier League, on top of having to mediate between a more diverse set of owners, he'd find himself in a constant jostling of power with the Football Association, which oversees the broader game in the land, including the national teams and its own FA Cup that Premier League clubs compete in; the English Football League, which runs the lower divisions and hosts another separate Cup; and UEFA, Europe's regional governing body for the sport, which has its own rules and regulations (including over financial matters) and puts on the most prestigious tournament England's biggest clubs all strive to compete in. Then, of course there's FIFA, the global governing body, which is always intruding on your calendar by setting "international dates" when you must pause your league play and release your players to go off and represent their countries in international competition. Plus, you are having to compete against other formidable domestic leagues across Europe—in Spain, Italy, Germany, and France—to recruit the world's best players.

And if all that weren't enough, for the past few years the English government has been considering the establishment of a new public regulator for football.[34]

The NFL's socialism has flourished in one country, thanks in part to its hermetically sealed system over which it can assert full control. But flourishing in one country is not enough for a twenty-first-century American mediatic and cultural phenomenon, and so Goodell does want to go to London and beyond, dragging the NFL along with him, even as some of his league owners are also buying into the world's other football to hedge their way onto a global stage.

It's unclear whether the NFL will be more successful in exporting its alluring game or its influential socialistic sports business model. Today's NFL owners pay lip service to their club's "Any Given Sunday" mantra, but do they really believe that parity is an essential ingredient to any sporting venture's success?

How the NFL leaders, and outside investors seeking to ape their success, answer that question will help determine how much of a revolution fans around the world are in for in the coming years. Because in truth, we don't quite yet know what Americans will do when they do have the power to reshape global sport.

3
Away Games

Philadelphia Eagles fans sing "Fly, Eagles Fly," but the truth is their team doesn't always travel well.

The Eagles were scheduled to play the National Football League's first-ever game in Mexico on Sunday, August 11, 1968, a preseason matchup against the Detroit Lions. CBS was set to televise the game, and 70,000 tickets had been sold before Mexican authorities abruptly canceled the game midday Thursday, some 72 hours before kickoff.[1] The Eagles scrambled to host the Lions instead at the University of Pennsylvania's Franklin Field, and a *Philadelphia Inquirer* account of the game played before 12,176 fans noted that it had been "booted out of Mexico City by a threat of riots." The Eagles lost 20–3 and lost their quarterback Norm Snead to a broken leg.[2]

The "threat of riots" in Mexico, meanwhile, had been the political unrest brewing in advance of that nation's Olympic Games, scheduled to take place in October. Mexico's authoritarian, one-party regime was confronting massive pro-democracy student protests determined to counter the image the government wanted to project of itself as an enlightened, efficient, and amiable Olympic host navigating its proud nation toward modernity and First Worldliness. Sport's soft power, it turns out, can be a two-way street. Ten days before the opening ceremony, on October 2, tragedy struck: government security forces gunned down hundreds of protesting students in a bid to silence their movement before Mexico's moment in the global spotlight.

A decade later, on August 5, 1978, the Eagles finally did play the NFL's first-ever preseason game in Mexico (two years after the league had played one in Tokyo), against the New Orleans Saints. The Eagles put in a sloppy performance and lost 14–7.

Their diplomatic performance was even worse. In the lead-up to the game, all Coach Dick Vermeil could talk about was wanting to avoid "Montezuma's revenge." In the days after the game, which was plagued with logistical mishaps, Eagles QB Ron Jaworski penned an article for the *Philadelphia Daily News* that opened: "After two days in Mexico City, I now understand why there are so many revolutions down there. Our game against the Saints was being staged by the government, and if this is how they run a football game I can imagine how they run a country."[3]

Jaworski's undiplomatic dispatch said Mexico City contained some of the "worst slums" he'd ever seen, not to mention some of the worst drivers and laziest airport workers. He was the rare visitor to leave unimpressed with the food, claiming to have lost weight during his visit (8–10 pounds over two days!). He called the experience "one of the worst weekends I've ever had in my life," caused by "one of [then-league commissioner] Pete Rozelle's market missions and we were the guinea pigs who had to carry it out."

As a twelve-year-old kid with little fondness for the Eagles, I was entertained by the fervor with which Mexican TV subsequently vilified Jaworski, who conjured up all the worst tropes of the imperious "ugly American" abroad. Mexican sportscaster Fernando Von Rossum shared the Eagles' office address on the air, and thousands of fans mailed letters complaining about the national affront. But one undiplomatic QB wasn't about to derail Rozelle's "market mission" or constrain the NFL's growing popularity in Mexico.

These were the late seventies, after all. I know the classic period of any sport is when you are about twelve, so call me biased, but come on, there was something especially compelling about that Pittsburgh Steelers dynasty of Mean Joe Greene, he of the Coke-for-jersey exchange, Terry Bradshaw, Franco Harris, Lynn Swann, Jack Lambert, and their rivalry with America's [supposed] Team, the Dallas Cowboys of Staubach, Dorsett, Pearson, and "Too Tall" Jones.

Von Rossum agrees. "That rivalry, coming when it did, was instrumental in growing the popularity of the game in Mexico," he told me in a Zoom interview in August 2024 from his home in Ensenada.

Von Rossum was the Al Michaels of Mexico in those years, the silky, knowledgeable chronicler of the NFL on Mexican TV, who was awarded the NFL's coveted Ralph Hay Pioneer Award at the league's Hall of Fame induction ceremony in Canton in the summer of 2024. The award has only been presented to ten other individuals since 1972, for "significant innovative contributions to professional football." In presenting Von Rossum with the award, Hall of Fame President Jim Porter said: "he took a game that was totally foreign to most of his television audience and helped build the National Football League's presence in Mexico to a point that international games became part of the country's sports landscape."[4]

Von Rossum was a chemical engineer when he started calling games for a Monterrey station in the mid-1960s. He'd acquired a love and deep knowledge of the sport on visits to relatives in San Antonio, where he remembers being transfixed as a teenager by the NBC broadcast of the "greatest game ever played," the 1958 Championship game between the Colts of Johnny Unitas and the Giants of Frank Gifford that is often cited as the moment football overtook baseball at the pinnacle of US sports. Separately, he gained an appreciation for the masterful cadence of game announcing perfected by the likes of Jack Buck, whom Von Rossum could listen to calling baseball games on those evenings when his radio in Monterrey managed to pick up the distant AM signal emanating from KMOX-St. Louis.

What Von Rossum and his fellow Mexican announcers over the years pulled off was impressive, locked in a cramped studio talking over the audio that came with the US broadcast feed, seeking to convey a sense of immediacy and drama to these games being played in another country, all the while establishing a new language for the sport (so that, for instance, quarterbacks became *mariscales de campo*).

I pressed Von Rossum on what made that Steeler-Cowboys rivalry so riveting, as if seeking validation for my childhood. "Just think about those characters," he said, "from Terry Bradshaw, Franco Harris, and Mean Joe Greene to Jack Lambert, the linebacker whose aura was only magnified by his habit of taking his teeth out. And on the other side you had the Cowboys captained by their Navy vet Roger Staubach and the Doomsday defense." Von Rossum said the very first Monterrey-based channel to televise the NFL in

Mexico exclusively broadcast Cowboys games, so the Cowboys were already Mexico's team before they were christened "America's team" in 1978 by NFL Films producer Bob Ryan.[5]

By the mid-1970s, Mexico's state-owned Channel 13 network and the private Televisa behemoth had deals to broadcast NFL games. Channel 13 aired National Conference games, including the Cowboys; Von Rossum's Televisa had rights to the AFC and its ascendant Steelers. "So, we had this added dynamic of competing networks essentially championing and representing the two dynasties they aired most Sundays," Von Rossum said. (As a kid, I didn't appreciate how fortunate we were to be free of any local broadcasting restrictions—the Mexican networks could pick whatever games they felt were best.)

Sports rivalries can be gripping purely on their athletic merit, but the truly epic ones acquire added resonance and heft when they also represent a clash of competing worldviews, cultures, or geographies. Think Barcelona versus Real Madrid, or those US versus USSR Olympic clashes.

Steelers versus Cowboys was an NFL Classic versus New NFL, the league's 1960s prodigy child born to fend off competition from Lamar Hunt and his American Football League. This was a Depression-era franchise versus the contemporary and corporate glitz of the sport's TV era. This was Rust Belt versus Sun Belt; blue collar versus the moneyed banking and oil tycoons that would literally turn Dallas into a gripping primetime soap opera. The Cowboys unveiled their cheerleaders wearing iconic white go-go boots and hot pants back in 1972; the Steelers still don't have any (and never will). The Cowboys wear stars on their helmets; the Steelers appropriated the "Steelmark" logo of the industry they represent but only wear it on one side of their helmets, as if they cannot afford it on both.

Von Rossum remembers a day when he took a cab in Mexico City to a dinner after a rare Steeler loss in 1978, and being worried by how upset his driver seemed. When Von Rossum asked him if he was OK, the cab driver said no, not really, he was very upset because his team had lost. He then unzipped his jacket to show off a Steeler shirt. "I remember that day well, as it hit me that this esoteric thing we had been doing in a closet was having an impact, this sport was really penetrating and spreading among our Mexican audience."

Von Rossum estimates that by 1980, some 80 to 90 percent of all NFL followers in Mexico were either Steeler or Cowboy fans, with smaller factions of Dolphins and Raiders aficionados sprinkled about (somehow, one of my best friends in middle school in Chihuahua had fallen hard for the Buffalo Bills, though none of us could figure out why).

Later years would bring droves of 49ers, Packers, and Patriots fans, each dominant team in its moment onboarding a new generation onto their bandwagon, luring them in with their winning ways, setting them up for the long-term trials and tribulations of true fandom—the lean years. The Cowboys reportedly had about 15 million followers in Mexico in 2023 (out of some 42 million NFL fans in the country, according to the league), but the fact that the team hasn't won a Super Bowl in three decades would explain why its fan base skews older.[6]

Jason Garrett, the former Cowboys player and coach, is appreciative of the NFL's international forays: "Some of the best football experiences I had, looking back on them, and having little to do with what happened on the field," he told me in an interview.[7] Garrett recalls attending bullfights in Monterrey, with the Kansas City Chiefs during a week when they met down there for a preseason matchup, and the bonding that a trip to Tokyo accomplished for the team. In Mexico City, for a sloppy game the Cowboys lost 0–6 to the Houston Oilers in 1994, some on the Cowboys coaching staff advised players to guard against supposedly unclean water in their five-star hotel entering their "orifices" while showering. All part of the cultural experience. That preseason game, in which Garrett came on near the end as the third-string quarterback to complete six of six passes, still boasts the record attendance at any NFL game ever—112,376 fans.[8]

"What I remember most is fans having this amazing response to the kicking game," Garrett told me, "When the ball was kicked off, a roar; extra points, a roar; punts would go up in the air, and the crowd went wild." Crowds and kickers alike might have delighted in the fact that the ball would travel more in Mexico City, given the altitude.

Garrett started his playing career with the Ottawa Rough Riders of the now-defunct World League of American Football, and after playing for the Cowboys and New York Giants, his coaching career culminated with him being the head coach of America's team—or is it Mexico's team?—for a decade. And now he is working for the network that is heavily invested in bringing English football to the United States while also expanding the reach and cultural impact of its prime asset—Sunday Night Football. Garrett has experienced the globalization of football from every vantage point.

"It's been a decades-long endeavor by the NFL to grow this game, which is different than basketball, which already has such an international presence. This truly is America's game."

But Garrett appreciates that the league and more entrepreneurial club owners are eager to share his game with the world; he noted how fans overseas respond not just by cheering on the teams playing in international games, but celebrate the NFL as a whole:

> I remember being in London for one of our international games and being struck not only by the fact that there were a ton of Cowboy fans, and a ton of Jacksonville Jaguar fans, but also a ton of other football fans, a lot of people with Patriots jerseys, Steelers jerseys, Texans jerseys, fans just repping their favorite teams and players. People love American football, and so it's a really good thing for us to keep pushing and trying to make this a worldwide game.

You can witness the flip side of what Garrett is describing at summer exhibition games between European football clubs in the United States, where American fans show up wearing jerseys of their favorite teams regardless of who's playing, rivals' jerseys even, that you'd be well-advised not to wear to the same match across the ocean. Each football has a fifth column in the other's home, and these determined fans' appreciation for a foreign sport is often inextricably bound to an impassioned cultural affinity with the other sport's home country.

I once sat next to a Denver Broncos fan up from Southampton at an NFL game at London's Wembley Stadium. The Broncos were not playing, but they were all he wanted to discuss with me, assuming that as an American I would be a font of endless, nuanced knowledge and analysis about every Bronco roster move. I disappointed him with my lack of Broncos intel and pivoted to ask him what he made of his hometown club's prospects of avoiding relegation from the Premier League that season and what the atmosphere was like at St.

Mary's Stadium. He made it clear he had zero interest in discussing the English variety of football, which he had clearly opted out of for this exotic import.

As Ubiratan Leal, an ESPN Brasil Major League Baseball and soccer analyst, told me in advance of the NFL's game in São Paulo in September of 2024, younger Brazilians are more connected to the United States than their elders, and following the NFL is a clear way to signal one's affinity with the States and one's "cosmopolitanism."

Or take Roger Bennett, the perceptive *Men in Blazers* podcaster and transatlantic interlocutor for football. A Liverpudlian by birth, Bennett wrote in his *(Re)Born in the USA* memoir that one of his earliest beliefs was of being "an American trapped in an Englishman's body."[9] As a teenager, Bennett worshipped all things American, particularly all things Chicagoan; a geographic choice advanced by family lore, friendship with an exchange student, a generation of high school films set in Chicagoland, and, of course, the Bears of Mike Ditka, Walter Payton, and William "the refrigerator" Perry. Bennett, an avid Everton fan in his local football, writes of falling in love with the exotic American football thanks to a weekly NFL highlight show launched in 1982 by Channel 4, a "maverick start-up network."[10] If the Cowboys and Steelers still loom large in Mexico given when the league started appearing on TV in that country, it's no coincidence that the Bears still have a disproportionate following in Britain, given when Brits started tuning in.

The NFL's immense popularity in Mexico can be ascribed to proximity and to our two neighboring nations' overlapping, shared cultures. American football was first brought back to the Universidad Nacional Autónoma de Mexico by a couple of Notre Dame grads eager for their UNAM's Pumas to play in blue and gold (which they do, to this day, in both footballs) as far back as the 1920s. The NFL's popularity then spread across Mexico in the 1970s thanks to television, long before the NFL had much of an international strategy. The top spectator sport in the United States was always going to have a spillover fanbase in Mexico.

But the scale and profitability of that fanbase, coupled with the success of the NFL's games in London over time, have encouraged the league to think globally and grow the game beyond America's shores. The NFL has been more successful than any other sports venture anywhere at monetizing its fans, but it has been slower than many other sports at crossing borders to gain adherents. Unlike such other American cultural blockbusters as a Marvel movie or a Taylor Swift concert, the Super Bowl is still watched by far more people within the United States than outside it.

Commissioner Roger Goodell is focused on changing that, focused on turning the NFL into a global game, and he is empowering some of the bolder franchises to do some of this international proselytizing on their own. The league, which traditionally hasn't allowed individual teams to market themselves beyond their hometowns, created a Global Markets Program that enables teams to pursue marketing deals in specified overseas markets. So, for instance, the Los Angeles Rams cannot buy a billboard promoting themselves in Las Vegas, or to make a deal with a Vegas pizzeria to be the "official pizza of the Rams," but they can now do either of these things in Mexico City under their league-awarded Global Market rights for that country. Teams can choose what countries they want to treat as an extension of their home market. The league initially hoped to divvy up the world with no more than two or three countries claiming a particular country, but their tidy plan had to give way to the reality of many clubs wanting access to the Mexican market (you can now go to a number of Steeler-themed KFCs in Mexico City); the Bears, naturally, were eager to claim the UK.[11]

Television, of course, remains the main gateway to overseas fans, and to expand the game's reach to more and more foreign screens, Goodell is focused on bringing NFL games to more countries, viewing these overseas games (or "market missions" as the Eagles' Jaworski called his memorable Mexican weekend) as the most effective trailer possible for all subsequent attractions. All NFL club owners pay lip service to this global aspiration, but plenty have balked at sacrificing one of their precious few home games to go proselytize overseas for the league. For years it tended to be the less storied franchises going through rough patches or struggling to sell out their stadiums that were most willing to sign up for international duty.

In 2021, Goodell managed to expand the long-established sixteen-game season to a seventeen-game regular season, to free up teams for more international duty. In its 2024 season, the NFL played its first-ever game in

South America, in São Paulo, plus three games in London and one in Munich (it skipped Mexico as the Estadio Azteca in Mexico City was being refurbished for the men's 2026 FIFA World Cup). In 2025, the number of international games ticked up to seven, including my Steelers facing off against the Minnesota Vikings in the first regular season game ever played in Dublin (Steelers owner Dan Rooney had been President Obama's ambassador there). The Chiefs played the Chargers in the second annual São Paulo game, and in addition to the customary three games in London, the league also played its first game ever in Berlin's historic Olympic Stadium and in one of the other football's most sacred grounds, Real Madrid's Santiago Bernabeu Stadium, which to those of us of a certain age feels a bit as if a visiting Protestant congregation took over St. Peter's Basilica in Vatican City for the day. And Melbourne, Australia, has been announced as an NFL debutante in 2026. Goodell is pushing for an eighteen-game regular season, featuring sixteen international matchups each year, and he has refused to rule out the possibility of a Super Bowl being played overseas in the foreseeable future.[12]

It's worth noting that the English Premier League, the most globalized domestic sporting league anywhere, lacks such an ambitiously peripatetic plan. Years ago, Richard Scudamore, the league's chief executive then, floated the idea of a "39th game" (the 20-team league currently is set up where each team plays each other twice in a season, at home and away) to be played abroad, but the fans wouldn't have it—never mind how globalized the league is.[13] The Football Supporters' Federation, a nonprofit representing British fans, mobilized against what they termed "the outrageous desecration of our national game." To this day, fans of clubs like Manchester United and Liverpool in the United States or in East Asia only get to see their teams in person on one of their frequent preseason summer tours or by traveling to the source.

To further highlight the NFL's internationalization, Goodell introduced a novelty for the 2024 season—a primetime, Friday night international game on opening weekend, sandwiched between what has become the traditional opening game hosted on Thursday night by the defending Super Bowl champion and the league's first Sunday slate of games. A federal law bars the league (in exchange for permission to negotiate their TV rights as a collective without running afoul of antitrust law) from playing on Fridays or Saturdays from mid-September through early December to protect high school and collegiate football attendance,[14] but the NFL scheduling masters saw an opening to squeeze this one in before that blackout period and extend its opening weekend.

The first of these Friday night international games was awarded to the massive metropolis of São Paulo, Brazil, much to the delight of the city's tourism authorities who'd been lobbying the league to come down. And the NFL picked a marquee matchup for the occasion: the Philadelphia Eagles against the Green Bay Packers.

Brazil has long loomed large at the NFL's Park Avenue HQ in New York City. A massive, sports-mad country with a population of more than 210 million and an expanding middle class eager to absorb American culture, Brazil already is home to an estimated 40 million self-professed NFL fans. The game has been on ESPN Brasil since 1991, and in more recent years there has been an explosion of Portuguese-language websites, publications, and social media influencers devoted to following the league.[15]

Brazil, in other words, looks to the NFL very much like its next Mexico.

If Mexico was claimed early by the Steelers and Cowboys, the Packers have vied with the New England Patriots to be the most popular team in Brazil.[16] The Patriots might be slipping, though, with the end of the prolonged Tom Brady-Bill Belichick dominance and of the Tom Brady-Gisele Bündchen marriage.

As for Green Bay, its appeal in Brazil tracks why it is many Americans' second team. The Packers are one of the NFL's more storied franchises, tracing its history back to 1919, when its founder Curly Lambeau convinced his meat-packing employer (the Indian Packing Company) to pay for the team's jerseys. Representing the NFL's smallest market (and doing so competitively, as we saw in Chapter 2, thanks to the league's "Socialism in One Country"), the Packers are a throwback to the types of communities that gave birth to professional American football—Canton, Decatur, Muncie, Akron, and so on. Even back in the 1960s, when the Vince Lombardi-led Packers won five titles, the team was already seen as the league's throwback, nostalgia franchise, championing bygone values and tradition in an era of fast-changing mores. As David Maraniss described it in his biography of Vince Lombardi, *When Pride Still*

Mattered: "Green Bay was susceptible to appeals from the past, especially from Lambeau. It was an inward-looking town whose culture was rooted in the rituals of church, family, neighborhood tavern and the Green Bay Packers."[17]

For today's Brazilian fans, another attraction is the fact that the Packers wear Brazil's national colors.

Then there's the team's unique ownership structure. Mark Murphy, the president and CEO of the Packers who will retire in the summer of 2025, said before the trip down to Brazil that he assumed the team owes much of its popularity there to "our structure, you know that we're owned by the community, that we don't have a wealthy owner," but rather 550,000 shareholders. "Our main goal, number one goal," he continued, recording one of our Great Game Lab *Set Piece* conversations, "is to win championships, and number two is to make sure we stay in Green Bay."[18]

Murphy applauded the league's aim of making the game a "global property," and said the push wasn't without opportunities for personal growth for him, as well as his players. He said everyone involved with the team had a fantastic experience when the Packers played in London in 2022. And he was looking forward to going to São Paulo: "I have never been to South America, and I'm a 69-year-old man."

As for his younger players, many of them arrived at training camp without a passport, well before it was clear which of them would survive the roster cuts to ultimately be on that eleven-hour flight to São Paulo. Murphy ensured that all players going through training camp would end up leaving it with a passport, regardless of whether they made the team.

Murphy has also been impressed by the flip side of sporting globalization—the other football's inroads into the US market. He marveled at the sellout crowd of 78,128 that turned out in Green Bay to watch an exhibition game between Manchester City and Bayern Munich in the summer of 2022, adding that "it seemed a little odd seeing soccer played inside Lambeau Field, but people loved it."[19] Murphy was also surprised to discover how excited his own players were for that game, and how much they knew about the visiting football clubs and their players.

As for the Philadelphia Eagles, they still don't travel well.

In advance of the team's trip to São Paulo, Philadelphia's cornerback Darius Slay said on his podcast that he was looking forward to the start of a new season, "but, man, I do not want to go to Brazil," adding that he didn't understand why the NFL would "want to send us somewhere with a crime rate this high." Never mind that São Paulo's murder rate was considerably lower than Philadelphia's, Slay and other players were reacting to cautionary league instructions to avoid leaving their hotels unaccompanied.[20]

Several Brazilian reporters raised these comments at an Eagles press conference held at São Paulo's Neo Química Stadium that I attended on the eve of the Friday night game. Coach Nick Sirianni and his players who spoke deployed a charm offensive, expressing their gratitude for being able to represent their sport abroad and for the warm embrace of Brazilian fans. Siriani also talked about the significance of NFL players getting a rare opportunity to play before the "Friday night lights," as they once did in high school.

Quarterback Jalen Hurts expressed amazement that he, "a kid from East Houston," could now serve as an ambassador for his sport. Running back Saquon Barkley, the team's big offseason signing from the rival New York Giants, ingratiated himself with the hosts by unveiling a Brazil national team soccer jersey with his name and the number 10 on it.

But the player who acknowledged some of their teammates' smears against Brazil, and did the most damage control around them, was Tanner McKee, the team's third-string quarterback, who asked if he could speak directly in Portuguese, much to the surprised delight of the assembled reporters. People "are a little afraid of things they don't know," McKee said. "We're in a country where many of them haven't been, they don't speak the language, they don't know anything about Brazil."

McKee, who played at Stanford, had spent two years in Curitiba, Brazil, as a Mormon missionary. He assured us that most of his teammates had been very excited about the prospect of traveling to Brazil, wanted to learn more about the local culture, and were enjoying the trip. Unfortunately for the NFL's PR folks, McKee would spend the actual game on the bench, behind Hurts, but he still should have won an MVP award from Roger Goodell for his media appearance.

The NFL can't be blamed for the trope of the "ugly American" overseas, which has more to do with spoilt American tourists wanting everything to be just as it is back home than it has to do with young players who often come from underprivileged backgrounds suddenly being asked to engage in globe-trotting sports diplomacy. But the league's dire warnings to players to avoid engaging with their surroundings when traveling to Brazil (or Mexico in other years), however prudent from a risk-mitigation standpoint, run the risk of insulting the very fans being wooed with these international games.

I had flown down to São Paulo to witness the NFL's historic first game ever in South America and purposefully stayed with a contingent of traveling Packers fans at the Meliá Hotel near the border of the trendy Itaim Bibi and Jardim Europa neighborhoods. The hotel is surrounded by smart bistros (including the festive Vaca Vieja, or "Old Cow" steak place, which traveling Packers fans would colonize by week's end) and equally smart apartment buildings. Just a few blocks away, across the Avenida 9 de Julho (which I was told celebrates a failed attempt by the state of São Paulo to secede from Brazil in the 1930s), the high-rises gave way to a leafy neighborhood of mansions that you might need to be on a big NFL contract to afford. The hotel staff wore Packer jerseys and had redecorated the place; the elevator doors featured life-sized Packer stars for the occasion.

You could fit 213 Green Bays into the massive sprawl of São Paulo, a relatively young, gritty metropolis built on the wealth of nineteenth-century coffee trading and twentieth-century industrialization. São Paulo prides itself on its reputation for being a serious, unglamorous, hardworking place, content to leave all the stereotypes foreigners might associate with Brazil—think hedonistic samba-dancing beach culture—to Rio de Janeiro, its great rival, and that city's so-called Carioca residents. As Glen Goodman, an ASU colleague who is a historian of Brazil, put it to me: "*Paulistas* love to go to Rio as much as foreigners do, and they also admire its spectacular setting and beauty, but they certainly don't do so with a chip on their shoulder. On the contrary, they tend to visit Rio with an attitude of 'yeah, we paid for all this.'"

Like most great cities throughout the American hemisphere, São Paulo is a city of immigrants—Poles, Germans, Italians, Greeks, Portuguese, and Russians, blended in with waves of arrivals from the countryside and a massive influx of Japanese immigrants in the 1920s and 1930s that has bequeathed São Paulo with the largest ethnic Japanese community outside of Japan. This Japanese community is the nation's hub for another imported sport in Brazil—baseball. American expats brought baseball to Brazil around the same time that British expats brought their football to Brazil in the late nineteenth century, but it was only later in the twentieth century that the game acquired a broader popularity, thanks to the large Japanese-Brazilian community.

As for the competing footballs' migration stories, São Paulo's impressive Museu do Futebol offers plenty of reminders that NFL Commissioner Roger Goodell isn't the first football evangelist from abroad who tried to get Brazilians to become passionate about a game initially perceived to be a foreign elite affectation. The museum, which engagingly chronicles the development and importance of the world's football in Brazilian life, and Brazil's fabled achievements at FIFA's World Cups, is carved into the city's old art deco masterpiece of a stadium, the Pacaembu. Its main entrance's address—on Charles Miller Square—provides a nod to football's origins as an import.

No country on earth is more identified with the world's football than Brazil is (probably no country has been so thoroughly branded by any one sport), but that passionate relationship began only in 1894, thanks to the son of an expat Scottish railway engineer in São Paulo. That's the year young Charles Miller returned to Brazil from his boarding school in Southampton clutching a ball and the rules of the sport that was then taking the British Isles by storm.

Miller organized the first league in Brazil out of the São Paulo Athletic Club, and the Museu do Futebol has a room full of images depicting how posh the sport remained for its first couple of decades in Brazil. People dressed for games as they might for the opera, and match reports included breathless accounts of who among the elites had been spotted in the crowd. Hard to believe that this same game, within a few decades, would come to be seen as the proletarian *jogo bonito* of Pelé, Jairzinho, Carlos Alberto, and their teammates, whose triumphs advanced a novel multiracial national identity and social cohesion while transfixing global audiences.

I had been invited to participate in a museum forum on the relationship between our hemisphere's two footballs that was co-hosted by the US

Consulate three days before the NFL game. The other speaker was Cris Kajiwara, the president of the Brazilian Confederation of American Football. She had recently returned from the thirty-two-nation Flag Football World Championship in Finland, bullish about the sport's growth, especially now that it is slated to become an Olympic sport. The United States won both the men's and women's tournaments, beating out Mexico in the women's final. Brazil's women were knocked out in the Group of sixteen stage by Austria in a close 34–32 contest.

Kajiwara, who grew up in São Paulo's Japanese community, told a funny story about how she first came to be involved with American football in the land of the other football. On social media, she started following Corinthians, one of the city's massive clubs; but inadvertently, she had followed the club's American football feed, instead of its soccer one. Like Real Madrid or Barcelona in Spain and other clubs around the world, Corinthians is owned by thousands of members and fields teams in more than twenty sports, including all the footballs, basketball, handball, swimming, boxing, and something intriguingly called "beach tennis" which I need to check out.

Kajiwara was immediately hooked by what she saw on the feed she'd mistakenly started following. Among other things, she appreciated how welcoming flag football was to all genders, unlike the incumbent, traditionally male *futebol*. Our moderator, Marilia Bonas, the museum's technical director, mentioned that the museum has recently refurbished its exhibits to show the evolution of women's soccer, which is growing rapidly in Brazil despite some of that residual cultural resistance. She said it would be hard to overstate the influence of the United States in setting an earlier example for gender equity, both in soccer and in women's sports more broadly: "I know from my own personal experience, that my initial ideas about girls playing the game came from American culture, from watching TV programs and movies where it was happening before here."

I hadn't expected gender inclusivity to be among the NFL's pitches on its Brazilian mission, but then I hadn't expected the league to be such an avid promoter of 5-on-5 flag football. On the day after the forum at the Museu de Futebol, I attended a Philadelphia Eagles community event to which they had invited kids from across the country for flag football drills and scrimmages in

Eagles t-shirts, encouraged on by Eagles mascots and cheerleaders, the team's inescapable "Fly Eagles Fly" anthem, and the US ambassador to Brazil.

There I met Pierre Trochet, the president of the International Federation of American Football, organizer of the recently held World Championships in Finland. The fun fact I picked up was that the IFAF is not based somewhere in Ohio or Pennsylvania, as you might expect, but in France. "So, you're like the Gianni Infantino of American football?" I asked him, referring to the all-powerful head of FIFA, to which he laughed and responded, "Well maybe, but with a lot fewer resources."

IFAF is the Olympic-recognized governing body for flag football, which will be played for the first time at the Los Angeles 2028 Summer Games. Trochet's priority these days is ensuring that it isn't a one-off to humor that Olympic host's eccentricities, but rather a new Olympic mainstay. "We have some 20 million people playing flag football in 100 countries," he told me. "In Mexico alone, 100,000 kids pick up the game each year."

The NFL is itself organizing flag leagues around the world and featured Mexican player Diana Flores in its marquee commercial leading into halftime during the 2023 Super Bowl (the league again used this slot to promote its international reach during the Super Bowl the following year, when it highlighted its talent scouting and development program in Africa). Promoting the five-on-five flag version of its game helps the league overcome three obstacles to rapid global expansion at the participation level: there aren't the same brain injury concerns at play; the game is gender inclusive; and the prohibitive cost barrier to entry for the equipment-heavy full-scale tackle version of the game is drastically lowered.

The kids at the Eagles event seemed to be having a blast, and the gender breakdown was close to 50-50. I asked Fernando Ferreira, a coach from one of Corinthians' youth clubs who was running drills, whether it is hard to convince kids in the land of *futebol* to give American football a try. "It can be, but it is very easy to get them to play a second time," he told me. Plenty of kids love both footballs, he added, but for some who aren't tuned into the top sport for whatever reason, having another option, "a game they can identify with and find inspiration in, can be a gift."

It's about finding your people, I suppose, or finding a different way to connect with people around you. I asked a gaggle of boys waiting their turn to do a diving catch whether they liked futebol too. The verdict was 4-to-2, with the four immediately squabbling over which team they rooted for (Corinthians! No, Palmeiras! Santos!) and the other two sort of rolling their eyes and staying on message: "We're Eagles fans!"

Flag football was also a star attraction at the "NFL Experience" across town, at Parque Villa-Lobos, a veritable theme park set up by the league throughout the week, as it does in Super Bowl cities. Fans there could admire the Vince Lombardi trophy, try their luck at field goals, long snaps, precise throws, and some flag football, as well as watch some of the other games throughout the weekend on a massive screen. Fans milling about wore jerseys of just about every NFL franchise, though the New England Patriots and Miami Dolphins, two of the teams that have been awarded Brazil as global markets, were doing their best to gain converts with their own booths, activities, and giveaways. My favorite convergence-of-the-footballs indicator was the Panini hut, where you could create a trading card of yourself holding a football and get a free album and cards. Panini albums have long been a staple of World Cup culture for kids the world over, and I had no idea the Italian company was now trafficking cards in the American variant of the game.

Victor Romanelli, a Steelers-loving English teacher standing in line for his close-up with the Lombardi trophy, told me he first connected with the Pittsburgh team as a big Wiz Khalifa fan who wondered a dozen years ago what the rapper's "Black and Yellow" song was about. That's all it took.[21]

I was more surprised to see a couple wearing Arizona Cardinals jerseys (we don't see many of those even in Arizona) who explained they'd picked the team after their favorite vacation ever, to the Grand Canyon. "Larry Fitzgerald is my favorite athlete of all time, along with Neymar," Marisa told me.

At the game itself, what struck me the most were the choppers—the endless progression of helicopters coming and going from the edge of the parking lot at Neo Química Arena well before kickoff. The whirring sounds and sights of the progression of choppers touching down and immediately lifting off to make way for the next hovering arrival suggested a military base in a combat zone, rather than a sporting event. Sure, a handful of big shots at concerts and big sporting events anywhere in the world might arrive by helicopter, but this was something else. I stood in the parking lot, as the sun was setting, mesmerized, then anxious, at the sight. Who was coordinating all that traffic? Aren't helicopters deadly dangerous, or is it just a freak coincidence that I can think of about a half-dozen celebrities who've died in helicopter crashes in recent years, including Kobe, of course, and the owner of Leicester's football club in his own stadium's parking lot.

Small things you notice in passing can convey big truths about a place. This chopper traffic spoke volumes about the fact that there are quite a few people with a lot of money in this massive metropolis. And second, at the risk of sounding like a Philadelphia Eagle, this chopper traffic also testified to the fact that São Paulo's public infrastructure—in this case the road to the stadium—leaves a lot to be desired.

I went to the stadium from the Meliá on a bus with the traveling Packers fans, and it took us two-and-a-half hours to crawl the 17 miles. Once there, we were ushered to a tailgate party featuring plenty of caipirinhas, *batucada* percussionists, and scantily clad samba dancers. Roger Goodell might have chosen to bring the game to São Paulo, but our package tour operator was determined to give these Midwestern visitors the full Rio experience—a taste of what they expected from Brazil.

One of the things about my childhood that I don't have reason to bring up often is that my parents sent me to a camp in Rhinelander, Wisconsin, for three summers so that I could get to know my other country and spend time among my fellow Americans, speaking their language and learning their ways—which back then (much to my frustration) included ignoring soccer. Camp Algonquin was my mother's creative, some historians might say extreme, reaction to a previous summer's frustration at coming to pick me and my brother up at a camp in New Mexico (within driving range of Chihuahua) only to discover that we had befriended and hung out all summer with the other Mexican kids. This defeated the whole purpose of the adventure, in her mind, and so I was off to northern Wisconsin the next summer, to a camp where kids from anywhere south of Chicago were rare and exotic.

My Wisconsin memories and vague sense of the state's geography got more of a workout in Brazil than they've had in a long time as I sought to bond with all the friendly cheeseheads I met on the bus to the stadium and at the previous night's NFL season opener watch/samba dancing party at a steak hacienda. The guy seated next to me as we crawled our way to the stadium told me he didn't live in Green Bay, "or really that close," as he lived in Appleton, some 30 miles away. I had to laugh at that last bit, given we were then 5,380 miles away from Lambeau Field. He then laughed too and shook his head, as if reminding himself how nuts this all was.

More than one person I talked to reminisced fondly about how the Packers for more than half a century (until 1994) would play several games each year in Milwaukee, even as they insisted that there is nothing quite like attending a game at Lambeau, which is often ranked as the league's best gameday experience. I vaguely remember being confused by this as a kid, that some Packer home games would be broadcast from Milwaukee's Municipal Stadium. There must have been a recognition in those years that perhaps Green Bay, 120 miles up the road from Milwaukee, was indeed too small to claim an NFL team all for itself. Yet by the mid-1990s, as the sport became primarily a television production with its riches tied to that medium, the smaller, nostalgia-soaked community of Green Bay became one of the stars of the production. Indeed, after several renovations, Lambeau Field, the oldest continually operating NFL stadium, is now the league's second largest, with a capacity of 81,441, or almost 80 percent of the city's population. The spring after their Brazil adventure, Lambeau and the Packers would host the three-day extravaganza that is the NFL draft, and the tens of thousands of visitors it attracts.

The sold-out Neo Química Arena, the futuristic stadium built for the 2014 men's World Cup that is home to Corinthians (the soccer powerhouse, not its American football team Cris Kajiwara started following by mistake), cannot accommodate 80 percent of São Paulo's 20-million-plus population; it comfortably seats about 50,000. The atmosphere was electric as it prepared to play the role of Eagles' home ground—the NFL still designates a home and away team for these international games, so all the videos and announcements within the stadium presupposed we were sitting in a Portuguese-speaking Philadelphia, and both end zones proclaimed this was Eagles territory.

"Tickets were harder to come by than tickets for Taylor Swift last fall," ESPN's Ubiratan Leal had told me the day before. "But that's partly because she played three consecutive nights in São Paulo, and the NFL only played once."

Much like at the NFL Experience across town, and as Jason Garrett recalled from the international games he had played in, fans came wearing a veritable kaleidoscope of NFL apparel. About half of what I saw represented the two teams on the field, with the other half representing the rest of the league. Looking back from my seat at the rows immediately behind me, I spotted Seahawks, Raiders, Steelers, Chiefs, 49ers, Buccaneers, Dolphins, and Patriots shirts or hats.

I sat between a couple of Packers fans from Wisconsin who now live in Florida who "wouldn't have missed this for anything" and Jason, an intense, solo-traveling Eagles fan from Philly in his thirties who yelled and screamed obscenities at Packers fans and officials as if this was mid-December and a playoff spot was on the line. He did so with performative gusto, much to the delight of nearby Brazilian fans seeing a native Eagles fan in the wild. During commercial breaks, Jason switched off and became just another amiable American traveler overseas, trading sightseeing tips with the Packer couple before again acquiring his Philly gameday persona when play resumed.

Also nearby, I met a Packers fan who'd come up from Paraguay to watch the game, explaining he acquired a love for the NFL and for the Packers years ago while studying in the United States I heard a similar story from Hugo Monteiro and his wife Isabella, young Eagles fans living in São Paulo who'd picked up an allegiance for the team as graduate students at Temple University. When I asked them if they were fans of the other football too, they shook their heads and chuckled at the ridiculousness of my question. "Of course," Hugo said, "but that's the game of our hearts; this is the game we appreciate with our heads."

The game was on ESPN 2 in Brazil, as ESPN 1 is solely reserved for the earlier imported football, even for reruns of highlight/discussion shows. Unfortunately for the NFL, their first-ever game in Brazil had to compete with the national soccer team's World Cup qualifying match against Ecuador in Curitiba, televised on the country's largest broadcast network.

All in all, it's fair to say that Charles Miller, the boarding school graduate who brought the original *futebol* to Brazil, would have been impressed by the NFL's campaign to win over Brazilian hearts, minds, and eyeballs for its spectacle. Prior to the game, Commissioner Goodell and US ambassador Elizabeth Bagley saluted the bicentennial of US-Brazilian diplomatic relations as two massive, half-field-sized American and Brazilian flags were unfurled side by side. Then, after the singing of the American anthem, pop star Luísa Sonza offered a soulful, acoustic rendition of Brazil's national anthem that would be one of the game's highlights for fans. The gymnast Rebeca Andrade, who'd won four medals at the Paris Olympics the previous month, and three other Brazilian Olympians were also saluted in the pre-game festivities.

The game itself was a high-scoring and entertaining affair, featuring a mix of spectacular plays and opening day jitters. The Eagles turned the ball over on their first two drives, but the Packers failed to capitalize on those early opportunities with touchdowns, keeping the Eagles in the game, which then turned into a shootout with alternating momentum swings that ended in a 34–29 Eagles win. The field was slippery, raising questions among those watching back at home (though not really among the players and teams themselves) about whether the Brazilians and NFL had botched the turf issue. Normally, the NFL would love to have LeBron James call attention to its overseas games, but maybe not with his curt "Man this field sucks!!!" tweet.

Saquon Barkley was the standout player on the night, scoring three TDs and running for more than 100 yards on his debut as an Eagle. Clearly, waving the Brazilian national team's soccer jersey at the press conference had proven good karma for him going into the game and into a season in which he'd continue to excel (spoiler alert: Barkley would go on to set a new NFL record of 2,504 rushing yards in a season, including playoffs, and would set it on his 28th birthday, during the Eagles' win over the Kansas City Chiefs in Super Bowl LIX).[22] Green Bay quarterback Jordan Love's memories of the night might be less warm and fuzzy, as he left the game with a sprained medial collateral ligament in his left knee, an injury he sustained on the penultimate play of the game that would keep him out for the next two games.

Regardless of the loss and the uncertainty over the severity of Love's injury, most traveling Packers fans I debriefed on the long drive back to the hotel and over breakfast the next morning remained giddy about the overall experience. They were flabbergasted to have found so many impassioned Brazilian cheeseheads, who seemed to get what makes their club so distinctive. David Wallschleager, who started following the Packers on the radio and graduated from high school one year before the iconic 1967 "Ice Bowl" championship game, kept shaking his head, telling me what a kick out of this "whole scene" his dad would have gotten. It was his dad who started taking him to games, and Wallschleager still recalls how irate he was when they started charging $3 for tickets. He said he was also extremely impressed with what he saw of São Paulo and is fully onboard with Roger Goodell's plans for global expansion: "This was good for this city, this country, and our team. I can't wait to see where we go next."

When I had told them I was going to Brazil to witness the NFL's first game in South America, several friends of mine back home had scoffed at the NFL's foolish hubris in targeting such a soccer-mad market. But I wouldn't be so quick to dismiss the league's ambition, or to bet against its marketing genius. American football already has a considerable beachhead in Brazil, and it is a massive enough market to accommodate interest in two footballs. The NFL doesn't need to come close to the other football's popularity to be an enormous success in Brazil, much like soccer doesn't need to approach NFL levels of popularity to be a huge success in the United States.

And let's bear in mind that *futebol* itself is a relatively recent import to Brazilian shores, not some indigenous pursuit. The Corinthians team whose home the Eagles borrowed to host the Packers was founded in 1910 and named after the visiting Corinthians from England, a formidable club back then that traveled the world promoting fair play, sportsmanship, and amateurism. The Corinthian-Casuals still play in the lower divisions of regional English football and occasionally get flown to Brazil by their massive Brazilian offspring for exhibition games.

So, you never know. Maybe next century another sport will try to make inroads in Brazil playing in a borrowed stadium that normally hosts the São Paulo Packers, who will be seen as a hyper-local institution playing an inherently Brazilian game.

4

Mother England's Conundrum

Homegrown vs. #1

One of the more confusing moments of my childhood came during the 1974 FIFA World Cup. I knew the tournament was being hosted by Germany, but I wasn't prepared to turn on the small TV in my father's study in our Chihuahua home to find Germany playing against Germany in a group stage match. This was extremely perplexing, especially since the Germans playing in the white shirts and black shorts, the kit I vaguely understood to be the real German uniform, were referred to as the "Federal Republic," while the blue-shirted Germans were the "Democratic Republic." Being schooled in a nation that paid a great deal of lip service to democracy without being one, I felt compelled to root for the GDR. Surely, they must be the good guys. Dad popped in at halftime and set me straight, freeing me from the trap set by devious Communist propaganda. The hosts, the western "Federal Republic," were the good Germans, dad assured me, and they also happened to be the superior footballing power. The Commies won the game 1-0, as if to embarrass my dad, but the white shirts of Franz Beckenbauer and Gerd Müller went on to win the tournament, and I have rooted for them ever since, as if to atone for my confusion.

Sport fandom can be a wonderful geography instructor.

There may have been two Germanies in that 1974 World Cup, but there was no England. England had won the World Cup they hosted in 1966, the year I was born, and had lost a thrilling quarterfinal match to Pelé's Brazil in 1970 but then failed to qualify for those all-important tournaments held when I was eight and twelve. The birthplace of the sport had become one of its backwaters.

When England finally did reappear on our World Cup screens, in 1982, it was to deliver another geography lesson in Chihuahua. I was confused to watch some red-faced English fans in the Spanish summer sunlight flying a red-crossed white flag that was decidedly not the Union Jack. That necessitated the whole England-isn't-the-same-as-Great-Britain-and-then-there's-the-UK talk my dad had probably hoped to save for when I was of age. To this day, I am often reminding students (and myself) that England competes in international football, but it's Great Britain that goes to the Olympics, while it's the UK that's represented at the United Nations (and then reminding myself of the component parts of each). As Coach Ted Lasso famously asked, how many countries are in this country?

The reason England and the other "home nations" of the UK—Wales, Scotland, and Northern Ireland—compete separately in football is because they started playing the game before anyone else did, and the annual championship they contested among themselves as far back as the nineteenth century was the sport's first international competition. By the time FIFA was organized on the continent in 1911, the football associations of the four home nations were already well established, and each became a separate member of the international governing body. Indeed, the unique status of the British Isles in the global game is still reflected in the composition of the technical body charged with issuing and maintaining football's official rules: the International Football Association Board. IFAB has eight voting members that make all decisions, with four of the votes assigned to each of the British football associations, and the other four allotted by FIFA to the rest of the world's 200+ associations. IFAB, founded in 1886, also predates FIFA, and its organization reflects the fact that the international game evolved as a merger between the established game on the British Isles and its more fledgling organization elsewhere.[1]

But by the late twentieth century, the British faced an acute sporting conundrum, in many ways the opposite of ours. As described earlier,

America's conundrum is whether to be number one or to be left alone. England's conundrum is what to do about the fact that because it proved so wildly successful in propagating its sport to so much of the world, by the second half of the twentieth century the game's Britishness had faded into an all-encompassing universality. Much to the long-standing trauma of English fans, other lands (including Brazil, after being introduced to the game by São Paulo's young expat Charles Miller) took the game to new heights it hadn't attained in its birthplace.

In his celebrated memoir of supporting Arsenal, *Fever Pitch*, Nick Hornby recalls the awestruck shock with which he and his classmates in school, but really all Brits, watched what the Brazilians led by Pelé had made of their sport during the 1970 Mexico World Cup:

> It wasn't just the quality of the football, though; it was the way they regarded ingenious and outrageous embellishment as though it were as functional and necessary as a corner kick or a throw-in. The only comparison I had at my disposal then was with toy cars: although I had no interest in Dinky or Corgu or Matchbox, I loved Lady Penelope's pink Rolls-Royce and James Bond's Aston Martin, both equipped with elaborate devices such as ejector seats and hidden guns which lifted them out of the boringly ordinary. Pelé's attempt to score from inside his own half with a lob, the dummy he sold to the Peruvian goalkeeper when he went one way round and the ball went the other . . . these were football's equivalent of the ejector seat. . . . In a way Brazil ruined it for all of us. They had revealed a kind of Platonic ideal that nobody, not even the Brazilians, would ever be able to find again. . . . At school we were left with our Esso World Cup coin collections and a couple of fancy moves to try out; but we couldn't even get close, and we gave up.[2]

Every World Cup, English fans sing about "football coming home," some earnestly, many ironically. England bequeathed to the world its national pastime and then proceeded to become second-rate at it. England's only World Cup win took place when they hosted the tournament; meanwhile, Brazil has won five World Cups; Germany and Italy four each; Argentina three; and France and Uruguay two. Imagine how Americans would feel if the world does get hooked on our variety of football, and the day comes when Uruguay has won more of the Global Super Bowls than we have.

England's response to its conundrum of falling behind at its own game has been a radical removal of all barriers blocking access to its most cherished pastime and industry to outsiders. Brexit and the resurgence of populist nationalism in much of the world suggested we were rethinking globalization, but England has carved out an exception for its football. Desperate times, and all that.

David Edgerton, a historian at King's College London, published an influential book in 2018 entitled *The Rise and Fall of the British Nation: A Twentieth-century History*. Contrary to what you might expect from the title, Edgerton didn't set out to track the rise and fall of the nation's economic or military prowess and relative power, but rather the rise and fall of the idea and political reality of a Britain acting and thinking of itself as a discrete nation-state confined to the British Isles. In Edgerton's telling, the rise and fall of this national self-understanding occurred within a relatively short period, largely from the end of the Second World War until the 1970s and 1980s. Before and after, Britain has been defined by *non-national* periods of radical openness, though the earlier imperial period was defined by the extension of British capital and influence to all corners of the world, whereas the more recent openness has been about the importation of foreign capital and influences into the British Isles.[3]

This conjures up images of alternating tides and provides a useful framing for thinking about the relationship between the English and the global football worlds. England introduced the game to the world and was its indisputable master until it receded back into the background and was overtaken by others during its decades of insularity. But now the tides have reversed and outside influences—capital, business practices, playing and coaching talent, philosophies, you name it—have been drawn in to revitalize the English game and restore it at the center of global sport.

This may feel like a digression from our inquiry of how America connects to the rest of the world through sport to an exploration of how England does, but the two relationships are interconnected. Because of the transformation of England's football ecosystem to resolve its sporting conundrum, our mother country has become one of the most prominent venues for the resolution of our own conundrum. English football is now a global platform where multiple foreign agendas collide, including the pressing agenda of US sporting interests to shed their historic isolationism. England's Premier League is the Great Game's frontline in American efforts to start playing with, and against, others, and to close the gap between the global reach of other forms of American pop culture and the paltrier reach of American sports.

I have been to sixteen English football grounds, several of them on numerous occasions, to watch Premier League and Championship games, and so I can say with some authority that English football is as much of a head-scratcher as the NFL. Our football league's riddle is how it came to be the one place on Earth that perfected socialism; the riddle of English football is how a spectacle so culturally rooted in its idiosyncratic geography can simultaneously be the most globalized sports league on Earth, possibly the most globalized form of entertainment, avidly followed in all but three or four countries on Earth (the number went up by one on account of sanctions on Russia).

Take Wolverhampton, a fading industrial powerhouse of no more than 300,000 people in the English Midlands. In the fall of 2021, when fans were thrilled to be rid of the recent pandemic attendance restrictions, I found myself at a Monday Night Football game (thanks, NFL) in a frigid but rollicking Molineux Stadium. The hometown Wolverhampton Wanderers (who've leaned more into their alternative "Wolves" branding) were hosting Everton, Liverpool's original but now "other" club, in a matchup that is about as old school English as it gets. Wolves were founded by St. Luke's School in 1877, and Everton was founded by St. Domingo Methodist Church in 1878 (many of the English teams that date back to that time were founded by churches or workplaces eager to keep their young men out of trouble on their one day off) and so there we were a century-and-a-half later, watching them face off in a match that would be televised in all but four countries around the world. Built in 1899, Molineux oozes character, which is another way of saying it isn't a shiny, state-of-the-art NFL stadium; plenty of US sports teams complain about their facilities being old if they were built a century after Molineux. A few of the newer English stadiums could be confused with modern NFL stadiums, but most clubs still have quirky, non-symmetrical venues that contain a hodgepodge of stands of different heights that were built and refurbished at different times and are either named after the street they're on, a sponsor, or a club legend.

One Wolves club legend on the pitch that night happened to be Mexico's best player, Raúl Jiménez, who had suffered a serious skull-fracturing injury the prior year that nearly cost him his career, if not his life.[4] Against Everton, I watched him score his fiftieth goal for the club, a typically crafty chip over Everton (and England) keeper Jordan Pickford that proved the decisive moment in a 2–1 win that propelled Wolves into seventh place in the table. The crowd hadn't waited for Jiménez to score to show their adoration for the Mexican striker—already in the match's second minute fans were singing their *Si Señor* tribute to Raúl ("The best in the world and he comes from Mexico. Our number nine."), a song that will be repeated at least half a dozen times throughout the night, with extra gusto when he did score.

The whole scene was so wildly implausible. What was Raúl Jiménez doing playing across the Atlantic, not in Madrid or Barcelona like Mexico's all-time greats Hugo Sánchez and Rafa Márquez before him, but in Wolverhampton of all places? Adding to the surreal tableau of sport globalization was the fact that since 2016, Wolves have been owned by a Chinese conglomerate, Fosun, and have been the foremost outpost for Portuguese stars given a close association with Portuguese super-agent Jorge Mendes. And Wolves are a power in esports, too, with their players followed by more than 30 million online supporters in China. So, on the same website where I looked up details of a subsequent Wolves-Everton match in 2025, I could read that Wolves had also signed a new Rainbow Six Siege team that will debut in the Malta Cyber Series. Just like the deacons at St. Luke's mapped it all out in the 1870s, no doubt.

Earlier on the Monday when I watched Jiménez, I had a Thai lunch with Russell Jones, a Wolverhampton native who is the club's General Manager for Marketing and Commercial Growth. He recounted with a chuckle how the job has taken him to fashion shows in Shanghai—because the club had launched its own fashion label—and to create a record label with Warner Music to promote a stable of Wolves artists. Jones relishes the fact that his scrappy club isn't shy about trying new things.

When Jones started supporting his hometown club as a kid, Wolves were struggling near the bottom of the fourth division, facing possible extinction, but the club has a rich history on par with the biggest names in the game. They were one of the dozen founding clubs of the original Football League in 1888, and one of the dominant teams of the 1950s, when they won three titles and were proclaimed "Champions of the World" upon beating Ferenc Puskás' Hungarian powerhouse club, Honvéd, in one of the first games ever played at night. The sensation around that friendly televised by the BBC, and continental resentment at the English media's boast that their team was now world champs, were among the catalysts for the subsequent launch of European competitions that would evolve into today's UEFA Champions League.

Wolves can also claim to be a US champion of sorts, thanks to one of the strangest episodes in America's early faltering attempts to embrace the world's game. After being mesmerized by the 1966 World Cup, Lamar Hunt and other sports impresarios such as Jack Kent Cooke resolved to establish a domestic soccer league, the United Soccer Association, which would become the North American Soccer League. To kick things off, even before they had lined up their teams, they invited a dozen established European clubs to come represent them during their 1967 summer offseason. And so, Scotland's Dundee United moonlighted as Hunt's Dallas Tornado, and Wolves headed to Los Angeles to play as the L.A. Wolves. Mind you, this was back in the day when professional footballers earned middle-class wages, if that, and didn't spend their off months in places like Mallorca and the Maldives—and there were no foreign superstars in English football. A Wolves-produced documentary on their 1967 American escapade features aged alums from that squad still beaming at their good fortune of being assigned exotic LA, and all that was associated with it, as their summer base. None of them had ever flown before their adventure. What's more, Wolves won the title and were proclaimed US champions.

On the day we met for lunch, Jones was more focused on a neighboring North American country. The Raúl Jiménez phenomenon meant that Wolves suddenly had nine times as many followers in Mexico as in the UK. Wolves already pushed out content in many languages, including Spanish, but they hired a PR firm in Mexico to engage more directly with Mexican fans and organize events for them. When Jones visited Mexico and went to a domestic watch at the imposing Estadio Azteca, he was amazed to see street vendors outside the stadium hawking knockoff Wolves jerseys. "I know one is supposed to be annoyed, but I was also flattered and excited," he recalled.

Jiménez has been an enthusiastic ambassador for Mexican soft power in this part of the world. For one season, Wolves asked Adidas to design its alternate uniform to echo the Mexican national team's classic green jersey. The Wolves Foundation, meanwhile, partnered with the World Wildlife Fund on a campaign to save the endangered Mexican wolf that was spearheaded by Jiménez and engaged schoolchildren in both Britain and Mexico. Wolves also connected with *Sin Cara*, and when the popular Mexican-American wrestler visited Molineux for a match, Jones had a Wolves-themed luchador mask Jiménez had already popularized made for every fan in the stands that day. Jones noted that in addition to encouraging people in Mexico to follow Wolves, Jiménez was also helping the club expand its fan base among Latinos in the United States.

Sadly for Wolves, Jiménez struggled to regain his pre-injury form, when he was one of England's top strikers. He was his old self the night I attended Molineux, but those matches were no longer the norm, and in the summer of 2023, Jiménez would leave the club after five seasons and head to fellow Premier League club Fulham, in West London (where he eventually started looking like his old self, scoring twelve goals in the 2024–5 season). Many fans in Mexico have stayed with the club, but these days Jones is also trying to capitalize on Wolves fever in Korea, thanks to the exploits of the team's Korean attacker Hwang Hee-chan.

England wasn't always football's global hub, despite being its ancestral home. Not only was its national team second-rate in international competition when I was growing up, but its domestic league was too. We avidly followed the leagues in Spain and Italy; British football was insular and of less interest to outsiders. The country had become a net exporter of talent—top English players were keen to play for big Italian, Spanish, or German clubs. As the Premier League's own website notes: "In 1992 there were only 11 non-British or Irish footballers in the Premier League. These days there are, on average, about 70 nationalities running on the pitch in the Premier League."

So, what happened? What changed to make England the undisputed center of the footballing universe, at least judging by the success of its domestic league?

The answer entails a confluence of unbearable tragedy, exuberant globalization, and an unleashed Rupert Murdoch, all against the backdrop of the enduring cultural appeal and soft power of Anglo-American culture and our language.

Most immediately, the top division of English football rebranded and relaunched itself after more than a century as the new "Premier League" in 1992, influenced by the NFL's commercial success, as we learned earlier from Arsenal's Vice Chair David Dein, in response to tragedy and scandal. By the late 1980s, English football had become synonymous with hooliganism. English clubs were banned from playing on the continent for five years due to their fans' violent behavior. Back home, the sport had acquired a dodgy taint. Crumbling old stadiums packed fans into notorious standing terraces, where the atmosphere could turn rather menacing—certainly not a welcoming space for women, children, and anything approximating the type of corporate entertaining we equate with American pro sports.

Then in 1989, ninety-six Liverpool supporters were crushed to death in a horrific incident at Hillsborough Stadium in Sheffield—victims of shabby infrastructure and even shabbier policing, and the ticking time bomb of a generation's abandonment of the national game to its own toxicity. The fact that the Hillsborough tragedy occurred in the northern industrial city that had been the birthplace of English football's first professional club provided a handy reminder of some of the biases and prejudices that had led to this abandonment. Football was the working-class sport developed in the gritty northern industrial cities, and to the extent that cultural elites in London appreciated the game, part of what they appreciated and even fetishized was the game's spiky image, its association with toxic masculinity and violence. It wasn't the sport that Britain's governing class considered its natural habitat—those would be "public school" (in the confusing British sense of the term) games like cricket, rugby, squash, and crew. Football was for adventurous outings with the lads, or to watch from a safe distance on the BBC's *Match of the Day*, and to banter about to prove one's bona fides as a regular bloke.

One of the ironies of the class distinctions among Britain's sports is that the nation's ruling elite introduced the empire's colonies they governed to cricket, rugby, and squash—while more commercial British interests overseas introduced football to most other corners of the globe, including Raúl Jiménez's hometown of Tepeji del Rio in Mexico's state of Hidalgo, where the first soccer game in the early twentieth century was organized by a team of expat English engineers. To this day, some of Britain's former key colonies well into the twentieth century—cricket-mad India, especially—remain some of the places on earth least impressed with Britain's most popular export.

The Hillsborough tragedy forced a reckoning. Government and society stepped in to reclaim and reform the national sport, leading to massive investment in the game's infrastructure. Stadiums were refurbished, for instance, to do away with standing terraces. The game had fallen into disrepute under the stewardship of generations of owners who considered their clubs community assets like libraries or parks, which they kept afloat but couldn't prevent from deteriorating over time. Unlike in the United States, hardly anyone in English football prior to the late 1980s considered professional sports a serious commercial endeavor, and the game had therefore been starved of needed investment.

The difference in our respective media ecosystems offers one explanation for the different attitudes toward sport's commercial potential on either side of the Atlantic. As early as 1958, when Lamar Hunt was inspired to try acquiring an NFL franchise by watching that year's championship game between the Colts and Giants, there was a recognition (as he himself put it) that the game "televises well." And in a media environment in which numerous commercial broadcasters competed against each other to build and monetize audiences, investors like Hunt appreciated that the value of their sports teams would only grow alongside the growth of the insatiable medium of television.

The international varietal of football, with its continuous and uninterrupted flow over two 45-minute halves, was decidedly less ideal for an advertising-driven commercial broadcaster. Besides halftime, where do you stick the ads? But this was not an issue across most of Europe until late into the twentieth century given the prevalence of state-owned TV, whose reach and business weren't predicated on the selling of advertising.

Then along came Rupert Murdoch, around the same time that the game was undergoing its post-Hillsborough transformation. If media increasingly looms as the decisive factor in shaping the fate of professional sports, in the case of English football it was the urgent needs of Murdoch's media empire that helped catapult the Premier League ahead of its European peers. As *The Wall Street Journal* reporters Joshua Robinson and Jonathan Clegg masterfully recount in their book *The Club: How the English Premier League Became the Wildest, Richest, Most Disruptive Force in Sports*, Murdoch's pay-satellite Sky TV service desperately needed exclusive content to take on the BBC, and he bet heavily on the newly launched Premier League in 1992 to build his viewership—in the UK, but also, fortuitously, across Sky TV's Asian footprint.[5] Murdoch's largesse confirmed the belief of the new generation of American-influenced investors in the sport, including Arsenal's David Dein and Manchester United's Martin Edwards, that football could be a profitable enterprise. As for Murdoch, a year later he would again bet on sports to attain instant credibility and long-term viability for a fledgling media property when he bid a fortune to wrest a package of NFL rights away from CBS for his Fox television network.[6]

A third factor aiding the Premier League's stratospheric rise after its 1992–3 debut season was the opening of the British Isles to the outside world, and the broader embrace of exuberant globalization across much of the world. Britain's membership in the European Union meant former caps on the number of foreign players in the league were no longer enforceable, at least not against players from within the Union, who enjoyed the right to exercise their trade—be it bartending, banking, or ball-playing—anywhere within the trading bloc. Moreover, the late 1990s/turn-of-century Britain of Tony Blair attracted global investment with market-friendly policies and a slightly cringey (but apparently effective) "Cool Britannia" branding campaign. As a fashionable financial capital renowned for its strong currency and rule of law, London became a preeminent destination for deep-pocketed investors from East and South Asia, the Middle East, Russia and Eastern Europe, and even North America. They bought prestigious country estates and smart London townhouses, as well as many iconic English brands, including football clubs.

Owning and operating a football club promised foreign investors a shortcut to meaningful social status and public adoration. Every new sports owner who has been wildly successful in other pursuits initially believes they will succeed in football—because, really, how hard can this be?—and thus will be adored by their club's fans. Mohamed Al Fayed, whose son was dating Princess Diana at the time of her death, was a classic example of a wealthy outsider seeking to buy his way into the firmament of Britain's establishment: the Egyptian businessman famously acquired the posh Harrods department store (where he has been posthumously accused of sexually assaulting and harassing several employees) and, less famously, Fulham Football Club.[7]

Fulham's West London rival, Chelsea, was acquired in 2003 by Roman Abramovich, a Russian tycoon who'd made his billions by being at the right place at the right time when Russia's considerable energy assets were being privatized after the demise of the Soviet Union. Abramovich was the league's ultimate game changer, as an owner willing to plow whatever resources he needed into the club to win trophies—which he did in spades. During its two decades under Abramovich's patronage, "Chelski" (as the club's own fans, who often flew Russian flags and signs reading "Roman's Army" at matches, cheekily referred to themselves) won five Premier League titles, five FA Cups, and two European Champions League trophies. Abramovich became the model "sugar daddy" owner, for whom money, or profit-loss statements, were no obstacle in the pursuit of sporting success. Fans loved his largesse and couldn't care less where the money came from. The league, for its part, had a "fit and proper" persons test to determine the suitability of prospective owners, but this was merely designed to filter out, and protect against, speculative owners who might not have the significant resources necessary to support the club and might thus pose a risk to the long-term sustainability of a community asset. If your bank accounts were bulging, you would pass the "fit and proper" test with flying colors. It took Russia's 2022 invasion of Ukraine, and the subsequent sanctions against Putin's regime and Russian oligarchs aligned with it, for the British government to decide this community asset shouldn't be in Russian hands after all. A group of US investors who also owned the Los Angeles Dodgers swooped in to acquire Chelsea in a government-supervised sale of the club.[8]

All things being equal, an English-speaking sports league (or any other cultural offering) will always have a built-in advantage over competition from elsewhere, and once the English Premier League sorted itself out, it was always going to be hard for Italy's Serie A, Spain's La Liga, or Germany's Bundesliga to stand a chance against it. The combined legacy of the British Empire and the American Century is a world in which the English language has become a lingua franca. Beyond sport, we often think of the United States as the world's indisputable pop culture trendsetter; but it may be more accurate to think of the trendsetting as a joint Anglo-American venture. Dominic Sandbrook's entertaining book *The Great British Dream Factory: The Strange History of Our National Imagination* argues that Britain became even more culturally influential in the aftermath of its postwar imperial decline, wielding more soft power once its hard power had evaporated.[9] It is certainly hard to argue with the reach and impact of the Beatles, James Bond, Harry Potter, and so on. Sandbrook's book doesn't even touch on sport, but nowadays the EPL would be at the top of the list of cultural exports. At a Business of Football Summit in London in the spring of 2025 hosted by *The Financial Times*, the Premier League's Chief Executive Officer Richard Masters claimed that 1.4 billion people around the world feel that the English Premier League is an important part of their lives.

The realms of American and British sport stand worlds apart, but when they seek to win over hearts and minds in third nations, they both benefit from the hospitable foundation already laid by British and US power, our language, and the seductive lure of our popular culture. This fertile ground is there for the NBA and EPL alike.

Only since the 1990s has English football opted to leverage these built-in advantages in taking on Europe's other leagues seeking to grow their global audiences, and the Premier League has now pulled far ahead of the others. According to Deloitte's Annual Review of Football Finance 2024, English Premier League clubs collectively pulled in €6.97 billion in revenue during the 2022–3 season, compared with €3.83 billion for German Bundesliga clubs and €3.5 billion for Spain's La Liga clubs. On average, English clubs pulled in €348 million each, compared to €213 million for German clubs and €177 million for Spanish clubs.[10]

Although a far cry from the socialist paradise that is the NFL, the Premier League spreads its TV riches among its clubs more equitably than other European leagues and has become more competitive as a result. On its own website, under the "What We Do" tab, the Premier League touts this relative parity as a comparative advantage:

> Many of the most famous clubs in world football play in the Premier League and, thanks to our distribution model, which is the most equitable in top-flight European football, the League is incredibly competitive, unpredictable and exciting.
>
> In recent seasons, the battles for the title, UEFA Champions League places, and to avoid relegation have been the tightest and hardest fought on record.
>
> Some of the biggest names in world football play in the Premier League every week: from Erling Haaland to Bruno Fernandes, Mohamed Salah to Martin Odegaard, Emiliano Martinez to Virgil van Dijk. The world's best players come to England to play in a compelling league competition, in front of passionate full houses and matches that are seen all over the world.[11]

Another widely followed annual Deloitte report on international football finances, its Money League Table, revealed in January 2025 that Real Madrid had become the first club in world football to break the €1 billion barrier in annual revenues (€1.045 billion). Of the ten clubs that brought in revenue of between €500 million and €1 billion, six were English. The rankings show that despite the rise of England's Premier League, clubs like Real, Barcelona, Bayern Munich, Paris Saint-Germain, and Juventus remain global brands, thanks in part to their success and visibility in European competition.[12]

But these massive clubs on the continent have outgrown their domestic leagues, which they dominate to unhealthy degrees given the disparity between their resources and those available to their competitors. The number of strong, competitive teams in England fueled by formidable TV income and deep-pocketed foreign investment keeps growing, whereas it seems to be shrinking in other leagues. "Smaller" English clubs outside of what are considered the Premier League era's "Big Six," the likes of Bournemouth, Brighton, and Aston Villa, can now outspend all but the top two or three clubs in Spain, Italy, and

Germany to attract the world's most talented players and managers. Thanks primarily to its cut of the Premier League's TV riches, for instance, Russell Jones' Wolves rank twenty-ninth in the world on Deloitte's Money League Table, with €206.9 million in revenue.

The continental giants' unease at the inexorable rise of the English Premier League led to one of the most audacious if ham-fisted attempts to disrupt the sport. In the spring of 2021, the top clubs of England, Spain, and Italy announced they would secede from existing European competitions (in which the top teams from all countries compete) to create their own select European Super League that would play mid-week primetime matches featuring the game's perennial giants raking in massive TV riches, regardless of their performance in any one season. Within days, the Super League would join the infamous "New Coke" of the 1980s as one of the more disastrous marketing flops of all time. The plan was soon abandoned in the face of nearly unanimous and vociferous opposition from fans, governments, sponsors, and the sport's governing bodies across the continent.

One of the interesting aspects of the episode was the haste in some quarters to blame the fiasco on uncouth, greedy American owners who have no respect for the game's culture and traditions and will go to any lengths to improve their operating margins. It's understandable why that narrative would prove irresistible, but it is one that sold the English game short.

The reality is that the primary drivers of the Super League project were Real Madrid, Barcelona, Juventus, and Inter Milan, big clubs outside England concerned about being stuck in their underperforming domestic leagues. They knew the gap in resources and reach between the English Premier League and every other European League was growing by the year, and that if they stood aside and did nothing, they would continue to witness the Premier League's transformation into the world's actual Super League. Hence their desperate roll of the dice. The English clubs involved, willing with varying degrees of enthusiasm or reluctance to go along with this scheme for fear of being left out—Arsenal, Manchester City, Manchester United, Liverpool, Chelsea, and Tottenham—dodged a bullet when the project quickly fell apart; their Premier League has already won.

But is the league that plays on the island that invented the game a truly domestic league, or a global all-star league that happens to use England as its venue?

The question gets at the conceit, or trick, which allows the EPL to resolve globalization's tensions and flourish. It attracts the deepest-pocketed investors from all over the globe, who then attract the world's best players and coaches to offer up the highest-quality version of the game to fans everywhere. That is the familiar bonanza for consumers that occurs when trade and migration barriers are removed in any market, and they have access to the best from everywhere. But the EPL simultaneously sells a game that is still somehow "locally sourced" and authentic, in a way that a new global all-star league could never be. Imagine if the same foreign investors, from the Persian Gulf, China, elsewhere in Europe, and increasingly from America, had come together to create a super global league with entirely new clubs with snazzy uniforms—get excited to root on the New York Titans, the Frankfurt Bankers, and the Tokyo Samurai!—featuring the same amazing constellation of players and coaches they signed for their English clubs, and thus featuring the same level of outstanding play. Would that league have as large and as impassioned a following as English football does?

If you are inclined to think not, as I am, those singing Wolves fans I sat amongst, whose families have been going to Molineux for generations, are a big part of the reason. English football is equally compelling content to television viewers in Arizona, Vietnam, Sweden, and Rwanda, because we are all craving authenticity and originality—and this literally is the original source of the sport we all love, never mind that it has required the intervention of foreign players, coaches, and owners to resuscitate it. The local fans are as much protagonists of the spectacle being peddled overseas as the players are; their communities and stadiums, especially the fading older ones, are the spectacle's set. It's not all artisanal, exactly, but this "product" oozes authenticity and originality. The rootedness of a league whose clubs are typically more than a century old is a refreshing antidote to that unmoored sense of dislocation that often accompanies globalization. The league itself would never use the clunky academic term of "glocalization" (the simultaneous ability to reflect local sensibility and global appeal), but that is exactly what it is pulling off.

Mother England's answer to its conundrum of either opting for the homegrown or reclaiming the status of #1 at times can strain credulity, or at the very least offer up some surreal juxtapositions. Crystal Palace's cozy, century-old stadium of Selhurst Park in South London, which plays the role of Richmond FC's home on *Ted Lasso*, is a case in point: squeezed tightly into the surrounding neighborhood, Selhurst Park feels more like a community facility than the venue for a big-time professional sports league, let alone a globally followed one. But during a match my son Seabass and I attended there a few years back, many of the billboard ads ringing the field were in Chinese, a tell that this spectacle was primarily intended for an audience halfway around the world. Moreover, Palace's jersey sponsor was for an Asian betting company, and it featured Chinese characters that most local fans wearing the same jersey wouldn't be able to read. Nor could they make bets on the advertised site, one of several such offshore gambling sites buying Premier League sponsorships to target the Asian market. Imagine, I ask my students back in Arizona, going to your local ballpark and cheering on your team, whose jersey says something you can't read unless you are fluent in Mandarin, while being served up ads in a different language for products you can't access.

As an aside, the number of Premier League clubs that sign sponsorship deals with Asian gambling sites of questionable repute (and often opaque provenance) to maximize short-term profit (Wolves are another of these clubs) is another reminder of how much the EPL still stands to learn from the NFL in terms of managing and enhancing a sport's long-term brand value. The league is phasing in a ban on such gambling sponsorship deals over the next few years, but it feels years too late.

Manchester City presents one of the starkest case studies of how iconic Premier League clubs that date back to the nineteenth century navigate the conundrum of retaining their local street cred while projecting themselves globally.

And in Man City's case, my mind always comes back to the door to the Chairman's Club at the Etihad Stadium, where I was invited to watch a City match against Barcelona in the Champions League in the fall of 2016. My live sports experiences usually take place in the cheapest seats in the house, but this was on the other end of the scale. We were served a fancy multi-course dinner in the luxurious clubroom prior to kick off, with a chance to mingle with the club's leadership, some of its past legends, and sponsors; then we migrated to the adjoining leather seats near midfield and dashed back in at halftime for coffee and dessert, and then again after the match for more drinks and snacks. Not a bad way to experience a match.

But back to the door that let us into this lavish experience, because that's what impressed me the most on the night. The wooden door is a replica of the original door to St. Mark's Church in the Groton area of east Manchester, about a mile south of today's stadium. That is where, in 1880, the church established a football club to keep young men out of trouble that would change its name a few times before incorporating itself formally in 1894 as Manchester City FC.

The club would go on to become the scrappy underdog in the shadows of cross-town rival Manchester United (a team technically based in the city of Salford across the river, as "City" fans are always quick to point out) in the latter decades of the twentieth century, bouncing between the first and second divisions. Alex Ferguson, United's longtime legendary manager who won thirteen league titles over twenty-seven years and was knighted along the way, would famously refer to City as "the noisy neighbors."

The noisy neighbors won the Emirati jackpot in 2008, forcing it to shed its hardscrabble underdog image and start hoarding trophies and overtaking United as the dominant force in English football. Within a few years of Sheikh Mansour bin Zayed bin Sultan Al Nahyan's acquisition of the club, City became the gold standard within England, and arguably within all of football, for how to invest in short- and long-term success, and for how to build a well-oiled sporting machine with a global following. Manchester City's supporters joined Chelsea's fanbase as one whose club had found its "sugar daddy" to deliver them from mediocrity and take them to the promised land. City won its first Premier League title under new ownership in the 2011–12 season and went on to win six more in the next dozen years. In the 2022–3 season they culminated their ascent into the world's elite by winning their first European Champions League title.

There is much to admire about the City project, despite some of the controversies hovering around it, which I had an opportunity to observe up close over the course of an extended visit with the team's communications team in 2018. For starters, the Club has invested considerable amounts in the development of its east Manchester community, far beyond its own facilities, and has an active, highly admired foundation.

You need deep pockets to achieve sustainable success in European football, but money doesn't guarantee success, as any sports fan can point to plenty of examples of incompetence or hubris undercutting any edge provided by resources. But City's ownership team and leadership combined their resources with political, commercial, and footballing savvy. That wooden church door to the Chairman's Club is a sign of the Emirati ownership's political savvy; they installed it.

The worst sin foreign owners can commit when buying into English football is to disregard, or seek to alter, their acquired club's existing identity and history. The Emirati owners at City were careful to do the opposite, to outdo their predecessors in honoring the club's legacy and memory, understanding that it is a large part of the enterprise's value. Hence the door that so impressed me, and the intentionality of the club's philanthropy in the community, and engagement with former Man City legends. In its stadium shop, City even offered a line of St. Mark's swag with the church's Maltese cross on it.

Under the leadership of Chairman Khaldoon Al Mubarak, an Emirati business leader who also serves as CEO of one of the nation's sovereign wealth investment vehicles, City was thoughtful and systematic about investing in its facilities, squad, and on- and off-field talent. They essentially ceded the footballing operation to the best and the brightest in the business from Barcelona, wooing Ferran Soriano to be the team's CEO and then his countryman Pep Guardiola to become the team's manager (or coach, in American footballese).[13] Widely acknowledged to be the sport's greatest coach ever, the former Barcelona player and manager has been at City since 2016, mesmerizing supporters and opponents alike with his harmonious, possession-based brand of fluid football. And loads of trophies.

On the commercial side, City was quick to learn from the American sport and entertainment worlds, hiring marketers from those worlds, and executing on Ferran Soriano's vision, first expressed when he was at Barcelona earlier, that football needed to think of itself more as an entertainment offering, more akin to Disney than to a public community asset or a religious ritual. The club sold a minority stake to influential US investment firm Silver Lake and was first to embrace innovative media and marketing partnerships. Most intriguingly, Manchester City became the hub of City Football Group, the world's first self-proclaimed "truly global football organization," acquiring and operating thirteen clubs across five continents, including NYFC in America's Major League Soccer.

On its own website, CFG states that its purpose is to "empower better lives through football," and its ambition is to "be the world's best sports entertainment organization." The website's aspirational language also claims that "the CFG approach ensures that every club remains authentic to its fans and community, plays entertaining football and benefits from being part of a global organization that applies the world's best expertise on and off the pitch."[14]

Manchester City and its Emirati owners aren't alone in seeking to develop a multi-club transnational football conglomerate, though they are probably the most ambitious attempt out there. Red Bull, operating New York's other MLS club, would be another example. The theory of a consortium of clubs sharing a philosophy of football and benefiting from synergies in the scouting and development of talent, and across their marketing efforts, sounds great but has yet to be fully proven. And as City's own language suggests, concerns about a club retaining its authenticity within its own community is a concern once they join such a conglomerate. City has proven more adept than most at navigating this conundrum, but there are other examples of fans resenting foreign owners who might treat their club as a second-tier "feeder club" within a multi-club organization (this has been a source of friction, for example, in Chelsea's ownership of French club Racing de Strasbourg).

In Manchester, City's owners have worked hard to embed their project in the community and win over fans. Winning has a way of doing that to a certain extent, but City has also done so by investing in its foundation, its Academy, and in the women's game. Contrary to what people might have expected from its Persian Gulf owners, City has been among the most progressive forces in the league when it comes to promoting the development of clubs' women squads, which not long ago were treated by most English clubs as an offshoot of their youth or philanthropic organizations. On my first visit with the club, City executives boasted of being among the first clubs in England to change the terminology from "Ladies" to "Women," and to include news of the women's team in the main social media feed offered up to supporters following the club. This annoyed some older, less enlightened fans, but Man City was adamant that if you support the club, you support both its men's and women's teams. This has become the prevailing attitude across English football but was a less entrenched view when I was first hearing it from City in 2016.

Hogwash, would reply some of the Emirati ownership's persistent critics; or sportswash, more likely. "Sportswashing" has become a common term since the criticism surrounding Qatar's 2022 World Cup to convey the perceived laundering of certain political regimes' reputation through sport. In the case of Manchester City, the core allegation from the time of the 2008 purchase, vehemently denied by the club, is that this is all essentially a branding exercise by a petrostate. City insisted, and the Premier League has always accepted, that this is not the case, that despite being a member of the country's ruling family, this is a personal investment on Sheikh Mansour's part.[15]

The question of whether Persian Gulf interests have a place at the Premier League table is part of a broader debate over the extensive investments coming from the region into global sport, particularly football, which came to the forefront with the Saudi takeover of Newcastle in 2021 and the Qatar World Cup the following year, and to which I will return in the next chapter.

Beyond the provenance of City's riches, a related controversy is whether clubs should be able to leverage their owners' wealth to catapult themselves to the top of the game. This is an interesting one, with persuasive arguments on either side, given that unlike in the NFL context, these clubs have never competed on an even playing field, and in some cases the injection of new riches can be seen as a means of remedying historic inequities.

Manchester City isn't the first club whose fortunes changed overnight upon a change in ownership—Chelsea under Roman Abramovich was an equally dramatic case, and there have been others. What's more, City didn't just start winning because they were the richest club in England; they made smart investments and built a coherent team with a long-term strategy and a shared vision, while plenty of other big English clubs (including their cross-town rivals in its post-Ferguson era) were wasting plenty of money. Indeed, in the years between 2015 and 2024, when Manchester City became the dominant power in the league, Chelsea spent by far the most among English Premier League clubs on transfer fees to attract players (€2.78 billion). The two Manchester clubs were virtually tied in second (City at €1.96 billion, United at €1.95 billion), but had drastically different results to show for their investments (City won six titles in that period, United none). Even more telling, when you factor in offsetting revenue for player sales, City's "net spend" on transfers for the period drops to €703 million, nearly half of United's, and below the corresponding figures for Chelsea, Tottenham, and Arsenal. This proves City hasn't been operating in an economic bubble all its own and suggests the club has been both better than its peers at developing talented players and more disciplined about parting ways with some of them for the health of its business.[16]

So far so good. But City has long been accused (both by UEFA, Europe's confederation that organizes the Champions League, and by the Premier League) of improperly boosting its revenues through accounting tricks, often involving inflated related-party transactions to grow the club's revenues to help it get on more equal footing with the likes of Chelsea and United. There have been a series of years-long legal cases brought against the club involving these issues, which have placed an asterisk on their success in the eyes of many fans of rival teams. Sports fandom being tribal, City fans tend to believe the club's denials of any wrongdoing and resent what they perceive as a campaign to protect the old status quo and unfairly prevent City from becoming one of the game's "big clubs."

To understand the context of the cases against City, and the underlying rules involved, bear in mind that English and European football have a long history of football clubs being driven into bankruptcy by owners who turned out to be terrible fiduciary custodians of these assets—either because they were too indebted, too eager to roll the dice in pursuit of short-term glory by signing pricey stars, or because they never had the resources they claimed upon arrival, or lost them in hard times affecting their other businesses. Or sometimes, they were just crooks. Let's face it, sport attracts all kinds, and football leagues haven't always been the most adept at vetting their prospective members.

As a result of too many communities struggling with the potential demise of their cherished football clubs, and often having to bail them out, a raft of "Financial Fair Play" regulations has been introduced at the European level and across the various national federations (in England they're now known as

"Profit Sustainability Rules," or PSR) to ensure that football clubs live within their means. The key detail and distinction here is that they must live within the means of the club, not within the means of the club's owner. So even if you are the wealthiest person on earth worth a trillion dollars and you acquire one of the smaller Premier League teams, you can't simply deposit hundreds of millions into its bank account to go on a shopping spree to spend as much as the biggest clubs do on talent, or even to outbid them for some of the world's best players.

At least not anymore, though that is precisely what Roman Abramovich did when he acquired Chelsea two decades ago, and to a lesser extent what City did subsequently. The financial regulations have been tightened and more strictly enforced in recent years, so City faced more constraints, and ultimately more legal jeopardy, in navigating the chicken-and-egg challenge of not being able to invest directly to grow the club until it first increased its revenues. The handy shortcut City was accused of taking was commercial sponsorship deals with other Emirati firms ultimately controlled by the same ownership group, such as Etihad Airways, the Abu Dhabi-based carrier that pays a fortune to be the club's shirt sponsor and for naming rights to City's stadium.

Over time, City's success has translated into millions of new followers around the world, and the club nowadays would require no accounting chicanery to be among England's top-grossing clubs. Its in-house newsroom delivers content to supporters, more than 90 percent of whom are outside the UK, in more than a dozen languages. But the seemingly never-ending legal cases against the club involve the transitional steps the club took to catapult itself to this next level. More recently, the Premier League's Profit and Sustainability Rules limit the cumulative loss clubs can sustain over a three-year period to £105 million and have gotten serious about enforcing them, which has hampered the ability of Newcastle to reap the benefits of its new Saudi owners, as we shall discuss in the next chapter, in the same way Chelsea and Manchester City enjoyed their sudden windfalls.

If the ostensible purpose of these financial regulations is to safeguard the solvency and viability of clubs, you can understand why supporters of clubs like Newcastle and City are suspicious as to why they are enforced against owners with almost unlimited resources. The concrete suspicion is that these rules serve as a brake to impede more clubs from closing the gap with the traditionally dominant powers of the game, clubs like Manchester United, Liverpool, and Arsenal. And increasingly, beyond the high-profile cases of these two clubs with Persian Gulf owners, the new deep-pocketed investors buying into English football and having to navigate these constraints are American owners.

The nation's conflicting attachments to its multicultural reality (the United Kingdom has a larger share of people born elsewhere than the United States, and you only need to spend a day in London to realize this is diversity on a different level) and to a strong isolationist nostalgia play out every weekend in the shared ritual of football.[17] The game has broadened many fans' worldview and cultural empathy. The Egyptian striker and prolific goal scorer Mo Salah has been a hero in Liverpool for years, where fans love to chant that if he scores a few more, they will become Muslims too.[18] A multiracial English national team projects to the world, and to English youth, a profoundly diverse version of the country. But at the same time, the game is bedeviled by frequent racist abuse of players on the part of some fans who are more and more emboldened to resurrect behaviors we had assumed to be a thing of the past.

With all its radical and counterintuitive openness to the outside world in the Age of Brexit, English football also offers up fascinating metaphors and case studies of globalization and competing economic ideas. Mirroring debates in plenty of other nations (including Mexico), those we might call "football protectionists" have long argued that bringing in many foreign stars to raise the level of the domestic league ends up hurting homegrown players, as it diminishes the opportunities available to them, literally crowding them off the field and lessening their reliance on developing future generations of English talent. Indeed, when I attended an Arsenal versus. Manchester match at Old Trafford in March 2025, Manchester United did not start a single English player on the day, and no one seemed to notice. Across the Premier League's ten matches that weekend, English players accounted for only 29.5 percent of starting lineups.

Football protectionists believe this level of globalization might help the Premier League improve its standard, but at the expense of English football itself. England, they'd argue, has ended up with the world's best league but a second-tier national team, still a step below the game's perennial powers of Spain, Italy, Germany, France, Argentina, and Brazil, many of whose stars are now paid a fortune to play in England and keep English talent sidelined. The argument is akin to that of domestic steelmakers or carmakers seeking high tariffs to shut out foreign competition.

But the idea that England is being hurt by so many foreign players has lost much of its potency since the "Brexit" vote to leave the European Union in 2016, as English national teams in 2017 won the U-20 and U-17 FIFA World Cups for the first time. In 2018, England's senior team made its first World Cup semifinal since 1990, and they were runners-up in both Euro 2020 and Euro 2024. Losing back-to-back finals of Europe's championship might seem like nothing to boast about, unless you're England and hadn't even made a final previously.

England has an abundance of talent like never before, and each time the national team is selected, fans are upset that some star or another has been left out of the squad. England managers have struggled in recent years with too many good choices at too many positions, international football's version of a first-world problem. There may be fewer English players starting in the Premier League than ever before, but a higher proportion of them are world-class, because every week they must compete alongside and against the best from all over the world, while being coached by the world's best managers.

It's interesting to again resort to the Premier League's own website description of itself—under that "What We Do" tab—to see this theme addressed squarely, if not defensively:

> The global stars attracted to the Premier League help raise the playing standards of young English talent such as Phil Fodden, Bukayo Saka, Jordan Pickford, Trent Alexander-Arnold, and Marcus Rashford. Our clubs are producing excellent players, who take their place alongside international superstars on merit.

If young Nick Hornby was dazzled in another era by the glimpses he caught during World Cups of the world's best playing an exotically different game from what he was accustomed to from watching Arsenal, today's fans don't have that experience. They're watching those South American and continental stars play week in and week out in their English league, whose tactics and style are no longer insular, but rather a synthesis of all these foreign influences.

Brexit provided an opportunity for football's protectionists to reopen debates about the game's openness because players from EU countries no longer had an automatic right to work in Britain. The league could have reimposed earlier limits on foreign players; but instead, buoyed by the direction of travel, it doubled down on globalization by making it easier to sign foreign non-EU talent as well.

In short, if the NFL invites us to rethink and revisit socialism, the EPL is quite an advertisement for neoliberalism.

Eventually, it does feel like football, in the form of its ultimate trophy, will have to "come home," as the English fans like to chant, for all this radical globalization to be fully vindicated. Hence the hopes and pressure placed on this "golden generation" of English players leading into the 2026 North American World Cup.

All the best to them, and to their German manager.

5

Who Says No to Morgan Freeman?

December 2, 2010 was a dark day for what Winston Churchill loved calling the "English-speaking peoples" and for the more capitalist, less statist Anglo-American approach to sport. It was also a dark day for FIFA, and for the proposition that international sport is governed in the public interest, with an adherence to transparency and the rule of law. Because it was on that day, at the same meeting in FIFA's Zurich headquarters, that the executive committee of the governing body of the world's most popular sport voted to award its 2018 men's World Cup to Russia over England, and its 2022 World Cup to Qatar over the United States. Even the people who ran FIFA at the time knew these decisions would raise a raft of uncomfortable questions about how both bids had prevailed.

The choice of Qatar was especially dubious. The Persian Gulf nation had never even qualified to play in a World Cup before, which had previously been considered a prerequisite for hosting. FIFA's own unflattering technical evaluation of the Qatari bid noted that the place seemed too small, lacking enough cities for a World Cup, which are awarded to countries, not city-states.[1] Qatar's bid was also submitted under the false pretense that its World Cup could be held in the summer without disrupting the sport's worldwide calendar, thanks to newfangled heat-mitigation technologies the organizers would incorporate into all its venues. It would take another five years before the Qatari organizers and FIFA abandoned this pretense and announced they were indeed pushing the tournament to the end of the year.[2] Subsequent scrutiny would focus on Qatar's human rights record, but there would have been threshold questions about the suitability of this pick even if it had been the ultimate paragon of human rights.

It might have made more sense for FIFA to consider holding a regional World Cup in the Middle East and Persian Gulf that included a few games in Qatar, but also some in the United Arab Emirates, Saudi Arabia, and perhaps Egypt. The impulse to extend the reach of the game beyond its traditional Europe-Americas axis, and to bring the World Cup to new continents is laudable, but hadn't FIFA asked Japan and Korea to share the first one held in Asia? Awarding the tournament to Qatar alone was indefensible, and FIFA's own leadership knew this.[3]

On top of it all, in choosing Qatar over the United States by a 14-to-8 vote, FIFA's "ExComm" (two of its members were barred from voting due to corruption allegations) was defying the entreaties of not one, not two, but three US presidents. On the eve of the vote, each bidding nation for the two different World Cups made their final pitches, and Team USA's forty-minute "The game is in US" presentation included a recorded message from President Barack Obama, and addresses in the room from the bid committee's Honorary Chairman Bill Clinton, Morgan Freeman, Sunil Gulati (the head of US Soccer), and one of our best players, Landon Donovan. In what could have been a dramatic foreshadowing of things to come, US Attorney General Eric Holder was also in the room, as the government's lead representative on the bid committee.

Talk about a Dream Team. The current president reminded FIFA that its previous US World Cup, in 1994, had posted record attendance figures, and he assured the delegates that the passion for the game "burns stronger than ever." Former president Clinton talked about how he'd felt "something magical" taking place as he watched his daughter grow up playing soccer, as part of the first generation of Americans to have embraced the global game. Our greatest fictional president ever, Morgan Freeman (he's also played God, come to think of it) exuded much gravitas in saying, "Never has my country been more committed to bringing an event to our shores." A video he narrated that kicked off the presentation called the United States "the world's home away from home," and Clinton boasted that the United States could fill stadiums with supportive fans for almost any nation, even before anyone traveled for the tournament. Gulati's closing argument appealed to FIFA's interest in all the riches that remained for global football to extract from the United States as the game continued to gain in popularity. For all its popularity, he pointed out that soccer then still only accounted for two percent of all sports sponsorship spending in the country.[4]

Sepp Blatter, FIFA's president at the time, favored the United States bid for all these reasons, and he was as stunned as the US delegation was when he pulled "Qatar" out of the envelope containing the 2022 host nation.

Cataloging and assessing all the allegations of corruption surrounding the two votes on that day are beyond the scope of *The Great Game*, but it's worth highlighting a few key and at times misunderstood takeaways from all the subsequent charges, countercharges, and prosecutions—not to mention from what went on to transpire.

First, as we all know, Russia and Qatar did go on to host their World Cups in the end. This was not because the various probes into FIFA's inner workings after 2010 failed to uncover any corruption in the game. Quite the contrary. So much corruption was found surrounding almost every aspect of how FIFA went about its business—including the selection of previous World Cup hosts—that it would have been difficult to single out Russia or Qatar for any alleged misbehavior. Indeed, there was less of an evidentiary "smoking gun" for their selection than for some previous World Cup picks and rights deals. The most concrete case of corruption by a high Qatari official was unrelated to the World Cup host selection process, occurring a few months later when Mohamed bin Hammam, who ran the Asian Football Confederation, was challenging Sepp Blatter for FIFA's presidency at its 2011 Congress. Prior to the vote, CONCACAF's president Jack Warner arranged to have bin Hammam address Caribbean national federations in Port of Spain. To make his vision of FIFA's future more persuasive, bin Hammam brought "token gifts" for each federation—traditional manila envelopes stuffed with $40,000 in cash. Word leaked—cue scenes of Blatter's men in Zurich being shocked, shocked to find gambling in the casino—and bin Hammam had to step aside from the election, and he and Warner were banned from any further involvement with the sport.[5]

Second, the selection of World Cup hosts turned out not to be the main event in terms of FIFA corruption. That honor would belong to the management of commercial and media rights, and on that score, the original sin establishing the template for national and regional federations to follow was established by Adidas' CEO Horst Dassler in the early 1980s when he leveraged his close partnership with FIFA to create a sports media marketing firm ("International Sport and Leisure") which acquired the rights to sell FIFA's World Cup rights to broadcasters around the world, while providing lavish kickbacks to FIFA president João Havelange and others for the privilege of doing so.[6] Similar deals at the regional confederation and national federation level were at the heart of the US Department of Justice racketeering case, which would eventually result in charges being brought against more than fifty individual and corporate defendants from twenty countries. That years-long investigation burst into the open with the arrest of FIFA officials in May 2015 at their Zurich hotel.

Third, our regional confederation for North and Central America and the Caribbean (Go CONCACAF!) was as corrupt as any. FIFA's democratic structure, granting each member state one vote equal to all others, meant that CONCACAF, with thirty-five members (many of them small Caribbean nations) represented a mighty voting bloc within the global game, a voting bloc that in the years prior to the 2010 vote had been controlled by the Trinidadian Jack Warner and his charismatic American General Secretary Chuck Blazer, who famously resided in Manhattan's Trump Tower (where FIFA opened an office in 2025, with a lease pregnant with historical irony). The team of US prosecutors and FBI and IRS agents that spent years investigating FIFA lucked out when they discovered early on that Blazer had never filed a tax return. He thus became the investigators' prized informant and explained to them the two types of people involved in international soccer: "those who took bribes, and those who paid them."[7]

The Department of Justice claimed jurisdiction over the global racketeering case because so many of the illegal financial transactions went through the US banking system, but the question of whether this all amounted to overreach by Uncle Sam would become a contested political and legal question that defendants pressed with mixed success in appealing their convictions.[8]

The fourth and most important takeaway in understanding the influence-peddling of Russia and Qatar is the realization that cash-in-manila-envelopes corruption becomes anachronistic and wholly unnecessary when replaced by the finesse of high-stakes state diplomacy. Consider the decisive event in the Qatari campaign to overtake the United States bid to host the 2022 World Cup, a November 2010 lunch hosted by French President Nicolas Sarkozy for Sheikh Hamad bin Jassim al Thani, the Emir of Qatar, his son Sheikh Tamim bin Hamad Al Thani (who would succeed his father in 2013), and French football idol Michel Platini.

Platini was then a vice president of FIFA and the powerful head of the game's European confederation, UEFA. He was also one of the key votes on FIFA's 24-member executive committee, with much influence over other members. According to FIFA boss Sepp Blatter, the two men had earlier agreed to vote for Russia for 2018 and the United States for 2022. But something shifted at that lunch, and the following month Platini and thirteen fellow FIFA ExCom members voted in the fourth round for Qatar over the United States. Presumably, Qatar's 14–8 victory could have been a narrow loss but for this turnabout (there were three other UEFA members who were believed to be swayed by Platini), which would be amply investigated in the future, including by French law enforcement.[9] In the end, Platini, along with a half-dozen other FIFA officials who voted on the 2018 and 2022 World Cup selections (including Chuck Blazer and Jack Warner) would face corruption charges unrelated to the Qatari bid and be banned from the game.[10]

Platini has always maintained that the decision to vote for Qatar was one he made on his own, though he has acknowledged that the lunch impressed upon him that President Sarkozy was behind the Qataris and felt it was in France's economic interests to back the Persian Gulf state.[11] And indeed, within a year of being awarded the World Cup, the Qatari sovereign wealth fund had acquired Sarkozy's favorite (and financially beleaguered) team, Paris Saint-Germain, which would subsequently become one of Europe's biggest spenders, at one point signing Leo Messi, Kylian Mbappé, and Neymar. Meanwhile, the Qatari-owned beIN Sports network paid generously for the broadcast rights to France's Ligue 1. French-Qatari commercial ties only deepened from there. French elites have long resented America's cultural ascendance and dominance, so tripping up, or delaying, the Americans' bid to become the center of global football might have been an additional motivation for French efforts to tip the scales in Qatar's favor.

But as I often discuss with my students, it isn't clear that anything surrounding that fateful luncheon at the Elysee Palace amounted to outright corruption. At that rarefied level of diplomacy, explicit quid pro quos can be dispensed with once an alignment of interests is identified.

Ah, yes, it would be nice to rejuvenate a club of such importance to the community as Paris Saint-Germain, Mr. President, and we would love to explore what can be done together on that.

And as you know, we are pursuing the World Cup as a catalyst for our nation-building project precisely because we share your belief in the power of football to bring people together and create social cohesion.

Well, it is not for me as the head of the French government to tell FIFA how to conduct its business, but I for one applaud your desire to bring football to your people. Everyone deserves to participate and share in the global game.

And so on.

At some point over the course of the meal, the Qataris could have mentioned in passing, apropos of nothing other than the thought of traveling home, of course, how stressful it is to find enough top-notch aircraft on the market for one's fast-growing airline. By then, Morgan Freeman's rhetorical flourishes for Team USA would lose any remaining allure. The contours of an understanding would have been quite clear by the time the crème brûlée was served at the Elysee Palace.

Qatar has insisted throughout that it did nothing improper in pursuing its World Cup bid, and it's only fair to acknowledge that the whole system they had to navigate in pursuit of the tournament was extremely corrupt long before they arrived on the scene. As the tournament approached, questions over Qatar's baseline eligibility as a potential host, and the circumstances surrounding its selection, gave way to concerns over its treatment of its LGBTQ population and of the migrant workers building the tournament's infrastructure.

Morgan Freeman of all people played a starring role in the Qatari production. FIFA might have said no to his pitch to hold the 2022 tournament in America, but when the curtain was raised for the opening ceremonies in Doha, there was Freeman walking across the misty stage as a wise man from the West (or a nomadic deity?) who'd heard "the call to celebration" and engaged in a dialogue about tolerance with Ghanim Al Muftah, a Qatari influencer and activist for people with disabilities. If you read closely between Freeman's lines, the Qataris were clearly letting us know exactly what they made of all the fuss and opposition stirred up around their bid:

> I remember even after hearing the call, instead of seeing another way, we dismissed it and demanded our own way and now the world feels even more distant and divided.
>
> How can so many countries, languages, and cultures come together if only one way is accepted?
>
> What unites us here in this moment is so much greater than what divides us. . . . But how can we make it last longer than just today?

Qatar and Russia clearly wanted, and felt they needed, the World Cup far more than Britain and the United States did, and it's important to step back and appreciate that while Vladimir Putin and the ruling family of Qatar were operating in very different contexts, their bids both represented state-sponsored efforts to harness sport to advance national objectives. The practitioners of this state-sponsored model are the great rivals to US sporting interests in the Great Game to gain the upper hand in global sport. They are also our co-conspirators in accelerating the globalization of sport at a time when globalization is being reconsidered in other walks of life.

By contrast to this state-sponsored model, as discussed earlier in the context of Olympic geopolitics, we don't deem the performance of either America's athletes or our professional sports industry a vital public or governmental concern. Our global sporting ties and endeavors are driven by the cultural and business imperatives of private actors, with limited state involvement. Barack

Obama was happy to record a short video addressing FIFA's ExCom on behalf of America's World Cup bid, but the decision to pursue that bid in the first place was not his to make. Obama, Freeman, and Clinton could offer all "The game is within US" platitudes they wanted in Zurich and talk up the merits of the US World Cup bid, but at the end of the day they could not direct a big investment fund or an NFL franchise to go out and bail out a struggling football club in France. Nor could an American president pick up the phone and ask a major US media company to overpay for the rights to televise a league overseas to advance his foreign policy objectives.

American sporting power does not reside in the White House or the State Department. It is diffuse and radiates from the NFL offices on Park Avenue in New York, the Disney CEO's office in Burbank, the Electronic Arts complex in Redwood City, Coca-Cola's skyscraper in Atlanta, Nike's campus in Beaverton, the commissioner offices of the major collegiate athletic conferences, and so on. America's quest to conquer global sport—not only by continuing to expand the overseas reach of our Big Three domestic leagues but also by establishing ourselves as the improbable epicenter of the world's most popular sport—is taking place in classically American fashion, through a convergence of cultural, societal, and economic forces and uncoordinated decisions made by individuals in settings that range from corporate boardrooms to suburban family dinner tables.

Even in the absence of outright corruption, it isn't hard to see how these nations embracing state-sponsored sporting development would prove seductive partners to FIFA and the IOC, organizations that understandably love it when sport is a top priority for a regime wielding unlimited resources and political control. Democracies, with their overlapping jurisdictions and interest groups, independent media, pesky public opinion, and concerns over budgetary constraints and transparency, are more complicated partners in the organization of something as complex and massive as a World Cup or an Olympic Games. But an authoritarian regime—and let's face it, state-sponsored sporting projects normally are headed up by authoritarian regimes—eager to host a massive sporting event and brand itself through it is a dream partner for sporting authorities who can rest assured the bills will be paid, deadlines met, dissent muted, all while the proverbial trains run on time. If FIFA had any issues in its preparations for Russia or Qatar, it only needed to make one phone call to have them addressed.

A World Cup played across North America is a different type of dream for FIFA, delightful in terms of the commercial opportunities, but more of a logistical nightmare as it is forced to engage with a byzantine array of overlapping federal, state, county, and municipal jurisdictions. Whatever understanding FIFA might have with Washington is not going to compel the City Council in Los Angeles or San Francisco, or law enforcement agencies in Harris or Jackson County, to do anything they aren't keen to do.

That said, Donald Trump is no ordinary US president, and he understands the World Cup is no ordinary event. Trump, who owned the New Jersey Generals in the doomed USFL in the mid-1980s, is a creature of media who understands the power that comes from presiding over sport. In his first weeks in office during his second term in 2025, he rushed to New Orleans to attend the Super Bowl, the first sitting president to ever do so.[12] And he understands that the men's FIFA World Cup, to be played over a month as America celebrates its 250th birthday in 2026, will culminate in a final match with a global audience that is fifteen to twenty times larger than the Super Bowl's, as FIFA president Gianni Infantino reminded him at the first meeting of the White House's "World Cup Task Force" hosted by President Trump on May 6, 2025.

FIFA's novel Club World Cup that kicked off the following month provided a dry run for what might be expected next summer, with President Trump playing the part of avid aficionado. When Juventus played a match In Washington, Infantino had the players of the Italian club swing by the Oval Office to meet the president, who held an impromptu press conference on topics ranging from a Supreme Court ruling on trans rights to the possibility of a military strike against Iran while the athletes looked on uncomfortably. Then President Trump presided over the final at Giants Stadium on July 13. And more than aficionado, this time he could have been mistaken for Chelsea's manager, as he ended up lingering on the winners' dais as the London club celebrated their surprise win over Paris Saint-Germain. Moreover, the eye-catching (OK, blingy) trophy Tiffany designed for the tournament remained in the Oval Office months after the tournament, at which point FIFA clarified that the president had been given a copy for his successful hosting of the tournament.

The fact that an "America First" president whose nostalgia-fueled political project is predicated on a belief that globalization went too far is fully invested in FIFA's World Cup is a sign of how much the country's relationship with the global game has changed over the past generation. Not long ago, an American political leader with Trump's ideological profile would have been hostile toward FIFA. But Trump hosted Infantino in the White House twice in his first four months in office, and at the first meeting of his World Cup task force, he talked about what a big soccer fan his son Barron is and pledged to Infantino that the 2026 World Cup would be the "biggest, safest, and most extraordinary soccer tournament in history." Vice President Vance (who oddly quipped that all those visitors who come to the tournament should return home when it's over) and most of Trump's key cabinet members were also present at the meeting.[13]

Stylistically, Trump is closer to the state-sponsored sporting power leaders with whom Infantino is used to partnering. And as a showman, Trump may prove to be more solicitous of FIFA's needs, and more engaged with the details of the tournament than US presidents would normally be. Infantino looked extremely pleased to be hosted at the White House, and the following week he accompanied Trump on the president's trip to Saudi Arabia, which made him arrive late to his own FIFA Congress in Paraguay, much to the annoyance of European football officials, who staged a walkout in protest.[14]

Back in 2010, when the two World Cups were awarded to Russia and Qatar, the bloc of state-sponsored sporting powers appeared formidable rivals to the United States in the Great Game to conquer global sport. Russia, China, and the Persian Gulf nations were wholeheartedly in the game, mobilizing tremendous resources to host global sporting events, acquire overseas trophy assets, or compete successfully across a range of sports.

The Great Game had also expanded beyond the contest to occasionally host one of the big tentpole international sporting events, or to perform well in prestigious international competitions. Increasingly, these states wanted to become invested, embedded, and associated with week-to-week, year-round sports—in the same way that beer and car brands are. Why just host one-off big events when you could buy a permanent stake (fancy Chelsea, Manchester City, or Newcastle?) in the world's most followed league? Why not own the sports broadcasting platform on which millions of fans globally engage with their passion? Why not bring more and more routine but high-profile sporting events to your realm? Why not launch your own golf tour so the game's stars from around the world play under your auspices? In this age of state-sponsored sporting powers, my son grew up knowing of "the Emirates" and "the Etihad" as stadiums in England, well before knowing they were Emirati airlines based in Dubai and Abu Dhabi.

Over the past couple of decades, no world leader has valued sport more as a means of branding his regime and nation—even his persona—than Vladimir Putin. For the Russian dictator, excelling at sport and displaying the requisite vigor to do so, was the perfect antidote to any perceived decadence or decline (personal or national), much as it was for Teddy Roosevelt a century earlier. Hence the pervasive imagery over the years of Putin on the ice rink, playing alongside Russian hockey greats, horseback riding without a shirt, penning books about judo, swimming in icy waters, fly fishing, and allegedly dating former Olympians.[15] So you can imagine how painful it must have been for him to watch a Russia-free Summer Olympic Games in Paris and a Russia-free men's World Cup in Qatar. Such a contrast from a decade ago, when Putin had hosted the 2014 Sochi Winter Games, looked ahead to hosting the next men's World Cup in 2018, and was feted by IOC and FIFA mandarins as one of sport's greatest benefactors. Indeed, he was the guest of honor at the opening ceremony of the Beijing Winter Olympics in early 2022, as his troops were assembling near Russia's border with Ukraine.

St. Petersburg was to have hosted the European Champions League final later that spring of 2022. Gazprom, Russia's state energy behemoth, had become the number one sponsor of European football, whose defending club champion as Putin sat watching the Beijing Olympics was Chelsea, owned by his former associate Roman Abramovich, who'd earlier chaired Russia's bid to land the 2018 men's World Cup. Russia had also obtained a coveted Formula 1 Grand Prix for Sochi and become a consistent provider of top talent for the glamorous tennis circuit.

But then all of Russia's accumulated soft power through sport was wiped away; the country was even banned from participating in the Eurovision Song Contest. The British government, as discussed earlier, moved to force a sale of Chelsea as part of its sanctions against Russian oligarchs, and that represented a pickup for Team USA in the Great Game as the club was acquired by another American ownership group. FIFA's top brass, for their part, might not have moved on their own against Putin, their 2018 host with whom they got along famously, but UEFA members like Poland, Sweden, and the Czech Republic forced international football's hand by refusing to play scheduled World Cup qualifiers against Russia.[16]

The *vozhd* in the Kremlin must have been surprised by the suddenness and vehemence of Russia's expulsion from international sport in the aftermath of his "special military operation," given that the trend in recent years (under the banner of not politicizing sport) has been toward inclusion and participation, regardless of geopolitical differences and regimes' off-field misbehavior. The Olympic "movement" lives in fear of a return to the 1976–84 period, when three consecutive Summer Olympic Games—Montreal, Moscow, and Los Angeles—were affected by three different boycotts that kept a substantial number of countries from participating.

Mindful of this history, the IOC's sanctions against Russia were cautiously crafted to minimize their precedential value for other countries and political controversies. At a press conference prior to the Paris 2024 Olympic Games' opening ceremony, Thomas Bach, the president of the IOC, said he had turned down a Palestinian request to bar Israel from the Olympics because it would infringe on the IOC's political neutrality, adding that if the IOC were to "approve exclusions on the basis of nations that are at war with one another the number of Olympic committees in Paris [206] would probably be cut in half."

But Russia had committed transgressions against the Olympic movement itself, and that was the principal reason it was being sanctioned. Its state-sponsored doping excesses had already landed Putin's Russia on an Olympic probation of sorts at the Rio de Janeiro and Tokyo Summer Games, where Russian athletes had to compete under a "Russian Olympic Committee" flag and the nation's anthem wasn't played during medal ceremonies.

The post-invasion sanctions imposed on Russia in 2022 were also framed as a response to Olympic misconduct, rather than a judgment on unrelated world affairs. One of Russia's grievous sins meriting an escalation of the preexisting doping sanctions was its annexation of regional Ukrainian Olympic federations in Russian-occupied territory. Also, in the immediate aftermath of Russia's February invasion, Olympic officials made much of the fact that Putin had violated the "Olympic truce," the call to refrain from any conflict during the period covering the Olympics and Paralympics, plus the week prior and after.

As a guest of honor at the Beijing Winter Games in early 2022, Putin was not going to embarrass his important Chinese allies by launching his invasion during their athletic celebration. He instead waited until four days after the Games were over. Or so he thought: He didn't consider the Paralympic Games (perhaps that's on brand for him). And, in any case, the truce extends seven days, not just four, after a Games' conclusion.

It's equally deplorable, surely, to invade your neighboring country two weeks after an Olympics than two days after, but for purposes of the IOC sanctioning Russia in such a way that didn't open up Bach's feared Pandora's box stuffed with "but what about X, Y, or Z country?" inquiries, the more the sanctions were framed as infractions against sport and the Olympics themselves, the better.

But either way, Putin's own goal had sidelined Russia from being a Great Game protagonist during a critical period, when American efforts to acquire more of global sports were intensifying.

The case of China is more mystifying. A decade ago, China would have figured prominently in any analysis of the Great Game to gain a controlling stake in international football. But then, almost as quickly as China had spent its way into becoming a formidable state-sponsored force in the game, it took a drastic U-turn and retreated back into its corner.

President Xi Jinping has made no secret of his fandom for the game, and for Manchester United in particular. He asked that a state visit to Britain in 2015 focus on Manchester instead of London, and Prime Minister David Cameron hosted him in the northern city. While there, the Chinese delegation also visited with Manchester City, which would soon thereafter welcome Chinese investors acquiring a minority stake in the club. China has only ever qualified to play in one men's World Cup (it is much stronger in the women's game), back in 2002, but within months of his visit to Manchester, President Xi announced that the country would seek to host the men's World Cup in 2030 and become one of the sport's superpowers by 2050.[17] The Chinese government issued ambitious plans to invest in the game at the grassroots level and signaled it was eager to see China's conglomerates and state enterprises create one of the world's top domestic leagues, as well as acquire some of Europe's top clubs.

For a couple of years, Chinese investors were among the biggest spenders in the game, acquiring clubs like West Bromwich Albion, Southampton, Wolverhampton Wolves, Aston Villa, and Birmingham City in England; Atlético Madrid and Espanyol in Spain; and the two Milan giants, Inter and AC, in Italy. Chinese clubs also spent lavishly on signing big stars away from European clubs, in a way the Saudi league would do a few years later.[18] In 2016 alone, China's domestic Super League clubs, many of them owned by the country's high-flying commercial real estate firms, spent $450 million in player transfer fees.[19]

Soon thereafter, China's leadership made its U-turn, with a series of measures and policies whose consistent theme was a refusal to cede control. The government imposed a hefty tax on the previously encouraged transfer fees, and President Xi's regime began leveraging corruption investigations to rein in companies and tycoons who were amassing too much power in the eyes of the Communist Party. Xi began to talk up the goal of "common prosperity" and the virtues of a more equitable distribution of riches and an abstinence from Western ostentation. The crackdown on the autonomy and growing cult of personality surrounding some of China's more charismatic billionaires came in late 2020 when the government scratched the initial public offering of Jack Ma's Ant Group, a fintech darling, and imposed a multi-billion-dollar fine on his other major company, the Alibaba online retailer.[20]

President Xi was clearly worried that if not reminded of their subservience to the state, China's tycoons could become a competing power base to the Communist Party. He is also ever mindful that Chinese public opinion has little patience and tolerance for corruption, which includes the scourge of match-fixing and ostentation often found in international football. [21]

As much as he might be a fan, President Xi and his top advisors must have worried about the difficulty of exerting any control over the nation's footballing fortunes. In contrast to China's meticulous and systematic analysis of major and niche Olympic events with an eye toward maximizing the nation's yield of medals, the country's rulers could very well spend the next few decades boasting that China is on the verge of footballing greatness without actually knowing for certain whether they could ever deliver on that promise.[22] Chinese football, remarkably given the stakes, has not yet produced its Yao Ming, a bona fide superstar to represent the country in the world's top leagues. The country failed to qualify for the men's 2026 World Cup, even with the expansion in the number of participating nations from thirty-two to forty-eight.

The freewheeling off-field culture of overseas sports leagues may have given Chinese leaders further reason for pause. In the fall of 2019, Chinese authorities had to contend with two critical tweets from people associated with Western sports teams that are extraordinarily popular within their country. Houston Rockets General Manager Daryl Morey tweeted an image supportive of protesters in Hong Kong, followed within weeks by Arsenal's talented German midfielder Mesut Özil tweeting out a strong statement denouncing China's treatment of its Uighur Muslim population in the western province of Xinjiang.[23]

In both cases, Chinese authorities lashed out at the clubs (who rushed to distance themselves from their employees' views) and leagues involved, betraying a thin-skinned unpreparedness to participate in global sport. Perhaps best for now to focus inward on developing sport at the grassroots level and continue to challenge the West for Olympic supremacy in that more controlled environment of nation-state face-offs.

And so, the last few years have seen a hasty selloff of European footballing assets by Chinese investors. Russell Jones' Wolves, owned by the Fosun Group, remain for now the last English club in Chinese hands, with most of the others having been sold to American owners. Italy, meanwhile, provided a stark illustration of China's retreat and America's advance in the Great Game when control over Inter Milan changed hands in May of 2024 from Suning to Oaktree Capital Management, a Los Angeles-based investment firm, after the Chinese conglomerate defaulted on a loan.[24] Inter would then make the Champions

League final the following year, though they were humiliated in it 5–0 by Paris Saint-Germain on the day the Qataris at last won their European prize.

It's hard to imagine that China will not be a player again someday in the Great Game, but for now, for different reasons and in different ways, China and Russia, who looked poised to play such large roles in the game's outcome a decade ago, are both taking a breather on the bench.

Which pretty much leaves the Persian Gulf States alone on the Great Game's field with Team USA, as the world's other primary sports globalizers, carrying the banner of the state-sponsored model.

Back when FIFA said no to Morgan Freeman in 2010 and handed the 2022 men's World Cup to Qatar, the two deep-pocketed Gulf states investing heavily and successfully in sport were Qatar and the United Arab Emirates. Saudi Arabia, inspired by its smaller neighbors, only joined the Great Game in the intervening years, coinciding with Russia's and China's retreat.

Faced with the conundrum of being young, unimaginably wealthy but small nations facing uncertain futures in a turbulent part of the world, the UAE and Qatar, to a lesser extent, emulated Singapore's strategy for cementing their place on the map by becoming respected regional hubs and safe havens. The formula included a technologically advanced port with ample capacity; an embrace of free trade and commercial and legal protections for investors; a wealth of amenities to induce these investors and their families to stick around; and a world-renowned airline to leverage all these assets, wave your flag around the world, and complement your port in making you a global connector. These Persian Gulf emirates followed the Singaporean recipe faithfully (on a visit years ago with Foreign Ministry officials in Abu Dhabi, I learned they all had to read Lee Kuan Yew's memoirs as part of their training) but added the additional ingredient of becoming associated with prestigious international sport, both by hosting high-profile events and by sponsoring competitions, teams, and venues elsewhere. Manchester City and Paris Saint-Germain are owned by Emiratis and Qataris, as discussed earlier, and plenty of other major European clubs like Arsenal, AC Milan, and Real Madrid advertise Emirates, the airline, on the front of their jerseys. Emirates' name is also attached to

England's FA Cup and the NBA's mid-season tournament, as well as a host of tennis, golf, horse racing, rugby, and sailing competitions.

Until fairly recently, Saudi Arabia did not share its smaller neighbors' ambitions to be cosmopolitan entrepots—playgrounds even—where foreigners of all stripes could feel at home whether in pursuit of business or pleasure. Unlike Qatar and the UAE, the Saudis had a considerable population (closing in on 35 million in 2025), a sizable land mass, and were believed to control the world's largest proven oil reserves (until that honor went to Venezuela). Saudi leaders had long wanted to keep foreign influences at bay to preserve their conservative, theocratic rule and culture, and saw no reason they shouldn't do as they pleased. Things changed with the generational shift within the Saudi ruling family, and Crown Prince Mohammed bin Salman's "Vision 2030" masterplan issued in 2016 for a Saudi future predicated on the three pillars of a "vibrant society," "thriving economy," and "ambitious nation."

Modernizing autocrats who look to the West for partnership in adopting many of modernity's trappings and dragging their societies out of feudalism—from Peter the Great to Deng Xiaoping and the Shah of Iran—typically end up perplexing their Western partners when the limits of their modernization plans become clear. In Saudi Arabia's case, epochally meaningful changes have been introduced in short order that upset traditionalists. In 2017, for the first time, women were allowed to drive and join women's gyms, and policies were established to encourage their participation rate in the workforce, which soared to 36 percent by 2025. The regime did away with the roaming religious police. The first movie theaters in the kingdom opened in the spring of 2018, debuting with *Black Panther*. Young people in Riyadh now attend rock concerts and hang out at malls, like their counterparts in Dubai or Doha do, or in Phoenix for that matter. When it comes to football, women have gone from being banned from attending men's matches as spectators to being able to play in their own professional league.[25]

But "MBS," as the Crown Prince is known, has driven this transformation with an iron fist. Dissidents and critics have been persecuted and jailed, and in the fall of 2017, many investors, including many of his relatives, were bizarrely locked up at a Ritz-Carlton in an ostensible crackdown on corruption while MBS and his ministers impressed upon them who was in charge.[26] The following year's horrific murder of Jamal Khashoggi, a Saudi columnist for *The Washington Post* who was critical of MBS, during an appointment at the Saudi consulate in Istanbul, remains the most enduring stain on the Saudi rulers' reputation.

Embedded in Vision 2030 is a feverish embrace of sport at every level, from grassroots recreational leagues to elite spectator events that draw global audiences. It all seems fueled by a potent mix of envy, regret, and a sense of urgency to make up for lost time: envy of neighboring Gulf states Qatar and the United Arab Emirates; and regret that Saudi Arabia didn't emulate their transformative branding-through-sport strategies earlier. It's as if MBS has ordered his ministers—and Saudi's deep-pocketed sovereign wealth fund, the "Public Investment Fund"—to do all the things the Emiratis and Qataris have been doing, only more so.

That playbook includes launching one of the world's best airlines and branding it through sport, so even before flying its first passenger, the aspirational Riyadh Air was already the jersey sponsor for Atlético Madrid in Spain's La Liga and also a sponsor for Saudi-owned LIV Golf. As I write this, Riyadh Air's website boasts of its planned top-notch service, the planes it has ordered, the retro uniforms its flight crews will wear, and the fact that it will fly to more than 100 destinations . . . by 2030.[27]

The Saudis have invested heavily in developing their own domestic league, where fans have been able to watch the likes of Cristiano Ronaldo, Karim Benzema, and Neymar. In addition, the Saudis have acquired two of the most prized trophies in the Great Game: an English Premier League club of their own, as well as the right to host the men's World Cup in 2034. FIFA awarded the Saudis the 2034 tournament at its same December 2024 gathering that agreed to send the 2030 edition to an eclectic combination of six countries representing three confederations—Spain, Portugal, Morocco, Argentina, Paraguay, and Uruguay. The South American countries will each only host one match, to commemorate the 100th anniversary of the first World Cup held in Uruguay, but the net effect of FIFA's move looks suspiciously like clearing the decks so that its Asian confederation would have first dibs on the 2034 World Cup. And lo and behold, the Saudis were the only Asian nation to submit a bid in time for the selection. The Saudi World Cup promises to be a reprise in some ways of the Qatar one, with the kingdom subjected to much outside scrutiny of its human rights record.

In the case of both Gulf states, critics charge them of engaging in sportswashing, and surely Qataris and Saudis, like every other big sporting event host and countless automakers and beer brewers, appreciate having their "brand" enhanced by an association with sport. But those of us in the West, and particularly in the United States, tend to exaggerate the extent to which other nations do what they do solely to influence or impress us. We tend to discount the influence of these other countries' domestic public opinions on events. MBS would likely be investing heavily in sport, whether we like it or not, because he is trying to materially alter his own citizens' understanding of where Saudi Arabia fits into the world and how younger Saudis should think about their lives in the kingdom.

We also mustn't fall into the trap of thinking these countries, or their World Cup bids, are interchangeable. Saudi Arabia is already a football-mad country of 35 million people with a deep history of playing the game at the international level. The Saudis had qualified to play in six men's World Cups, starting with USA '94, prior to being selected to host the 2034 edition, which is six more than Qatar had played in when it was selected. Qatar was an absurd choice even apart from any human rights issues; Saudi Arabia is not, though it does pose some of the same human rights concerns.

Human rights concerns also hovered over the Public Investment Fund's acquisition of Newcastle United in the English Premier League in the fall of 2021, which outraged much of Britain's media and fans across the English Premier League, except within the Toon Army, as Newcastle fans are known. For them, this was their chance to win the same "sugar daddy lottery" that had landed Manchester City and Chelsea unspeakably wealthy owners who transformed their long-term trajectories and netted them trophies in a relatively short period.

I visited Newcastle between the time the Saudi purchase had been announced and before the deal closed that fall of 2021. The black-and-white-striped club founded in 1892 has had its storied moments, but a fair amount of angst pervades even its better days. Newcastle is widely regarded as having fielded the best team not to win the Premier League in the modern era: the 1990s "Entertainers," a generation that included such stars as Alan Shearer, David Ginola, Les Ferdinand, and Andy Cole. Things have been far grimmer in recent years, including seasons spent relegated to the lower division, the Championship.

Newcastle's previous owner, Mike Ashley, who sold the club for $430 million to the Saudi-led group, was one of the few remaining English owners of a Premier League club. He'd made his fortune in discount retailing and was roundly denounced by supporters, fairly or unfairly, for lacking ambition and failing to invest enough to win.

But now the Saudis were coming, and Jim Burns was excited. I ran into him and his family—all decked out in their Newcastle gear—at the Chicken Coop restaurant in the center of town, a couple of hours before a three o'clock kickoff against Chelsea FC at St. James' Park, Newcastle's stadium. Burns has been going to Newcastle matches for six decades, since his father first took him when he was six. Supporting the team remained a family affair for him, as proved by his accompanying daughter, son-in-law, and two grandkids. "It is like a religion. Once you've been bitten, there is no going back," he said.

If you know Newcastle only dimly from reputation, then you know about the city's beer, and you might know about the foolishness of "bringing coal" to it. That expression stems from the city's pivotal role in economic history—an indispensable source of coal, and thus energy, for the industrialization of Britain and the growth of its empire. But Newcastle has reinvented itself as a cheerful, whimsical town of exuberant hills, stately architecture, and a scenic waterfront—a playground for its numerous university students, weekend visitors, and crazed football fans, all of whom can let their hair down and let go a bit, since they're practically in Scotland.

Newcastle United was struggling when I visited the city, in last place and in danger of being relegated at the end of the season. But with its wealthier owners coming to the rescue, Burns was looking forward to a turnaround. "I need to see them put their hands in their pockets and pull out the money," he said. "I expect them to do what Manchester City did, sure. Those are the least of my expectations."

When I asked Burns if he had any qualms about his club being associated with the Saudis, he gave me a bit of a "there you people go again" scowl, then let me in on a bit of a secret: The rest of the country, he told me solemnly, likes to conspire against Newcastle, "to keep us down." Burns said there was much hypocrisy and not a few double standards behind my question. "Why doesn't anyone care about Abramovich's human rights record?" True enough when he posed the question, though of course that would change a few months later after Russia invaded Ukraine, after which the Russian would be deemed unsuitable as a club owner.

Burns pointed out that the Saudis are welcome to invest in real estate and British companies, even to buy British armaments, and they have a strong relationship with the British government. But the minute they wanted to invest in Newcastle, suddenly everyone got all twitchy. This suggests to Burns that the outrage surrounding the deal is more about an aversion to the idea of Newcastle doing well than about the Saudis.

Burns' son-in-law, David Jones, was more measured, admitting there are things to be troubled about with the Saudi owners but that they're beyond the control of supporters. "And so, we have to distance ourselves from the politics, and focus on the sport in our community," he said. His wife Sarah offered this hopeful note about the Saudi takeover. "I think it can change things over there, in Saudi Arabia, as they come over here and become more familiar with our ways and experience more freedom," she said, making the classic Western pitch for the benefits of more involvement, rather than less, with troubling regimes. "Their desire to engage with the outside world, and the attention that comes with that could be good for people back there as well."

Walking the uphill cobbled pedestrian streets from the Chicken Coop to St. James' Park—which looms over the city's center, as any proper cathedral should—I came across the Back Page, a football memoir shop that lovingly curates old matchday programs, jerseys, and signed memorabilia from club legends. As I poked around for a couple of minutes, a boy came in with his father and excitedly bought a Saudi flag. "Large," he said when offered a choice. The salesclerk told me they had been selling swiftly and that he wished he'd had more earlier.

At St. James' Park, as is true across the entirety of English football, the anti-racism, anti-discrimination messaging is relentless, with signs everywhere advising fans to text stadium authorities to help them crack down on any forms of discrimination. The club's avowed values, the signs assured us fans, were "Diversity. Inclusion. Welfare."

United with Pride, Newcastle's own LGBTQ+ supporters' group, endorsed the Saudi takeover instead of joining other clubs' LGBTQ+ supporters' groups to protest against the new owners. United with Pride said in a statement: "There is potential to be a positive influence to improving the conditions of the LGBTQ+ community in Saudi Arabia and elsewhere," given that the owners will experience how minorities are treated elsewhere.[28]

Other clubs' supporters mounted protests over the Saudis crashing their league. The weekend before my visit, when Newcastle played away at Crystal Palace, fans there unveiled a massive banner mocking the Premier League for its vetting of prospective owners. The image showed an owners' test checklist that included terrorism, beheadings, civil rights abuses, among other atrocities, and a Saudi in traditional dress wielding a bloody sword.

I sat during the game at St. James Park next to Olly, an eighteen-year-old season ticket holder, who advised me to "come back in 10 years when we're top of the table." He was excited about the takeover and watched the day's lopsided loss to Chelsea with the equanimity of someone holding an uncashed winning lottery ticket in their pocket.

But he also acknowledged it would be "daft" to say that what happens in Saudi Arabia doesn't matter. "Of course, the situation in Saudi Arabia matters, and from what I hear it includes some horrible human rights abuses," he said. Echoing Sarah Jones and United with Pride, Olly added: "My hope is that this will help improve things there, bringing attention to the situation."

It's a tidy rationalization, but it seemed sincere: Newcastle could save Saudi Arabia while the Saudis save Newcastle.

David Taylor, a Newcastle native and lifelong United fan now working as a journalist in London, wasn't buying it. "I'm appalled that my club is being taken over by owners that don't respect human rights, and I'm honestly quite ashamed that more Newcastle supporters aren't speaking up," he told me.

Taylor feels a complicated mix of emotions. It isn't as if you can switch club allegiances as an adult, and an ownership group doesn't define the club or its history. "My view is it will always be our club, no matter which new owner with an agenda comes along," he said. "But if it is ours, and it is supposed to represent something we're proud of, we probably have to work to make sure the club stands for something that matters—and that's not just about football anymore."[29]

Who should be allowed to play the Great Game, owning stakes in global sport? Saudi Arabia's Public Investment Fund owns significant shares in blue-chip corporations like Disney, Citigroup, Bank of America, Uber, and Boeing. The Saudis, as Jim Burns pointed out to me at the Chicken Coop, are close allies of the UK. Should there be a higher standard for owning a football club? Once the English Premier League opens itself to outside buyers, is there a distinction to be drawn between US hedge fund billionaires and buyers from the Persian Gulf?

The Saudi purchase of Newcastle went through in the end, but from there things didn't unfold quite how fans had hoped. The club didn't go on an immediate, massive title-winning spending spree the way Chelsea and Manchester City did when they found their sugar daddy owners. Lionel Messi wasn't signed in that January transfer window to the biggest contract in sports history, though the new owners did sign the veteran right back Kieran Trippier and a few other useful players. It would have shocked most of the fans at St. James' Park on the day I was there to hear that some of the players they were watching in the black-and-white stripes would still be there three years after the takeover, but they were. And they were doing a lot better.

Newcastle fans might see it as the ultimate double standard leveled against them, but they weren't allowed to cash in their lottery ticket right away, as other clubs had. Unlike the 2000s and 2010s when Chelsea and Manchester City were transformed by their new owners, by the 2020s the Premier League has tightened financial regulations that require clubs to live within their means. Even if they wanted to, Saudi owners could no longer wire a billion dollars to Newcastle's checking account for player transfers and salaries. They would have to grow the club the old-fashioned way, increasing its revenues before they could increase spending.

And so, Newcastle United's ascent since the acquisition has been steady rather than spectacular, as much about the work of the team's earnest English manager Eddie Howe as anything else. He has improved the performance of players he inherited when he was hired by the new owners a month or so after my visit, and then successfully integrated smart signings like Trippier, Bruno Guimarães, and Dan Burn. The club has gone from fighting to avoid relegation to fighting for European places and made it to consecutive finals of the EFL Cup (named after the Indonesian energy drink Carabao), winning the trophy (the third most prestigious in English football) in spring 2025. It was Newcastle's first domestic trophy since 1955, and the town went understandably crazy.[30]

The fact that the club's fortunes have improved while operating under "PSR" (profit and sustainability) constraints has weirdly allowed Newcastle fans to occupy the moral high ground—even when owned by the richest sovereign wealth fund on earth!—vis-à-vis fans of the other big clubs in England who are allowed to continue outspending them.

As the most globalized of all sports leagues, the Premier League will continue to be where the global ambitions of America's sporting interests and their Persian Gulf counterparts compete and partner most directly, sitting around the same table as they jointly run a league on someone else's island. But it would be too simplistic to view a clash between US interests and Persian Gulf ones as a zero-sum game. This is not a Cold War proxy for a broader conflict, as US-Russian or US-Chinese contests can be. Persian Gulf rulers and investors are heavily invested in many of the same US funds acquiring English and European clubs and are mostly aligned with the United States in geopolitical terms. The Gulf states have seemingly infinite financial resources but pose no grand challenge or alternative ideological offering. They represent the most potent state-sponsored model of sport on the global stage these days, but one that is predisposed to act in concert with America.

Even the Saudis' audacious move to disrupt golf with the PIF-backed LIV Circuit—a case of not just luring one prestigious event to the kingdom, but of wanting to take over a prestigious sport's entire global organization—shows how intertwined Persian Gulf and American interests really are. When LIV debuted in 2022, the incumbent PGA's Commissioner Jay Monahan sounded much like Amnesty International in decrying the Saudis' lavish spending as an exercise in sportswashing. But within a year, he and LIV announced their intentions to come together, though they are still working on the details. All along, the foreign state-sponsored sporting rival to the PGA was allied with then-former and future president Donald Trump, who hosted LIV events at his golf courses—and it was the Biden-era Department of Justice that investigated PGA moves to quash LIV's rise, and then their planned association, for potential violations of antitrust laws.[31]

Though often portrayed in simplistic black-and-white terms, the intersection of sport and human rights poses difficult questions, trade-offs, and—to use a word seeping its way into most of our chapters—conundrums. And this is true even in the abstraction-friendly confines of the ivory tower and my classroom, a step removed from the real world. As I often ask my students, do we think participating in elite international sport is a right or a privilege? Does the answer differ whether we're talking about hosting international sporting events or merely competing in them? And do these rights or privileges belong to individual athletes or nations? And even if the answer is nations, do we mean their governments or their societies?

That last distinction has been poignantly made by Jamal Khashoggi's widow Hanan in several interviews, in which she has said she doesn't want Saudi Arabia to become a global sporting pariah (as South Africa's Apartheid regime was in the late twentieth century) because of what happened to her husband. "He would have been very happy his country got the opportunity of a World Cup," she told *The New York Times* in January 2025, "He didn't want his country to be a barrier. He wouldn't want his whole country to suffer because a small group of people took the life of an honest man," she said. She did express worry about the government using sport to deflect attention from its own mistakes and crimes, but called for event organizers to address that concern and even honor her husband's memory.[32]

A related conundrum is the question of whose values and standards sport's international governing bodies should reflect and enforce. This one constantly bedevils my idealistic college students. Many of them love sports and believe they are a force for good in the world, something purer than international politics or economic relations. Most of them are passionate about human rights, democracy, and decolonizing the world and its institutions to ensure a more representative and equitable international order. All laudable impulses and goals, but I do press them to appreciate that at times there can be uncomfortable tensions and trade-offs between them. For instance, the more inclusive and representative you make sport's international governing bodies (say, by giving every national committee an equal vote), the more you risk an erosion of standards as they settle for lowest common denominators between them. This is a problem faced by all multilateral governance institutions, starting with the United Nations' General Assembly.

You won't see a truly representative and democratically run international organization with more than 200 member states maintaining Scandinavian ethical and governance standards, but somehow, because this is about sports, that's what we'd like to imagine. But if a small Caribbean nation (to pick on our own CONCACAF region) struggles with corruption and a weak rule of law in its everyday governance, what reason is there to suspect it will overcome those vices when millions of FIFA dollars with few strings attached wash up ashore?

I have become more and more inclined to a "live and let live" attitude when it comes to sport, erring on the side of maximizing participation. Should we really bar a China or a Russia (at least when it isn't actively killing its neighbors) from hosting the Olympic Games because they don't respect their citizens' rights in the same way we do? If so, what's our response to others who might argue that the United States should also be barred on account of the death penalty? I don't want to go down this slippery slope that possibly leaves us with a sparsely attended intra-Scandinavian Olympics. That said, I can't deny that the decisions to allow Adolf Hitler to preside over the Olympic Games in 1936 and to allow Argentina's murderous military junta to preside over the 1978 FIFA World Cup were abhorrent and indefensible.

So, there is a line to be drawn. Somewhere.

I recently called up Michael Page, Deputy Director of the Middle East and North Africa Division at Human Rights Watch, to confess that I was at a loss as to where to draw this line, and that I am fearful of slippery slopes, even sand dune ones in the Persian Gulf. Who's to say which countries are beyond the pale, and which aren't, for sporting purposes?

Page was one of the leading critics of Qatar's treatment of migrant workers leading up to its World Cup, with HRW being part of a coalition of human and labor rights groups advocating for reforms to the Emirate's kafala system that deprived these workers of most rights because they were essentially indentured to one employer. Qatar did agree to some important reforms, though apparently abuses persisted in practice.

Page reassured me that it is OK to worry about slippery slopes and where to draw the lines. Even as a full-time human rights advocate, he doesn't believe we should hold out for perfection, pretending that we can leverage international football, however potent this "universal desire across all cultures," to solve all the world's human rights problems. He is also highly skeptical of "cultural boycotts" that seek to penalize countries for misdeeds. "When you ban Russia from a sports competition, you might be banning Chechen athletes who don't at all agree with the regime's foreign policy and might actually be victimized by it. So what are you accomplishing?" To Page, bans resulting from transgressions against the sport itself—for doping, say—make more sense.

What is so distinctive from a human rights perspective about the Persian Gulf men's World Cups, past and future, is the centrality of the human rights concern at issue to the execution of the tournament itself. It isn't as if groups like HRW went searching for tangential human rights issues to raise in these countries because a World Cup was headed their way. "The migrant workers we are talking about in the case of a country like Qatar are a majority of the humans in the polity and they are the ones who created the World Cup's physical imprint from scratch," he explained.

Page sounds more frustrated with FIFA than with any government, because it doesn't hold itself or its partner hosts accountable. In the years leading up to the Qatari World Cup, all the scrutiny and pressure on the nation's rulers on human rights came from outside media and human rights activists, not from the one body that might have had some leverage to force changes in what were essentially its own supply chains: FIFA. "FIFA's paramount concern throughout was not to embarrass the Qataris," Page said. And so, it failed to do what any responsible corporation does overseas, which isn't to clamor for fixes to all the world's ills it encounters, but to simply ensure that its own operations aren't compounding human rights abuses, environmental degradation, or other behaviors that are antithetical to its stakeholders' values.

In the aftermath of the Qatari selection and the corruption scandals that followed, FIFA pays a lot more lip service to its commitment to human rights, and to the fact that it holds host nations to certain human rights commitments. But it's hard to be optimistic that the organization will provide any more forceful oversight over its Saudi partners than it did over Qatar. Indeed, for all the talk of reform of FIFA in the wake of the US prosecutions of many of its top officials over the past decade, the opaque selection process for the 2030 and 2034 World Cup hosts seemed designed to hand the tournament to the Saudis with a minimum of fuss. And with all the sponsorship dollars flowing his way from the Persian Gulf, FIFA boss Gianni Infantino seems to view the region's rulers and their sovereign wealth funds much in the same way that Newcastle United fans do—as his ultimate sugar daddy.

FIFA's sprawling structure and multiplicity of missions, as another human rights group and even many within the sport have argued, also makes it difficult for the organization to hold partner hosts accountable for anything. There's an inherent conflict of interest in setting yourself up as a business (owning and operating those World Cups), the promoter of the sport worldwide, and its ultimate regulator. The new Club World Cup FIFA introduced in the summer of 2025 annoyed regional confederations like CONMEBOL and UEFA, who saw in it a FIFA money grab, a new tournament to compete with their established continental cups, with the added twist that it was created by their ostensible regulator.[33]

American sports have a long history of navigating civil rights debates in our country, and a checkered record of at times being part of the solution and at times part of the problem—and most often trying to pass as an unwitting bystander to societal ills. The Great Game now forces America's sporting interests to reckon with the collision of sport and human rights issues at a global level and makes the governance of organizations like FIFA and the IOC as relevant to Americans as any shenanigans at the United Nations. And the fact that the US government and many in the corporate sector view the Persian Gulf as a sugar daddy of their own will continue blurring lines in the Great Game contest with their state-sponsored model. We might already be on the same team.

6

Big Media's Conundrum

"So much sports. This is all sports. What happened? We used to be so gay," Jimmy Kimmel quipped during his roast at the Disney upfronts in May of 2025.[1] The upfronts are a staple of the TV and advertising worlds, an annual springtime ritual in New York City that dates back to 1962. Over the course of a week, TV networks—both their executives and celebrities—put on a show to introduce and promote their upcoming season's programs to the advertising community and the media. It's always been a famously profitable week for midtown Manhattan's finest eateries, as there is much schmoozing involved in moving billions of dollars' worth of ad inventory to Madison Avenue firms and their clients.

Kimmel's quip reflected an inescapable reality apparent to anyone following the 2025 upfronts, and larger trends within the industry: We're witnessing the "sportification" of media, such is the importance of sport to media's current business and future prospects, coming on the heels of the "mediafication" of sport in the twentieth century.

The Disney session at which Kimmel spoke was itself kicked off by five men walking onto the stage: Patrick Mahomes, Saquon Barkley (he of the Brazil jersey at the São Paulo conference), the Manning brothers, and Disney CEO Bob Iger. Despite all its storytelling prowess and IP franchises spread across its ABC broadcast network, its cable channels, and its Disney+ and Hulu streaming platforms, what Disney most wanted to highlight was that it was going to air some primetime NFL games on ABC, as it has been doing since 1970, and on ESPN, as it has since 1987. Disney also announced details that week of its new ESPN app that would for the first time make available core ESPN live sports programming to viewers who don't subscribe to cable.

As if to underscore its status as chief TV programmer across a number of media properties, the NFL timed the unveiling of its 2025 season's schedule to coincide with upfronts week, allowing the league's media partners—NBC, Fox, ABC/ESPN, Amazon, Netflix, and YouTube—to boast of the games they'd landed. The league was especially eager to promote its slate of seven international games, and excited to announce that the second annual Brazil game (an appetizing Chargers vs. Chiefs matchup) would again be played on the Friday of its opening weekend, but this time (free to viewers) on YouTube.

It's another sign of the times that disruptive streamers now also participate in this venerable legacy media institution of the upfronts. And that the presentations for two of them, YouTube and Netflix, starred NFL Commissioner Roger Goodell, whom influential Hollywood journalist Matt Belloni often refers to as "the most powerful man in entertainment," but during upfronts week referred to as "the belle at the ball."[2] The two platforms have limited NFL deals, and clearly Goodell is hoping they will want a much bigger serving next time the major rights are up for renewal.

Lamar Hunt's Chiefs are in high demand, so NFL schedulers featured the team in seven primetime games, more than any other team (the Cleveland Browns, New Orleans Saints, and Tennessee Titans were assigned no primetime exposure). The Chiefs were featured on both holidays, visiting the Dallas Cowboys on Thanksgiving and hosting the Denver Broncos on Christmas Day (you're welcome, CBS and Amazon Prime—and YouTube for your São Paulo treat). Defying the supposedly inexorable decline and fragmentation in viewership affecting all programming, the Chiefs' loss to the Eagles in New Orleans at Super Bowl LIX in January 2025 was the most-watched Super Bowl of all time, pulling in 127.7 million viewers domestically.[3]

The NFL's outsized cultural resonance is such that it can assert control over our nation's attention and sports news cycles even during its offseason. The league's staggered schedule reveals the week of the upfronts was a social media phenomenon, and its three-day draft in April—which in less creative hands might still be a press release—has become a three-day TV extravaganza attracting more viewers than any in-season live sports competing against it, as well as a massive tourism boon to the rotating cast of cities hosting it.[4] The NFL even arranged to have President Trump, flanked by Commissioner Goodell and DC mayor Muriel Bowser, announce from the Oval Office that its 2027 draft would be in the nation's capital.

The NFL might be top dog, but it isn't the only sport that is vitally important to TV broadcasters and streamers. Over at the NBC upfronts at Radio City Music Hall, Jimmy Fallon welcomed everyone by joking: "Good morning. I'm glad to be at the NBA upfronts—I mean the NBC upfronts." NBC was most excited to pitch to advertisers that this fall it would offer live sports on three nights in primetime: NBA on Tuesdays (as of October), college football on Saturdays, and the NFL on Sundays (to be replaced by a second NBA game once football season is over). The rest of the network's schedule, being less enthusiastically promoted, was a mix of reality shows and Dick Wolf procedurals (five by my count, including Wednesday's three-hour block of Chicago calamities—Med, Fire, and P.D!—and Thursday's two Law & Orders). This lineup almost feels like an acknowledgment by the NBC Entertainment folks that they are just waiting for their NBC Sports colleagues to acquire more sports rights to slot into those other nights, when these shows can then be shifted onto the conglomerate's Peacock streaming service.

Beyond the fall, NBC was touting the seventeen-day period in February 2026 when it would be airing the Milan-Cortina Winter Olympics, Super Bowl LX, and the NBA All-Star Game as "the greatest collection of content that has ever been assembled by one media company."[5] Not long ago, NBC leaders at 30 Rock would have bristled at such a claim or at least added the adjective "sports" before "content." They considered such fabled "Must See TV" NBC primetime lineups as the one that included *Friends*, *Seinfeld*, and *E.R.* on the same night as "the greatest collection of content ever assembled by one media company."

That mid-1990s Thursday night primetime really was appointment viewing, each of those shows creating "water cooler" content for office chit chat across the nation on Fridays. For decades, there were actual TV shows, not just big football games, that you had to watch in real time to be able to join in the conversation and be up on the national zeitgeist. For the week of October 2–8 in 1995, for instance, Nielsen reported that the five most-watched TV shows were NBC's drama *ER* (with more than 23 million households tuned in), and its sitcoms Seinfeld (21.5 million), *Friends* (18.9 million), *Caroline in the City* (17.5 million), and *Single Guy* (17.2 million). *Monday Night Football* was the only live sport broadcast on the top ten list, as the seventh most-watched program that week (14.9 million households). ABC's *Home Improvement* sitcom was ranked sixth, outperforming the network's football game by nearly a million households.[6]

How times have changed. In 2024, as discussed in Chapter 2, the NFL accounted for 72 of the 100 most-watched programs. Add to that four college football games, one World Series game (ranked 84th on the list), one women's college basketball game, the Super Bowl pre-game show, and two Paris Summer Olympics telecasts, and sports accounted for 81 of the top 100. Of the nineteen non-sports programs on the list, none were scripted dramas or sitcoms of the type that dominated ratings in the mid-1990s. Sixteen of them were political programs during a consequential election year, and the three others included two award shows and the Macy's Thanksgiving parade.[7] The year prior, in 2023, when the NFL claimed ninety-three spots on the list (absent the competition from a presidential election), the only other sport to make the list was college football (with two games).[8] *Sportico* aptly called this a "hegemonic stranglehold" over the nation's sports imagination, echoing Professor Andy Markovits' formulation in Chapter 1 of what a hegemonic sports culture looks like. Intriguingly, the top 100 most-watched programs on US TV for 2022 did include three of the men's World Cup games from Qatar (ranked thirty-eighth, fifty-ninth, and ninety-third) and not a single baseball game.[9] What's the over/under for the number of 2026 World Cup games that will appear on the top 100 chart for the year, and the over/under for the World Cup's highest slot on the list?

The Super Bowl has inhabited a category of its own, reigning over all TV ever since Lamar Hunt christened the first championship game in 1967. It's a cultural phenomenon that uniquely transcends its sport to become the nation's one annual civic holiday, whose observance requires you to tune into the TV network on duty for anywhere from four to eight hours. But for regular season games to receive the kind of reverential buzz and hype they do now at upfronts would have been unthinkable prior to the last decade. Earlier, as those Nielsen figures from 1995 illustrate, plenty of other programming could command audiences of 15–20 million viewers, often more easily than regular-season NFL games could. Indeed, back in the late 1980s, ABC had abandoned an experiment with Thursday night games because they were getting crushed in the ratings by *The Cosby Show* and other sitcoms on NBC.[10] And earlier, in 1970, NFL Commissioner Pete Rozelle was unable to get either CBS or NBC interested in airing a Monday night game, because they didn't want to give up their popular primetime programming (NBC's *Monday Night at the Movies* and *The Carol Burnett Show* on CBS), which is what opened the door to the scrappier, less established ABC landing *Monday Night Football*.[11]

By the time Howard Cosell, "Dandy Don" Meredith, and Frank Gifford presided over *MNF*, the NFL, NBA, and Major League Baseball had all established themselves as solid TV fare, pulling in large audiences, with desirable demographics often underrepresented in the networks' other programming, and deep-pocketed advertisers over the weekends. Sports also came to provide indispensable content to media conglomerates' extremely profitable (but now declining) cable channels. But there was always a sense that all things being equal, sports programming might not be as valuable to media companies as their scripted shows, which they could fully own and retain a longer shelf life. David Zaslav, the CEO of Warner Bros. Discovery, has been making this point over the last couple of years to explain why his company was unwilling to overpay (in his mind) to retain its NBA rights: "With sport, we're a renter. That's not as good of a business."[12] Zaslav's comments revealed widespread if seldom voiced anxiety among executives at traditional media companies, that they can spend fortunes to acquire sports rights for a few years, then spend additional fortunes to market them and do a fabulous job bringing them into your living room (or onto your mobile device), only to then be outbid in the next round of media rights auctions by deeper-pocketed tech streamers wanting to crash the party and take that desirable sports content you've helped build up off your hands.

It's a conundrum, all right. Because the need to offer live sports—ideally including some NFL—as part of your programming is as dire as ever for any media company seeking to routinely aggregate large audiences to sell to advertisers in real time. Sports seem to be the last type of programming that can do this, which is one reason the valuations associated with popular professional sports (player contracts, new stadiums, franchise ownership, sponsorship deals, media rights, Super Bowl commercials, you name it) continue to rise at a stratospheric pace.

As Joe Ravitch, the legendary Hollywood media and sports investment banker who founded the Raine Group and has managed the sales of both Manchester United and Chelsea, put it when he visited my class in early 2025: "You've seen the value of sport go up exponentially, as evidenced by the tripling of the NBA rights deal and vast increases for the NFL, in a world where it gets harder and harder to capture audiences. You need live. You need passion. You need dedicated audiences willing to pay to subsidize the cost of these events."

"The value of sport is only going to increase," he added, "I buy and sell a lot of teams around the world and have created a lot of leagues and the value of these franchises has only gone up in the 30 years I've been doing this." Ravitch also mentioned that every time there is an economic crash or recession, people invariably come to tell him the bubble has burst, but invariably the value of sport programming keeps going up, given the scarcity of the IP and its value in a fragmented media market. Now, the fact that sports leagues can make considerable additional revenues from new business lines like gambling and the sharing of fans' data only adds rocket fuel to sports valuations.

None of this is to suggest the death of high-quality scripted TV programming anymore, or the demand for it. Quite the contrary, there's never been more compelling TV content of all types available to consumers. It's just that live sports, news, and some reality shows that have sports-like attributes, such as competitions with winning and losing bakers, singers, or bachelors, are the only programs we still need to watch together, when first aired. For the rest of TV, including many shows that would have merited their own water cooler in the past, the audience is far more fragmented, choosing to watch on their own time. I only recently watched *Breaking Bad*, and it was as riveting to me as it was when it first aired a decade ago. But nobody's going to stream the 2014 Super Bowl, the 2012 presidential debates, or the Academy Awards from years past. These events demand to be watched live, together in the moment, and that's what makes them so desirable to advertisers.

Big media needs sport to retain its audiences much in the same way that a half-century ago sports realized they needed media to retain their viability and cultural salience. Hence the ongoing transition from the "mediafication" of sport to the "sportification" of media.

Given where we are more than a century later, it's fitting that it was sport that provided the new medium of radio its first mass audience sharing a big experience together, the 1921 Georges Carpentier vs. Jack Dempsey heavyweight championship fight broadcast from Jersey City. By 1938, an estimated two-thirds of all American households tuned into a broadcast of Joe Louis knocking out Max Schmeling.[13] Baseball and football were initially wary of both broadcast mediums—radio and TV—for their potential to depress attendance at ballparks. For this reason, some baseball teams did bar play-by-play radio transmissions of their games. And then attendance did dip impressively—as it did for most forms of public entertainment, including moviegoing—with the advent of television in the 1950s. By 1956, Major League Baseball's overall attendance had dropped a third from its 1948 levels.[14] In the NFL, the Los Angeles Rams saw their attendance fall from 205,109 throughout their 1949 season to 110,162 fans in 1950, its first season on TV. Attendance then bounced back the following year when the NFL instituted blackout rules for local broadcasts.[15]

The NFL and television would grow up together, and as discussed in Chapter 2, it would be America's football that would be the first sport to fully embrace the new medium, not as a nuisance to be reluctantly accommodated, but as its principal showcase. It was on TV, the NFL soon understood, where games needed to dazzle and be at their most compelling. It was on TV where the biggest financial upside lay over the long haul, and it was TV, somewhat counterintuitively, that would drive demand for gameday tickets over time by making the NFL America's most popular entertainment. This didn't all happen in a straight line, and for many years it required the aid of federal legislation regulating the pooling of TV contracts (the Sports Broadcasting Act of 1961 discussed in Chapter 2) and local blackouts, but we've now arrived at a point where the NFL is dominating TV ratings while selling 98.3 percent of its seats, having mostly done away with local blackouts.[16]

Benjamin Rader's influential book *In Its Own Image: How Television Has Transformed Sports*, which contains some of the historical attendance figures noted above, lamented the extent to which TV had "trivialized the experience of spectator sports ...sacrificed much of the unique drama of sports to the requirements of entertainment," and capitalized upon the public's love of sports by swamping viewers with "too many seasons, too many games, too many teams, and too many big plays. Such a flood of sensations has diluted the poignancy and potency of the sporting experience." Hitting closer to home, given how many hours I spend watching the EPL on NBC rather than focusing on games closer to home, Rader also bemoaned that by "leading viewers to expect only the best, television sharply attenuated the traditional sporting experience." [17]

What's amazing about reading the professor's critique is that it dates back to that Orwellian year I graduated from high school: 1984. For many of us, those were still halcyon days when sport was purer and scarcer on TV (certainly in the case of the other football). Prof. Rader had no idea what was coming, though perhaps in comparison to what might have been for him the halcyon days of the 1950s or the 1960s, 1984 might have already resembled a preview of the twenty-first century. What is clear is that the process he described, of TV transforming sports, has now been turned on its head. TV became so dependent on sport after altering it to fit its needs that it is now sport's turn to transform media and shape its future.

Remarkably, it isn't just legacy linear TV, the traditional broadcast networks and cable TV, that are clamoring at all costs for sports rights to cling to their audiences. Following in the footsteps of Rupert Murdoch in the 1990s and satellite providers like DirecTV, today's newer disruptive media—the streaming services—are also craving live sports and ancillary sports storytelling to grow their subscriber base and gain some of the gravitas and credibility that comes from partnering with blue-chip sports leagues.

This is a relatively new development. Not long ago, the general entertainment streaming platforms unattached to legacy broadcasters— Amazon Prime, Apple TV+, and Netflix—professed little interest in, or need for, live sports content.[18] That has all changed with the adoption by two of those platforms of an advertising-based tier and a recognition by all of them that in a highly competitive media/streaming ecosystem with a glut of seemingly interchangeable offerings, sports content can be a key differentiator driving subscriptions. I don't need to subscribe to yet another streaming service with a strong lineup of movies and old sitcoms I don't have time to watch, but when Paramount Plus acquired the rights to the European Champions League, I knew they had me. And they knew they had me. Just to watch Arsenal in the various competitions it plays in each year, I have to fork over money to Peacock, Paramount Plus, ESPN+, plus Cox Cable to access the USA Channel, which seems to be all Law & Order all the time, punctuated a few times a week by English football.

I have an especially intense relationship with the Comcast Corporation and its NBC Universal subsidiary, and for a long time, I have thought of it as a fabled laboratory straight out of a Gabriel García Márquez novel or another work of Latin American magical realism. It's a place that has conjured up a means of coexisting in and managing all times simultaneously: past (the NBC broadcast network), present (cable channels like Bravo and USA), and future (the Peacock streaming service). This time lab has also created an indecipherable algorithm that dictates in which of these time frames to serve Martinez up his next Arsenal or Wolverhampton Wanderers league match.

You wouldn't expect things to proceed in a predictably linear fashion in a *Macondo*esque time lab, and so Comcast is dealing with the plot twist that the past is proving stickier than the present, or maybe it's that the more recent past is proving more ephemeral than its past. Put less fancifully: cable is toast. In 2010, there were 105 million cable subscribers in the United States, but by the end of 2024, the number was below 50 million.[19] Sport has been one reason many of us have clung to cable, but the proliferation of sports on streaming services is only accelerating the cord-cutting craze. Companies like Disney have to walk a fine line, because it doesn't want to prematurely forego all the money ESPN still makes from cable operators. At the same time, it needs to prepare for the inevitable future, and in that regard, its new app that offers the games you used to only get on cable can be seen as an escape pod from the doomed Death Star, to cite IP from elsewhere within the Disney behemoth.

Cord-cutting is not a new story, except for the surprising resilience of the original broadcast networks. If anything seemed more doomed and more anachronistic than cable a few years ago, it was broadcast TV. But those networks are still hanging around, still going strong with sports, and offering a powerful flagship to combine with a streaming service. So, Comcast is spinning off its declining cable channels and planning for a TV future that is all about the interplay between its original broadcast network and its Peacock streaming service. Maybe rabbit ear antennas will even make a comeback.

In the meantime, sport is a must-have for all platforms, whether they are defending their incumbency or staking out new frontiers. The NFL is an essential offering for the traditional networks; it's hard to imagine at this point a CBS, FOX, or NBC without the NFL. The league obliges by offering all of them a slice of cultural salience: Monday nights to ABC/ESPN, Thursday nights to Amazon Prime, Christmas Day to Netflix, and (in what could be a precursor to a package of its international games) Brazil Friday to YouTube. Apple TV+ has no NFL, but it is a relatively recent entrant in the sporting world, having acquired rights to some MLB Friday night games and to Major League Soccer.

Amazon has been ambitiously doubling down on sports beyond its NFL deal, outbidding TNT in the contentious renewal of the NBA's media rights for the next eleven years starting from the 2025-6 season. Amazon joined NBC and ESPN as the basketball league's three media partners that collectively ponied up $76 billion, investing in documentaries about English clubs to sign up Prime subscribers in Asia, and acquiring some rights to EPL games within Britain.[20] In addition to the Champions League, Paramount Plus has acquired rights to some NWSL matches (shared across the streaming service and its flagship network, CBS), the English Football League (meaning the divisions below the Premier League), and Italy's Serie A. Spain's La Liga and Germany's Bundesliga were on ESPN+ last time I checked.

Bill Gates used to say that people tend to overestimate technological change over the short term and underestimate it over the long term, and something like that may be happening with the conventional wisdom around the relationship between sport and media.[21] People who follow this all closely are impressed by the resilience of TV networks and the advertising model, and the fact that the industry is still doing upfronts in New York where late-night talk show hosts are still cracking jokes about how we're still doing this, which leads to a temptation to conclude that we overestimated how much things would change, say in the five years since Covid. But seemingly modest shifts simultaneously occurring within that familiar framework do hint at more seismic transformations, which in a decade or so we will marvel at how we could have underestimated them. And for those, it's worth focusing a bit more on Netflix, Apple, and a guy who's extremely passionate about the Philadelphia Eagles (I can't seem to be able to shake them).

Netflix and Apple TV+ have very short histories in the sportscasting business, and neither seems entirely convinced they should be there (no one is quite sure what Apple's strategy is for its streaming service overall, let alone in sports). But both have already done something that the incumbent US sports broadcasters never could have done: they've gone global.

In 2022, Apple struck a $2.5 billion deal with Major League Soccer, acquiring exclusive worldwide rights to all the league's games for a decade, starting with the 2023 season. MLS ratings had been modest previously, with a mix of media partners, and the league seemed relieved and excited to partner up with the world's most admired consumer tech brand in an unprecedented—because of that word "worldwide"—deal.[22] International media rights for domestic leagues, be it the Premier League outside of the United Kingdom or the NFL outside of the United States, are typically sold country by country, reflecting broadcasting's national boundaries. So, when I grew up watching the NFL in Mexico, I was watching Fernando Von Rossum on Televisa, not the originating broadcast on NBC Sports. Similarly, here in the United States, NBC Universal has the rights to the English Premier League, but within Brazil it is ESPN and my friend Ubiratan's colleagues who broadcast Arsenal as well as the NFL, while in Mexico it's HBO Max and Fox Sports that have the EPL rights. And no, the fact that these American companies serving these other markets are acquiring these rights over there doesn't mean they can slip them onto consumers' platforms back in their home country. NBC would want a word.

But MLS and Apple made a deal for the whole enchilada. Global rights. Now, this was relatively easy to pull off because there weren't that many broadcasters outside the United States offering the league top dollar to air MLS games in their countries. America's domestic soccer league wasn't even the most-watched soccer league within its own country, so it isn't surprising it attracted scant attention elsewhere. MLS is no EPL or NBA.

Still, the deal itself was revolutionary, and if Apple's intentions here were a bit of a head-scratcher, they became clearer the following summer when it was announced that Leo Messi, the greatest player of all time, was coming to play in MLS, in Miami. It was as if Apple had greenlit a production before going out and hiring its leading man and offering him points, the way a studio might offer Tom Cruise points on the back end to star in its action thriller. That's how Messi ended up turning down the hundreds of millions in salary he was reportedly being offered in Saudi Arabia and how people in many parts of the world, especially Argentina, came to learn that the United States has a soccer league, which they could pay to watch on Apple TV+. Messi, who reportedly gets a cut of Apple's MLS Season Pass subscription revenue, was signed by Apple as much as he was signed by MLS or Miami.

The Messi phenomenon has proven a big boost to MLS, but there is only so much one player, and his friends Miami hired to play alongside him, can do. Either way, given the nature of how Apple TV+ runs its business, we don't know how many people are or aren't watching MLS these days. What we do know is that the production values are outstanding, and Apple seems very committed to the league, but it is harder for casual viewers to stumble on a sport that for the most part takes place within a streaming service's gated community, a community that is far more exclusive than the densely populated Netflix and Amazon Prime ones. It's hard to create buzz for a sport that is siloed in just one media outlet, no matter how fine a job that media company might be doing with it. The genius of the NFL is that it has all the major TV players hyping the league and thus reinforcing the value of each other's rights. Well into the third season, Apple and MLS were making adjustments, seeking other outlets and partners to sublicense games to, and they both publicly claimed to be satisfied with their arrangement. But many independent analysts and experts, including Joe Ravitch when we talked to him, are ready to proclaim the deal a bust.

For MLS, it's probably a close call. As a TV offering, it doesn't seem to be closing the gap with the more entrenched US sports leagues, or even with

European football leagues in our own media ecosystem. But to categorically proclaim this alliance a mistake is to gloss over the difficulties MLS was having well before Apple showed up. It isn't clear what their next play with traditional partners was going to be, or how those would have closed the gap or attracted Messi. The Apple deal, for all its limitations, did bring a measure of global cachet and needed runway for the league to keep developing.

For Apple, a company that booked nearly $400 billion in revenue in 2024 and has reportedly spent about $5 billion a year on original content for its streaming service since its launch in 2019, it's fair to say the stakes of its deal with MLS aren't all that high.[23] Whether its number of MLS Season Pass subscribers is meeting or exceeding expectations is less significant than what the company is learning. About being in the sports business, responsible for curating an entire league on its own, and offering a package of live football content globally. The MLS deal is Apple's sports media skunk works, where it can learn a bit unobtrusively given the league's relatively low profile. That's what companies like Apple do. It may learn that this isn't for them after all, or it may learn that it wants to someday make a bid with an additional zero for other global football rights. Who knows.

Regardless, the precedent of a global rights deal has been established, and it's one the NFL embraced for its 2024 Christmas Day deal with Netflix. For the first time ever, one media partnership gave the NFL instant global reach, in this case to Netflix's more than 300 million subscribers in more than 190 countries who got to see Lamar Hunt's Chiefs blow out my Steelers and the Baltimore Ravens blow out the Houston Texans. Naturally, the audience peaked during the second game's Beyoncé halftime show. Most heartening to the NFL, the domestic audience figures Netflix shared looked about what you might have expected those games to post on network TV, meaning there was none of the slippage seen when games have been shifted to Peacock. But of course, in this case, you also had the rest of the world thrown in for good measure.[24]

Netflix is the NFL of the streaming world these days, a juggernaut able to command more resources than any of its competitors and to influence the culture in profound ways through its programming choices and algorithmic weighting of them. Its *Drive to Survive* docuseries on Formula 1 is largely credited with creating a whole new fanbase for the sport in the United States, and a flood of investment in other top-notch sports docuseries. Not burdened with the legacy of a sprawling "Netflix Sports" division mandated to come up with X number of hours of live sports inventory each year, the company has the luxury of picking its spots by approaching sports in a way that marries gameday coverage with evocative storytelling. Netflix acquired the US rights to the 2027 and 2031 women's World Cups, and it will be interesting to see how it approaches that assignment and leverages the tournaments to create ancillary content in ways we might not have seen before. Julia Alexander at *Puck News*, one of the brightest thinkers out there on media trends, has floated the idea that Netflix should lean into women's sports and make that a hallmark of its brand, which would allow it to benefit from, and accelerate, the explosive growth in women's sports, while being responsive to the demographics of its subscriber base.[25]

Netflix likes to think of itself as being in the "event" business more than the "sports" business, and millions of its subscribers streamed its freakish Mike Tyson vs. Jake Paul fight (or "event?") in late 2024. The open question going into the next round of bidding for NFL media rights at decade's end is whether Netflix sees an entire league season as something it can "eventize," or whether it will be content to focus on special slivers, such as the Christmas Day NFL package. Perhaps a Premier League Boxing Day special to go with that? Commissioner Goodell is no doubt eager for Netflix to come in for more; there is a reason he showed up wearing a Santa robe to the Netflix upfronts in New York.

Increasingly, sports rights holders face the conundrum of how to continue amassing large audiences in a universe of endless choice and Balkanization. They're navigating the opposing forces of globalization and ever-greater customization, and in that context, there is much peril for the middle tier of sports leagues and content providers. This is the best of times if you're the NFL, the EPL, or a whacky new sport that just got invented and is looking to be on a screen somewhere, anywhere, but for the entire middle class of sporting titles (such as MLS before Apple came along, MLB's smaller-market games, or France's Ligue 1) that once had somewhat guaranteed audiences, these are anxious times. And even for those bigger leagues, it isn't clear whether the best way forward is to lean on new direct-to-consumer platforms and apps you control entirely (such as the NBA Pass), to continue holding country-by-country rights auctions with traditional partners, or to enter into global distribution deals similar to what MLS has done with Apple TV+ and the NFL's Netflix Christmas deal.

In the long term, much will depend on the appetite Netflix, Apple, Amazon, and YouTube have for live sports content. Unlike the NFL's legacy network partners, these four players can provide global reach and greater viewer customization, and if they want to commit to pricey sports content, they all have access to more and cheaper capital than their traditional media competitors. They've all taken modest steps in the direction of embracing sports as part of their brand, but the verdict is still out on whether they will ultimately feel—as Persian Gulf States, beer and auto brands, and traditional media do—that associating themselves with sports' soft power is an existential need.

I know what wager I'd make on that one, though an interesting question going forward is where I would make that wager. Gambling has not featured much in our Great Game inquiry; its impact on the future of sport and sport media deserves its own tome. When we talk about the underestimated transformations shaping sport media in the longer term, customized betting that is seamlessly integrated into the viewing experience will rank high. Sports betting is a big factor driving engagement and contributing to the appreciation in values of all things related to sport. You can bet on whether the Lions will come back in the fourth quarter against the Vikings; you can't bet on which guest will die before checking out of the White Lotus resort.

And for the record, I should add here that while I am critical in other chapters of the Premier League for partnering with some dodgy offshore bookmakers and splashing their logos on club jerseys, I have nothing against responsible betting for entertainment purposes on licensed, regulated apps, or spending a weekend afternoon at a Vegas sportsbook. But we all need to be mindful of the powerful vulnerabilities sports betting does create for potential addiction among sports fans and for potential manipulation of the games we watch and bet on.

ESPN's CEO Jimmy Pitaro told Dylan Byers on *The Grill Room* podcast shortly after the 2025 upfronts that ESPN's forthcoming new app and streaming offering would give his company an opportunity to close the gap with leading sports betting companies by having ESPN Bet (a partnership with a bookmaker) offer users "more personalized bets," and make "betting much more integrated into the experience including the live game experience."[26] Previously, ESPN had a distinct sports betting app from its general sports app (which didn't used to stream content airing on cable), then it allowed you to link accounts, but now spectating and speculating will coexist on the same platform. Millions of ESPN viewers historically had no direct relationship with the network (accessing it via their cable subscriptions), but as that changes over time, the network can look to increase the profitability of its sports betting partnership to offset any declining revenues from cable fees or advertising.

The Magic Media Kingdom that Cinderella and Mickey Mouse built hasn't always felt comfortable going into the gambling business (there is no Disney Resort Casino in Vegas or casinos on Disney cruise ships), but given where consumers are in these roarin' 2020s it's no longer considered feasible to be in sports and not be in sports betting.

Leagues and their stadiums have taken their own tentative steps toward being more directly involved in the sports betting business they used to assiduously shun, at least in the United States. Like ESPN, they could decide on further steps to assert more control and revenue over betting. But none of these choices are without potential pitfalls, and there are plenty of arguments for keeping the betting on a proverbial second screen.

In terms of other forms of customization, YouTube may be the most intriguing prospective sports media partner out there. If Netflix is the NFL of TV, YouTube would have to be FIFA, with a commanding lead in all streaming viewership. In April of 2025, Nielsen reported that YouTube claimed 12.4 percent of all TV viewing, compared to Netflix's 7.5 percent, Disney+'s 5 percent, and Amazon Prime Video's 3.5 percent (collectively, streaming services now account for 44.3 percent of all TV viewership).[27] We traditionalists often don't think of YouTube as being in the same category as the other media companies, given their reliance on user-generated content, but that's a powerful place to be coming from if the imperative is to find new ways of blending customization with global reach. That's what makes YouTube's initial deals with the NFL, for the Sunday Ticket package and more recently for the 2025 Brazil game, particularly interesting. That and YouTube's deep—as deep as Alphabet's—pockets. We have seen early signs of customization on traditional outlets, such as ESPN's ManningCast for its *Monday Night Football* games and CBS's Nickelodeon simulcasts, but you can imagine YouTube taking things to a different level, starting with its legion of influencers hosting watch-along rooms for various sports leagues, in a way it and Twitch perfected with video games. For those of us of a different demographic, I could see YouTube offering EPL games where you can choose which Hollywood superfan you want to watch along with . . . Leeds with Will Ferrell, Aston Villa with Tom Hanks, Manchester United with Julia Roberts, Arsenal with Kim Kardashian, and so on.

For the purposes of our Great Game inquiry, it is worth taking a step back and appreciating that all these media platforms we are discussing are based in the United States. This is certainly true for the big tech players, as well as some of our legacy media companies with subsidiaries that offer in-country sports content elsewhere, such as ESPN Brazil, Mexico's TNT, or even Britain's Sky, which, as we have discussed, has been so instrumental since its Murdoch-owned days to the Premier League's growth and success. Sky is now also owned by Comcast.

The United States is the world's sole mediatic superpower, and that gives us a huge advantage in the Great Game to control global sport. The twin Qatari efforts of Al Jazeera and beIN Sports are state-sponsored media efforts by a nation that embraces a state-sponsored model of sport to chip away at America's near monopolistic control over multinational media, with limited and fading results. And it's not like there are many people around the world, outside of China and Russia, relying on CCTV or the All-Russia State Television and Radio Broadcasting Company for their favorite sports programming. TikTok is the one non-American media phenomenon that transcends its home market and binds millions together across borders and around shared passions. The company has deals with most sports leagues and teams to connect them to younger fans, but pursuing exclusive rights to show games hasn't been its thing, as of yet, though if that were to change, I am sure the Roger Goodells and Gianni Infantinos of the world would eagerly take that meeting.

The United States, being the world's media hub while being obsessed with homegrown sports that have limited global reach, has always been an odd glitch in the design and architecture of the world's pop culture order. Think about how much money a fabulous movie about international football would make globally. And yet, how many truly great Hollywood epics about soccer can you name? Any at all? Me neither. Conversely, how well do you think all those fabulous baseball movies Hollywood has made over the years have done overseas?

In a globalized market, our media conglomerates face the same global imperative we discussed in Chapter 1 for the likes of Coca-Cola and EA Sports. Back in the day, NBC, CBS, and ABC didn't have global aspirations, so the NFL could be their end-all, but the global audience and reach of streamers like Netflix, Apple TV+, YouTube, and Amazon Prime will make them think very differently about the other football than their more traditional predecessors (though they too have shown recent signs of betting on the sport's growth among US fans, as seen by NBC's investments in EPL coverage and Paramount+'s in the Champions League).

It's past due I call out Coach Ted Lasso, the Jason Sudeikis character created by NBC to promote its first season of English Premier League football in the fall of 2013. Then a cast member on the network's *Saturday Night Live*, Sudeikis played a goofy American football coach taking the reins of Tottenham in a series of hilarious short skits where he was befuddled by such things as the absence of playoffs and the abundance of ties in the other football. Seven years later, of course, the character resurfaced as the protagonist of what would become Apple TV+'s first breakaway hit.

When the acclaimed comedy that mines for laughs the cultural gulf created by America's sporting exceptionalism and our transatlantic football schism won seven Emmys in the fall of 2021, I wrote a guest essay in *The Los Angeles Times* calling the show a "match made in globalizer heaven." "It took a U.S. media/tech platform," I added, "to make an iconic show about English football, and it took English football to make Apple TV+ a legitimate global media player."[28] This marriage of the world's default sport with its primary storytellers was long overdue, and it's one that should prove a strong union. The success of *Ted Lasso* predated Apple's acquisition of MLS rights and the signing of Messi, and I am not saying that the fortunes of one scripted show might dictate what a sophisticated tech platform would opt to do in the live sports space. But *Ted Lasso*'s huge success couldn't have hurt the cause of Apple executives making the internal case for soccer. Either way, we are likely to continue seeing more and more international football content on streaming (and other media) platforms with global aspirations. And this, in turn, will also continue to grow the sport's popularity within the home market of all these media companies.

Which brings us to a notorious Philadelphia Eagle fan and another cultural milestone in Hollywood's mission to help America shed its sporting isolationism: Rob McElhenney and *Welcome to Wrexham*.

The FX docuseries chronicling how McElhenney and his buddy Ryan Reynolds buy an aged and ailing Welsh football club and how things go from there once they own it provides the most revolutionary high-concept case study of media's sportification atop sport's mediafication. And while the show's impact on club, town, Hollywood friendship, and football in Britain has been considerable, its most lasting legacy is a further blurring of the lines between media and sport, and inspiring an avalanche of more such hybrid works.

As with *Ted Lasso*, there's a sentimentality to *Welcome to Wrexham*'s Covid-era origins. McElhenney, the brilliant writer and actor of *It's Always Sunny in Philadelphia* and *Mythic Quest*, is a diehard Philadelphia sports fan, and he's the first person to acknowledge that he grew up paying little attention to the world's most popular sport. He was all about the Eagles, Phillies, 76ers, and Flyers. But while on the set of *Mythic Quest*, which he produced, McElhenney became intrigued by Humphrey Ker's rabid support for his beloved Liverpool. Ker and McElhenney would watch games together, and during the Covid lockdown Ker recommended to his friend that he watch the *Sunderland 'Til I Die* docuseries to appreciate how deep and meaningful the relationship between a sports team and a community can be. I would have seconded the recommendation—it's absolutely brilliant, in part because of its unfiltered authenticity. More polished docuseries like the *All or Nothing* seasons on Manchester City and Arsenal promise behind-the-scenes access but feel like tightly controlled narratives in the end. *Sunderland "Til I Die* is more of an all-access pass to a veritable shitshow, which is to say things do not go to plan for the recently relegated club that is starting a new season angling for an immediate promotion back to the Premier League. Some of the behind-the-curtain scenes at the club are cringey enough that I almost felt at times I should offer the folks on screen a minute to themselves to sort things out while I step out. But throughout, the real stars, providing the emotional core of the *Sunderland* docuseries, are the club's fans, and the community, and their relationship with the club.

I certainly didn't sit through *Sunderland 'Til I Die* thinking "Gosh, this seems like it would be a lot of fun," but that was Rob McElhenney's takeaway after bingeing the series. Or at least that this was something he had to do. For them, those suffering fans. Not necessarily in Sunderland, a port city in the northeast of England suffering from waves of deindustrialization, but in *a* Sunderland. Or a Philly, another place where a sports team can mean so much to working-class fans. So, he set about finding a club to buy, and because the saga of promotion and relegation features prominently in *Sunderland 'Til I Die*, McElhenney knew he could buy a club in a lower division and work to get it promoted, and he knew that journey would make for good TV.

Covid wasn't THAT long ago, which makes it all the more remarkable that since his lockdown epiphany, McElhenney, along with Ker and their co-conspirator Ryan Reynolds, did sell a docuseries about acquiring and running a football club, then went out and found themselves one (in that order), acquiring Wrexham AFC in northern Wales, the world's third oldest football club, for $2.5 million from its Supporters Trust. And since then, they've already accomplished something no one else had ever accomplished in the (rather long) history of football in Britain: three consecutive promotions.[29]

Wrexham was languishing in the fifth tier of the game, "the National League," when the Hollywood duo arrived, but by the fall of 2025 they were playing in the Championship, as the second division of English football is confusingly called, just one step below the promised land of the English Premier League (Welsh clubs, unlike Scottish ones, play in England). One more promotion and Wrexham will be facing the likes of Manchester United and Arsenal and will be worth several times its current estimated value of more than $150 million.

The accompanying FX docuseries *Welcome to Wrexham* is in its fifth season, chronicling the team's meteoric rise within the football pyramid.

But wait. Is it more accurate to say the club has an accompanying docuseries, or to say that this major media production has an accompanying football club? The unprecedented—and highly improbable—footballing success of these celebrities who are new not just to running a sports team but to being interested in the sport itself is plenty fascinating, but what is most fascinating about the Wrexham phenomenon from our Great Game Lab perspective is what it represents in terms of the ongoing convergence of media and sport.

McElhenney and Reynolds were refreshingly candid throughout about their intentions, and in an odd way, their honesty about the centrality of the TV show might have reassured local fans in what an *Associated Press* story called the "tired-looking city" of 40,000 people that the two Hollywood celebrities weren't just doing this on a lark.[30] Or at least that it was a bigger, more profitable lark, perhaps worth their while and sustained attention. Either way, the club was in dire straits after previous financial implosions, so fans didn't think they had much to lose when they voted to hand control of their club over to the Americans.

The show aims to be various things at once. It is a fantastic explainer of British footballing culture, including the alien concept to American sports of the dramatic promotion/relegation system; a humorous depiction of the McElhenney/Reynolds dynamic, complete with an episode on bromance; a straightforward summary of the team's week-to-week fortunes on the pitch; and a loving portrayal of the town and its fans, in which characters like the proprietor of The Turf pub become part of the cast.

McElhenney told NPR's *Fresh Air* that the idea all along was to marry the "power of storytelling with the power of sport" and that "the whole point of the documentary is to get you to fall in love. It is at its core a love letter to working-class people." He had asked consultants, he explained in the same interview, to look for a "working-class club that has fallen on hard times and help me find people who love their team as much as I love the Philadelphia Eagles."[31]

One of the reasons so many wealthy Americans are crossing the Atlantic to invest in European football clubs is because there is a certain romance to rescuing those clubs with amazing histories and passionate fanbases that've fallen on hard times, of which there are many. And the prices seem reasonable to Americans because that specter of relegation depresses valuations. One terrible season that relegates you out of the Premier League can cost you hundreds of millions of pounds in lost revenue over the next decade. Everyone wants to orchestrate a *Sunderland 'Til I Die* with a happy ending, which is a lot harder to do than it looks. Well, at least we thought it was, before McElhenney and Reynolds waltzed into the game.

Normally, remarkable sports stories are captured after the fact by storytellers taking you beyond the matchday reports and coverage, but Wrexham is doing all this in real time. The football probably wouldn't be happening without the show (at least not under Reynolds and McElhenney's auspices), but it's also true that the riches generated by the show are fueling the sporting success. On *The Town* podcast early on in this journey, McElhenney explained the novelty of the experiment to host Matt Belloni like this: "The idea of telling a story and getting people invested in the story and you're watching as the story is also feeding into the building of the infrastructure of whatever the business or project is really fascinating."[32]

Still, it all sounds like a Hollywood stunt that could have gone awry, but somehow, it's all worked beautifully. A top executive at another club in England confessed to me that he was obsessed with the show and in awe of how well the two celebrities have navigated the business. They've been appropriately humble and collaborative in their dealings with fans, always talking about themselves as "stewards," not "owners." They have wooed a caliber of sponsors and hired top-notch executives and footballing talent—both coaches and players—that would have normally been beyond the reach of a club of Wrexham's size. The club and its show have developed a flywheel effect where they each benefit the other. Even the town is experiencing an economic upturn from all the attention.[33]

The challenge for Wrexham, the actual football club, will only get steeper from here, as it is notoriously difficult (and costly) to make that last jump from the Championship to the Premier League, though at this point I wouldn't bet against the charmed Hollywood duo.

They even got my in-laws Amy and Bill, fierce Ohio State vs. Michigan alums and rival football fans (but that's a whole different book), into the world's game in a way no previous coaxing or inducements from less charismatic enthusiasts of the game, who shall not be named, ever did. I mean, they never showed much interest in going to watch Arsenal while on preseason tour in America, but they took it upon themselves to go watch Wrexham get clobbered by Chelsea at the University of North Carolina. They had season tickets to Michigan football at the Big House for forty-one years, but this was the first match they ever attended of the other varietal of football. Go figure.

7
How Women Americanized the World's Game

There is a tender but telling scene near the end of *For The Win*, Amazon Prime's docuseries charting the 2024 season of the National Women's Soccer League. Two months after beating the Washington Spirit in the NWSL Championship Match at Kansas City's CPKC Stadium, three Orlando Pride players are relaxing by playing golf. It's the type of scene that makes such behind-the-scenes documentaries compelling for fans. We get to see three friends on the team just chilling together in their civilian lives. As they're about to get started, Haley McCutcheon tells Kerry Abello and Ally Watt: "We are just celebrating being world champs by doing something we're not really good at."[1]

World champs. I love that moment and all that's packed into that one line. I am sure for Haley it was just an amusing bit of commentary for the camera. But it captures how women in our growing pro sports leagues have downloaded the cultural quirks and swagger of the professional male athletes they grew up watching. And one of those quirks, going back to our Chapter 1 discussion about America's sporting conundrum and our national exceptionalism, is that if you win a domestic league in the United States, you feel entitled to proclaim yourself "world champion."

It's a habit that used to perplex me, as I mentioned about my old Steelers pennant, but in this case, it made me chuckle appreciatively. These accomplished athletes are basking in the fact that as the first quarter of the twenty-first century draws to a close, they have a strong soccer league of their own, and they get to do the thing they love.

Haley's appropriation of the term from male sports is also funny because, of course she and her teammates are playing a game that truly is global, unlike baseball or American football, whose winners coined that designation. It makes a lot more sense to think of there being a world champion in this sport, but also takes more hubris to proclaim yourself it knowing there is stiff competition out there and a way to settle the question of who is best.

Well, sort of.

Traditionally we think of "world champions" in terms of international competition between nations at World Cups and Olympics, and so we have feted the likes of Mia Hamm, Julie Foudy, Megan Rapinoe, Alex Morgan, and Trinity Rodman as world champs for their conquests on behalf of Team USA in these competitions. But FIFA, jealous of the money its confederations make from international club competition (especially UEFA, with its Champions League), unveiled a new men's Club World Cup in the United States in the summer of 2025. Previously, FIFA had merely hosted underwhelming tournaments between the winning clubs of each of the six confederations to determine a club "world champion."

On the women's side, FIFA is haltingly trying to create a parallel universe, and as of now the (delayed) plan is to organize the first women's Club World Cup in 2028, and in the meantime to hold a Champions Cup in 2026 between the winners of each confederation. It will be fascinating to watch how the top NWSL teams measure up to the top European clubs over time. It should be extraordinarily competitive, much in the way international play on the women's side has become more competitive in recent years. And in both cases, that heightened level of competition American women face is itself a tribute to what they accomplished in growing the sport globally.

So, although a bit hubristic in the best traditions of American exceptionalism, let's endorse the spirit of McCutcheon's passing "world champions" golf course boast. Let's also note that however ingrained such thinking is in our sporting culture, on the men's side, MLS champions do not go around calling themselves "world champions," presumably not even when they are goofing around a golf course in their own downtime. That claim would be too patently absurd.

The CPKC Stadium in Kansas City, where the Pride won their championship against the Washington Spirit itself stands as a monument to American leadership in the women's game and to the momentum of women's sports more broadly. Opened earlier in 2024 as the $140 million home of the Kansas City Current on the banks of the Missouri River, CPKC Stadium is the first stadium purposely built, anywhere in the world, for a professional women's team.

I had a chance to attend a game at the stadium with the Leonards in the spring of 2025, two days after my Opening Day outing with Chris. We caught a comfortable 3–0 Current win over the Utah Royals before a sellout crowd. The score flattered Utah, such was KC's dominance, but by halftime the locals seemed content with the lead they'd obtained thanks to goals from Michelle Cooper, Brazilian midfielder Debinha, and the team's unstoppable striker from Malawi, Temwa Chawinga. And this time Chris had no important Zooms he needed to rush off to join.

The venue is spectacular, with its impressive views of the river on one end and of the downtown skyline on the other. There isn't a bad seat in the house (none of the comfortable teal mesh seats are more than 94 feet from the field) that only has a capacity of 11,500. It's as if the Current wanted there to be excess demand for tickets from the get-go, though part of the novelty of watching a game there is that you've never seen a more luxurious smaller stadium. MLS has built a generation of extremely pleasant soccer-specific stadiums over the past two decades that typically seat 20,000–25,000 but the Current has doubled down on the trend by going even more intimate and more upscale. It's like being on a smaller Ritz-Carlton Yacht instead of a massive cruise ship.

The stadium has high-end hospitality suites (though we were in the cheap seats), including a "tunnel club" like the ones at Manchester City's Etihad Stadium and at the Dallas Cowboys' AT&T Stadium, where fans can eat and drink and high-five the players as they make their way from the locker room onto the field. Although one difference is that neither Cowboys nor City players walk past tiles in the club spelling out the thirty-seven words of Title IX, the federal legislation that proved so pivotal to the rise of women's sports and of soccer in the United States. The Current's luxurious locker room, which co-owners Angie and Chris Long showed off on a CBS News feature on the eve of the 2024 Championship Match, is an exact replica of Manchester City's oval-shaped locker room at the Etihad.

The gameday crowd was starkly different from the crowds I have communed with at matches in England. So many young kids. So many families. So many mixed-gender groups of young friends. And, quite movingly, some older gay couples I saw just soaking it all in, as if in disbelief. But mostly, what stands out after such a heavy dose of English Premier League action are all those kids. Where did they all come from? MLS also skews more family-friendly than football elsewhere, but this was something else. I was also struck by the market penetration of the sharp Current merch (their teal jersey with the KC city map in the background tracing the river is one of the top five I have ever seen). The pre-game atmosphere was also lighter and more festive. Current players were even signing autographs for ecstatic girls at a tent an hour or so before the game.

On the CBS News feature, the Longs talked about how they considered a world-class stadium and equally impressive training facilities "table stakes if you want to be competitive in professional sports."[2] Which is admirable, because of course that hasn't been table stakes in the women's game before now; this is more of a new gold standard. I can recall not that many years ago going to the boonies of Maryland to what felt like a field with high school bleachers to watch Rose Lavelle and the Washington Spirit, before they started playing their matches at DC United's Audi Field. On the Amazon Prime series, Angie Long appears with Brittany Mahomes, who played soccer in college and professionally in Iceland and owns a stake in the club along with her husband Patrick Mahomes. To all the accolades for their stadium project, Long's reaction turns a bit more pointed: "None of this is new in sports—it's sadly only new for women's sports. There is a very clear model for how to have and build and grow a successful franchise. We want everyone to walk in here feeling that it is a best-in-class environment."[3]

Mission accomplished.

It's appropriate that it was Kansas City that pioneered an NWSL-specific stadium. What made the Truman Sports Complex, where I'd watched the

Royals on Opening Day two days earlier, so revolutionary, after all, was its insistence that games that are important to our society, in that case baseball and football, deserve a ballpark of their own, designed for their own needs. After decades of baseball and football teams sharing stadiums, at the Truman Complex, all the Chiefs and Royals had to share was a parking lot. KC's MLS team has also built itself a stadium of its own, which the Current rented for a couple of seasons. In MLS' early days, I'd sometimes go to D.C. United and MetroStars (since morphed into NY Red Bulls) games in borrowed RFK and Giants Stadiums. I remember the eerie echoes from the vast empty expanses in the stands of those far-too-large stadiums and the feeling that we might all get kicked out at any moment if the actual owners of the stadium discovered we'd broken in to worship our heretical brand of football.

I jest, but part of what is especially poignant and historically significant about CPKC Stadium is that in many countries where football authorities clamped down on women playing the game (mostly out of fear that it was proving too popular), it was by denying them access to existing football facilities. In England, for instance, women's football grew in popularity during the First World War, and when the troops came home after the Armistice, the Football Association grew alarmed that women's games simply continued to grow in popularity. The male regulators of the game felt that women had performed their wartime service and could now head back home. Women's clubs, and their followers, understandably saw things differently. The FA couldn't quite make it illegal for women to play, but what it could do was ban women from using any grounds of FA affiliated clubs, and bar its clubs from having anything to do with women.[4] This form of a ban was tragically replicated in many other countries by cowardly football authorities.

Tom Proebstle, founding partner of Generator Studio, was the lead architect on the CPKC Stadium, and he told me later over a Zoom call that while he has gotten to work on such meaningful projects as the renovation of Lambeau Field in Green Bay, this was his "most personally rewarding assignment yet." He described stadium design as a balancing of engineering realities with aesthetic considerations, and a blend of learning from best-in-class facilities elsewhere and deferring to the uniqueness of a venue's location. Proebstle's

Current project was historic in anchoring both a new generation of women's sports infrastructure and Kansas City's recovery of its Missouri riverfront.

"Building a great stadium in the middle of nowhere is easy," he said, "but working with the constraints of a tighter urban site, that's where things get fun and interesting, and you find ways of making concessions to the environment to blend in and enhance what's already there. It's how you end up with iconic eccentricities, such as Fenway's 'Green Monster.'"

For the Current Stadium, Proebstle had to work with a tight seven-acre site scrunched between the Missouri River and a highway. One of the stadium's winsome eccentricities is its open north end providing the spectacular river views and a gate out to a riverfront walkway past the terraced bar where fans mingle and watch the action behind one of the goals. This horseshoe design might seem like an inspired choice, and it is, but it was also one imposed by an Army Corps of Engineers' determination that a stand couldn't go up on that end without impinging on the needed river levee.

In terms of incorporating learnings from elsewhere, Proebstle and his team sought to understand how some European grounds create such cauldron-like atmospheres. They determined that roofs over stands, prevalent across old English football stadiums, play a role not just in shielding supporters from the elements but also in retaining and reverberating the roar of the crowd. Greater verticality in the angles of the stands also helps on that score. Another trend captured in CPKC's design is how translucent it is, giving a sense of openness and light and of a structure that feels like a living riverfront organism. The functional spaces for the team itself were designed and allocated with the players' distinctive needs and lifestyle in mind. "Some of these incredible athletes are moms," Proebstle said, "and they do tend to want their families and support networks a little closer, with welcoming spaces."

That could be a metaphor for the stadium's larger role in the community. To be closer to its supporters. The stadium sits on the edge of Berkley Riverfront Park, and the Longs and others are developing a multi-billion-dollar residential and commercial district that essentially connects downtown KC to its riverfront origins and the stadium. Plans include extending streetcar lines to CPKC and creating, as Proebstle puts it, an ability to "march to the match on gameday, with stops at pubs along the way in a tight-knit urban fabric, as you see in Europe." The Leonards and I got a taste of that after the game, walking back toward downtown along the river in a teal-bathed stream of supporters, passing apartment complexes being completed and young people playing beach volleyball in the park.

Proebstle's Generator Studio office is only 3 miles from the stadium. His is one of a half-dozen or so firms that make Kansas City the undisputed global hub of sports architecture. He estimates that 65–70 percent of the world's new professional stadiums and facilities are designed by Kansas City firms, all of which are extremely busy and eagerly recruiting architects from the coasts to move to KC.

These firms will likely see a lot of business coming in from those inspired by the Longs' vision and the Current's success. Proebstle told me he got some gentle ribbing from some quarters about working in women's sports on a "flash in the pan," "one-off" project. But he will get the last laugh, as women's sport is about to benefit from a tidal wave of infrastructure investment. At a *Sportico* investment conference I attended in May 2024 in Los Angeles, the buzz was all about women's sports and the stratospheric returns on investment in the space. One of the speakers claimed that over the past half-dozen years, women's sports franchises had outperformed all other investment asset classes.

The vibes shift has been staggering. Not too long ago, a conference like that (whose audience still skewed broey) would have dutifully included a late afternoon panel about the importance of investing in women's sports as an exercise in corporate social responsibility. But here they were leading the day with women's sports with the same unabashed speculative glee normally reserved for things like Bitcoin or NVIDIA stock. In March of 2025, Deloitte issued a report predicting that women's elite sports would surpass $2.3 billion in global revenue that year, after exceeding $1 billion for the first time in 2024. Women's international football and basketball were the twin drivers fueling the explosive growth, with women's basketball revenues expected to leapfrog past women's football in 2025, from $710 million to $1.03 billion. Women's football revenues were anticipated to increase from $740 million to $820 million. Deloitte's top recommendation to enable the continued growth of women's sports organizations: invest in dedicated infrastructure.[5]

The milestones have been coming fast and furiously. The 2023 FIFA Women's World Cup final between Spain and England was watched by a global audience of 67.6 million viewers,[6] and later that summer the University of Nebraska set a new American record for a live audience at a women's sporting event in August of 2023, when 92,000 fans attended a volleyball match.[7] In spring 2024, boosted by the Caitlin Clark effect, ratings for the 2024 Women's NCAA championship game eclipsed the men's ratings, averaging nearly 19 million viewers.[8] That summer the International Olympic Committee touted the Paris Games as the first "gender equal" Olympics, with as many women competing as men. There were quibbles about that boast, but no doubting that the trends were all pointed in the right direction, and certainly no doubting the box office draw of such Olympic stars as Simone Biles, Katie Ledecky, Sha'Carri Richardson, and Sydney McLaughlin-Levrone.[9]

Days before the Paris Olympics, the NWSL's Angel City FC announced that Willow Bay, the prominent journalist and Dean of USC's Annenberg School of Communication and Journalism, and her husband Bob Iger, Disney CEO, had acquired a majority stake in the club at a stunning $250 million valuation. Earlier that same year, an investor group acquired an NWSL expansion franchise in San Diego for roughly $110 million. Two years earlier, NWSL clubs had been valued at under $50 million, and five years prior, they had been in the $5 million ballpark. It was as if the business of women's sports had compressed the meteoric growth of men's sports over the decades into a few years.

This growth is a global phenomenon. In May 2025, Reddit co-founder Alexis Ohanian acquired a minority stake in Chelsea Women that valued the club at £245 million.[10] Ohanian has been an evangelist investor in women's sports for years; he and his wife Serena Williams were also among the founding investors in Angel City. Along with a phalanx of other celebrities that included the actress Natalie Portman, they paid the league a $2 million franchise fee to launch the club in 2020.

Unlike the standalone NWSL, the dozen teams that currently play in England's Women's Super League are extensions of the larger clubs that also field men's teams and run academies. This is the pattern across Europe and in much of Latin America. Most countries in these regions were slow to embrace the women's game, but once they did, their clubs leveraged the built-in identity, branding, and followings they had built up over a century in the men's game, much as US colleges leveraged their fans' loyalty for their women's sports in the aftermath of Title IX. It would be as if Angie Long in Kansas City were running not her own organization, but the Kansas City Chiefs' women's side, or Sporting Kansas City Women if we want to avoid having NFL teams cross-pollinate footballs (an admittedly intriguing idea).

What's most telling about the Chelsea deal was that the club adjusted its structure to allow for investment directly into the high-flying women's club, as Ohanian presumably wasn't looking to buy a stake in the overall club, which is valued northwards of £4 billion. And that itself speaks to the revolution in attitudes (and in financial realities) surrounding these women's teams. Women's teams that developed as charitable appendages within these clubs may come to be seen as the business unit some investors might want to assign a higher multiple to, if only they could be spun off.

Up until 2014, as I mentioned in Chapter 4, Manchester City fielded a "Ladies" team overseen by its community foundation, not a full-fledged women's analog to the men's side. The WSL had launched in 2010, the 2012 London Olympics further bolstered interest in the game within Britain, and so two years later Manchester City Women were properly organized alongside the men's team and the academy. Nowadays City, along with Manchester United, Arsenal, and Chelsea—especially Chelsea, whose former manager Emma Hayes took over as USWNT coach in 2024—dominate the WSL and vie for top European honors (as their clubs' men's teams do) against the likes of Barcelona, Real Madrid, Olympique Lyonnais, and Bayern Munich.

It is notable how this "new" game on both sides of the Atlantic is picking up many of the cultural attributes of its geography's incumbent male sporting culture, and by that I don't just mean Haley McCutcheon's boast that her Orlando Pride were "world champions."

The NWSL has internalized the NFL's "Socialism in One Country" belief in parity and the mantra that any team should be able to beat any other team "on any given" day or compete for trophies in any given season. NWSL Commissioner Jessica Berman has called the league's parity its "superpower." And when the Kansas City Current finally suffered their first loss of the 2025 season in late April, against then winless North Carolina Courage, coach Vlatko Andonovski (a former USWNT coach) said: "This is just another example of how good this league is, and how you literally cannot relax even for a second regardless of who you're playing."[11] The league's last five seasons have produced five different champions.

Over in Europe, meanwhile, the women's game has also picked up the incumbent football's established norms. Guess which two teams dominate the Spanish Liga F? Wait, Barcelona has actually won the last six titles and are widely considered the best club anywhere, though Arsenal had something to say about that in the surprising Champions League final in 2025. But yes, Real Madrid was the runner-up in four of those six seasons. And if you are an Espanyol de Barcelona supporter on the other side of that city's divide, you now must worry every season about the possibility that your women's team might be relegated, much like you have long worried about your men's team facing that prospect. In neither case will you be expecting any trophies.

What's fascinating about these radically different approaches to competition is that, unlike the comparisons between our different varietals of football discussed in Chapter 2, there is no "Socialism in One Country" going on here. The NWSL and the European leagues are competing to attract the same global talent and to become the game's gold standard. Once the women's Club World Cups get going, we can expect to see heated transatlantic club rivalries develop, as we see between national teams. The competition won't just be between leagues and clubs, but also between approaches to life and sport. The NWSL's commitment to parity will be tested in ways the NFL's never has been, because there are no Barcelona or other behemoths lurking offshore for the NFL to worry about. Already, the NWSL has broken with American major league sporting tradition in one significant way: by ditching its college draft.[12]

For all their globalization, the fast-growing women's football scenes on both sides of the Atlantic are branches of the same tree, and they share the same roots of American intercollegiate athletics. The overarching story here for the purposes of our Great Game inquiry into how sport connects the United States to the rest of the world, is one of schools and colleges, encouraged by Title IX, turning the foreign varietal of football into an All-American pursuit and ultimately proving the salience of women's sports globally. Girls and women in the United States Americanized the world's game, and by wildly succeeding in that endeavor, they also globalized the emergence of women's sport.

People sometimes wistfully talk about wanting to travel back in time to experience the foundational days of certain things, or to buy certain land or stocks, knowing how much they'd be subsequently worth. What's fun about the staggering velocity of change and growth in this story of women's sports is that you wouldn't have to travel too far into the past for such encounters.

In that spirit, let me fire up my imaginary state-of-the-art time travel machine, a reliable Honda, and drop in on five past summers, all within my lifetime, that each tell a part of the story:

1) Summer of 2020 (Los Angeles): Sorry, I know we haven't gone very far, and I am already making a pit stop. I just want to try talking the original crew of Angel City FC investors into letting me in the group. If I can scrape together $10,000 to pitch in, that stake would be worth $1,250,000 five years later.

2) Summer of 1971 (Mexico City): I turned five then and was living large in Mexico City, but I had no awareness that a year after the famous 1970 World Cup that saw Pelé and his Brazil teammates win the Jules Rimet trophy, the Estadio Azteca across town would once again be sold out for a World Cup final, this time for the Denmark vs. Mexico final match of that summer's women's World Championship.[13] Though informally called a "Mundial" in Mexico and elsewhere, as the first such championship the previous summer in Italy had also been called, the tournament was not sanctioned by FIFA or any of its national associations. Quite the contrary, the sport's top authorities remained vehemently opposed to women playing the game. The English FA had only lifted its ban the previous year; France, Spain, and Brazil still had bans in place that would last for another four, nine, and ten years.[14]

There is a powerful *Copa '71* documentary about the tournament, released in 2023, that I share with my classes and have screened at public events.[15] In it, Mexico's Silvia Zaragoza (nicknamed "la Borjita," a play on the name of Mexico's male striker Enrique Borja) looks into the camera and talks about spending her childhood days playing *fútbol* on the street, at least until her father returned from work late in the afternoon, as he would either scold or hit her if he saw her playing. "He would tell me women were made for the home," she adds. It is such an intimate, painful memory delivered matter-of-factly and rendered all the more horrible by the knowledge of how commonplace Zaragoza's experience would have been among women of her generation. And not just when it came to playing football.

Chris Lockwood, one of the England players in the tournament, remembers that neither she nor any of her teammates had ever flown before going to Mexico, and that when they landed and made their way into the terminal, their flight was greeted by a gaggle of press and blinding camera flashes: "And I said, there is someone famous on this plane . . . but it was us." The story is endearingly like one Julie Foudy told me about her and her USWNT teammates' reaction to the massive traffic jam en route to Giants Stadium during the 1999 women's World Cup. Something big must be going on . . . Oh wait.

Copa '71 opens with a shot of Brandi Chastain, one of the stars of that 1999 US team, being shown images of the packed Azteca during the tournament. She initially thinks it must be for a men's game, and when she is let in on the fact that this was at a women's tournament held twenty years before the first officially sanctioned women's FIFA World Cup, she exclaims: "This is unbelievable. Why didn't I know about this? This makes me very happy and also quite infuriated if I am honest. I am almost at a loss for words." And she looks it.

I don't blame her. I had the same reaction when I first learned about the 1971 tournament, which I am ashamed to say was only within the last decade. I mean, I grew up in Mexico, obsessed with both football and history, and yet I had no idea this had happened. And that's a big theme of the documentary, the extent to which the tournament's very success, following patterns elsewhere, triggered a sharp counterreaction to shut it all down. What should have been the start of a new era proved a regression. The tournament was a success in part because it had the backing of some important media companies who saw the commercial potential of the game, but afterward these backers also turned against the sport when pressed to fall in line with the football establishment's clampdown on the women's game.

Toward the end of that same decade when I was in middle school in the northern city of Chihuahua, all my buddies and I were soccer-mad. We played and watched the game around the clock. But not a single girl in our class did.

This was a guy thing. Certainly, none of us had a clue that women had ever kicked a ball, anywhere, let alone in the Azteca before 100,000 fans (the crap team I rooted for in the league, Atlético Español, was lucky if it could get 10,000 fans in there). The first time I ever saw women play soccer was my first week of high school in New Hampshire, after I had left Mexico.

Girls played sports in my Mexican middle school; they could opt for basketball or volleyball. The idea that those sports are somehow more or less inherently "feminine" than soccer is of course absurd; these are all cultural determinations. Though in this case, it is a common determination around the world. American friends are always baffled when I tell them that girls were steered away from soccer and toward basketball, but to this day, despite tremendous progress, you still find a lot more resistance in countries like Mexico and Britain to girls playing soccer (which Brits call a "contact sport") than you do in the United States.

Both Mexico and England now have thriving professional leagues. In Mexico's case, the much-maligned FIFA deserves credit for playing a crucial role in recent years, pressuring First Division clubs to invest in a women's league. One of Mexico's best midfielders, Alexia Delgado, played for us at ASU and is now playing professionally in Monterrey, for Tigres, and for the national team. And yes, girls now play at the schools I went to in Chihuahua, though there's still some resistance.

In an interesting win for American soft power in the Great Game, flag football is the "cool" sport of choice among many girls in Mexico City schools, many of whom still view soccer as dad's sport. My Mexican step-niece, who is now in college, told me that in her Mexico City school, PE classes took place on a divided soccer field, with boys always playing soccer on one half, and girls mixing it up and playing whatever other games they wanted to on the other half. She remembers there'd only be one or two defectors from each side who'd want to opt in, or opt out, of the boys' *fútbol*.

In the United States, because of our sporting exceptionalism, we had a different incumbent "macho" varietal of football. Women taking up soccer in some countries is as culturally fraught as the idea of women playing tackle football is here. It's key to understanding the Great Game to understand how and why American women taking up soccer weren't going to face the same headwinds they would in much of the rest of the world, and what that would mean when, on the contrary, they suddenly enjoyed a powerful tailwind encouraging them to take up the game.

That tailwind wasn't there yet in 1971, and it's worth noting that the United States didn't even participate in those women's championships of 1970 and 1971, when international football was as foreign to American women as it was to American men. To explore what changed all that, let's make our next stop in our time travels, though we are just going to skip ahead to the next summer.

3) *Summer of 1972 (Washington, D.C.)*: I was six, still living large in Mexico and still very clueless about the great events of the age, including all the exciting happenings in President Richard Nixon's White House.

On June 23, Nixon signed Title IX, the thirty-seven words the Kansas City Current players walk past as they make their way to the field every home match, into law. The occasion merited one sentence in *The New York Times*, and it's safe to assume that Nixon wouldn't have been thinking about the Great Game, or the relationship between the world's two footballs, or Brandi Chastain taking her jersey off at a future World Cup final upon scoring the winning goal at the Rose Bowl, or about how he was in the process of creating that massive tailwind that would transform America's relationship with the world through sport.

Title IX, after all, says nothing about sports. What Congress dictated with this legislation is that no one "on the basis of sex" be "excluded from participation in, be denied the benefits of, or be subjected to discrimination under any education program or activity receiving Federal financial assistance."

And to be fair to Nixon, he had too much else on his mind that day to engage in such flights of future dot-connecting fancy. Some of his bumbling underlings had broken into Democratic National Committee headquarters at the Watergate complex six days earlier, and that same Friday morning of June 23, he held a conversation at 10:04 a.m. with Bob Haldeman, his chief of staff, that would come to be known as the controversy's "smoking gun" that would cost him the presidency when it came to light more than two years later. You know, the one where the two men discussed (on tape, no less) having the CIA order the FBI to back off from investigating the prior weekend's break-in at the DNC.[16]

But the chain reaction (the sports one at least) was inevitable. As part of long overdue societal calls for greater gender equity, girls and women had been demanding more opportunities to play sports in the years prior to the passage of Title IX. Meanwhile, one of those idiosyncratic aspects of America's sporting exceptionalism that most baffles foreigners is just how much of our sports takes place in our schools, including the sporting-industrial complexes we've nested into our universities, as discussed in Chapter 1, to provide the NFL with a feeder league in our national sport and develop our Olympic "amateurs" across many others. So, it should come as no surprise that within a short period of time, those seeking greater access to sporting opportunities for girls would see the power of reading sport into Title IX's "any education program or activity" language.[17]

Soccer was a handy sport for panicked school administrators at all levels to offer to girls to show they were complying with the law. What made it the most popular sport for boys around the world also made it popular among these administrators looking for ways to offset the opportunities they provided to boys in our homegrown football: the game was accessible and enjoyable to players of varying levels of skill and athleticism, and it was relatively cheap to organize for lots of kids to participate in.

An excellent *New York Times* story by Alexandra Petri pegged to Title IX's fiftieth anniversary in 2022 chronicled how the law wasn't merely a watershed for women's sports generally; it also proved a powerful boon for soccer specifically, relative to other women's sports. Petri reported that before Title IX passed, there were only 13 women's collegiate soccer teams with 313 players across the country. When women's soccer became a sanctioned NCAA sport (taking it over from the AIAW) in 1982, those numbers were up to 1,855 players on 80 teams. Then by 2020–1, in what the NCAA claims to be the most expanded women's sports program among universities in the last three decades, nearly 28,000 students were playing the world's game for 1,026 collegiate teams.[18]

Title IX is what imported the game into the country, and then over time the game was naturalized American by the women who took it up so prodigiously.

4) Summer of 1979 (Chapel Hill, North Carolina): Long before Bill Belichick showed up to coach the other football, long before my in-laws went there to watch their beloved Wrexham get clobbered by Chelsea, long before my wife Victoria spent four years there as a star history student and athlete, and not that long before Michael Jordan showed up to represent the school in a different sport, I attended the University of North Carolina's soccer camp over a couple of summers in the late 1970s. This was part of my American mom's ceaseless campaign—God bless her—to get me to know my other country.

I had done a more traditional camp in the Wisconsin Northwoods, as I bragged about to my Packer friends in Brazil, but the chance to stay in the air-conditioned high-rise dorm of Granville Towers, which had its own swimming pool, felt extravagantly posh and sophisticated by comparison. MJ would live here a few years later as an undergrad, and I'd like to think he was in the room I'd stayed in. And that he was as pumped as I was about those unlimited Coke fountain machines in the cafeteria. My first summer in Chapel Hill, we were taken to see a new movie out called *Star Wars*. I also discovered Pepperidge Farm cookies (I really thought the farm was a nearby quaint place), and the expressions "clueless" and "get a grip." And I acquired an exaggerated sense of my abilities on the field, because these kids hadn't played the game the way we did back home.

It'd be hard to find a more impactful American community in the Great Game than Chapel Hill, partly because of the aforementioned greats who made their way there after I did, but mostly because of the accomplishments of one of my camp's coaches. Because Anson Dorrance did a lot more than make sure we got to see *Star Wars* during its opening week.

Dorrance was a busy guy back then. He had been a star player for UNC earlier in the decade, then headed to law school while doing some coaching on the side for UNC legend Kip Ward's Rainbow Soccer camps. While he was studying law, UNC's Athletic Director Bill Cobey reached out in 1976 to tell him that the coach he'd played under, Dr. Marvin Allen, was retiring the following year and had recommended Anson as his successor, despite his scant experience. Dorrance served as an assistant the next season and then became the head coach in 1977, though as a part-time employee, still attending law school and coaching those fabulous Rainbow campers.

Then, as Dorrance told me during a recent phone call, "Bill calls me back into his office in 1979 and tells me that a women's club team on campus had petitioned for varsity status, and that because of the law Nixon had signed we had to take these seriously, and could I look into it and see what I thought." Dorrance did so, was impressed, and UNC women's varsity soccer was born, though initially it was a struggle to find teams to play against until the NCAA adopted the sport in 1982. "So when I reported back to Bill that they definitely deserved to be a varsity team," Dorrance added, "he of course asks me if I could also coach them, and the deal was I'd become a full-time employee if I coached both teams." All of this was transpiring the second summer I was in Chapel Hill, 1979, which makes me feel like a thirteen-year-old Forrest Gump, an oblivious extra to a grand historical moment.

Ultimately, law school had to give, and Dorrance coached both the UNC men's and women's teams until 1988, when he handed off the men's team to an able assistant. By then, Dorrance had also been named coach of the fledgling USWNT and was embarked on his lifetime crusade.

Anson Dorrance would become the winningest coach in NCAA Division I history, in any sport, winning twenty-one titles in his forty-five seasons as UNC Women's Coach. Dorrance retired in 2024 with a staggering 934–88–53 record. And of course, Dorrance led the USWNT—half of whom were Tar Heel players—to win the first-ever FIFA Women's World Cup in 1991.

"The Scandinavians, and Norwegians in particular, had been demanding a women's World Cup, but FIFA still wasn't too sure about it, worried it might tarnish their brand," Dorrance told me on our call, "so they hid this tournament away in Guangdong, China, which was the best thing that could have happened. Say what you will about authoritarian regimes, they can fill stadiums with enthusiastic fans waving flags they've been handed on their day off from the factory job. And FIFA was like 'this is great.'"

FIFA had come a long way since the women's World Championship held in Mexico twenty years earlier that it vehemently opposed, but it still remained reluctant to equate this tournament to its prestigious men's World Cups. That explains the tortured name and branding of "1st FIFA World Championship for Women's Football for the M&M's Cup." Also, FIFA limited the women's games to eighty-minute halves, as opposed to the men's ninety-minute halves, which led to US and Tar Heel captain April Heinrich's priceless quip: "They were afraid our ovaries were going to fall out if we played ninety."[19]

"The 80 minutes part actually helped us," Dorrance told me, because of our relentless style of play. We were aggressive and fit and were accused of cheating because we pressed when many saw that as a no-no in the women's game. We were always going to outrun and outduel the competition. Our tactical approach was to grab the other team by the throat and squeeze the air out of them. FIFA and the other teams were gobsmacked.

Dorrance's competitiveness comes across as visceral and core to his being, even in retirement over a long-distance phone call. "I was euphoric about beating the world at its own game," he said. He was born in Saudi Arabia and grew up overseas, the son of an oil executive, and I have heard Dorrance call himself a globalist but also acknowledge that being an American abroad made him an extremely patriotic one. There's certainly no overstating the centrality of his role in the Great Game, which he then spelled out for me: "Another way to think about it is that we were a catalyst for selling the world on its own game." Selling it to the other, initially excluded, half.

Title IX was the game changer that led to the massive growth in the women's game in the United States and the resources the game was able to command. It is hard to imagine an Anson Dorrance being able to choose to focus on a women's team at the expense of a men's team without Title IX, or that he would have had the ability to recruit so many great players to go play for him over so many years. Looking at things from across the Atlantic, *Guardian* sportswriter Suzy Wrack put it this way in her book *A Woman's Game*: "The head start and huge boost that Title IX provided meant that the US became the premier force in women's football almost overnight in the 1970s, and to this day remains a force that is extremely difficult to overcome."[20] Dorrance agrees that Title IX was the key to much of America's success in the game, but he pushes back against the familiar narrative that American women's soccer was born on the mountaintop and didn't have to claw its way up there. "There were all these other countries that had been playing for longer than we had," he said, "and many of them had professional leagues, which we didn't at the time. We were the ones catching up."

The legacy and impact of the NCAA and UNC women's game is everywhere. My call with Dorrance came days after Arsenal had upset Barcelona in the Women's Champions League final in Lisbon in May of 2025. Dorrance was ecstatic because the Gunners played three Tar Heels on the day: Alessia Russo and Lotte Wubben-Moy, who are both English, and the American Emily Fox.

"Imagine the satisfaction I get," Dorrance said, "watching these players we developed go out and beat Barcelona." He sees the Catalan team as arrogant and aloof, always resistant to consider promising players from US colleges. "They'll practically hang up the phone on us before we introduce ourselves," he said, laughing. Then his competitive drive came through again: "Barcelona hasn't produced the number of world-class players and world champions we have in Carolina." Spain is the current world champion with many Barcelona stars on the national squad, but Dorrance pointed out that if you combine all the women's world titles of the modern era—World Cups and Olympics—the United States has won nine of them, to eight for the rest of the world combined. And remarkably, one out of three players on those US champion rosters came through Chapel Hill, including Heinrichs, Mia Hamm, Carla Overbeck, Crystal Dunn, Kristine Lilly, Tobin Heath, and so many others.

US women's college soccer has been at the center of the world's game since Bill Cobey called Dorrance into his office in 1979, but there are signs the professional game is on the verge of leaving its college days behind. It was considered quite a gamble when Mallory Pugh Swanson skipped the college game to join the NWSL in 2017, but other stars such as Trinity Rodman followed in her path, and nowadays some of the most promising young players, like Riley Jackson, who had initially intended to play for Duke, are being wooed to sign with professional clubs straight out of high school or before completing their college careers.[21]

I asked Dorrance if the very success of Title IX-empowered NCAA women's soccer in incubating the modern professional game would ultimately sideline it from the game's highest levels. Would the women's game become more like the men's game, where the opportunity costs—not just monetary, but also in terms of developing your game—of playing in college would prove too high?

"Yes, we're about ten years behind the men's game," Dorrance replied, "but we shouldn't passively accept that what's best is to replicate the way things work or often don't work there, especially with the changes brought by NIL." He said the challenge is to figure out a new type of marriage between the professional and collegiate games, where players who've signed for pro teams might still be able to enjoy the benefits of spending time in college, getting an education, and maybe getting some playing minutes on some sort of loan arrangement. "Otherwise," he said, "we're forcing too many tough choices and compromises on these kids and their families. They need to be reminded to also enjoy life. No 15-year-old wants to spend all their time being chaperoned while they train and play day in and day out with 32-year-olds."

And with that, the ultimate Jedi of American soccer and of women's sports globally, responsible for my seeing *Star Wars*, told me he had to go. He was off to meet a former player of his who's playing professionally in Sweden and was taking courses in Chapel Hill over the summer term.

5) *Summer of 1999 (Giants Stadium, New Jersey):* Julie Foudy, the gifted and thoughtful midfielder who would go on to become a gifted and thoughtful sportscaster, podcaster, and author, described the moment when she visited one of our classes at ASU and recorded one of our Great Game Lab Set Piece conversations:

> First game against Denmark of the Women's World Cup. We had been trying to sell it to big stadiums and convince FIFA like this is the way we should go. And we had journalists and FIFA representatives telling us we were crazy. You shouldn't do it. No one's going to come. It's going to be an empty stadium. So, Andrés, you can imagine our excitement when we get stuck in traffic trying to get to that game, and we have no idea why there's traffic. Then we realize, oh my gosh! It's because they're coming to our game. What. And then we walk out of the tunnel. And it's like the perfect movie scene, you know. Tunnel. You see the light at the end of the tunnel, which is the field. You walk out, and the whole place gets on its feet, you know, and they said, it's the second largest crowd at the time, besides the Pope ... because, the Pope.[22]

My mom and I were at the end of that tunnel, with tens of thousands of other fans, cheering our heads off. Mom had given me so many opportunities to be connected to sports and anything else I was ever passionate about, including her country—I wouldn't have my blue passport if it weren't for her. She'd always been an agent for the fulfillment of others—her husband, kids, students, charities she volunteered at; in another time and place, she should have been in charge, like of everything, but throughout her life, she never thought she should be at the center of things. We all have known women like that, I know, but I am just glad I was able to bring one of them to a couple of those 1999 Women's World Cup games.

Oh, and I know Foudy would want me to add here that she scored the crucial second goal in the Americans' 3-0 win against the Danes.

Those were heady, end-of-millennium days, with Y2K barreling toward us, talk of the end of history, and an unbridled exuberance about where technology and globalization were taking us.

And women, that remarkable group of women on the US Women's National Team, were definitely at the center of things. That World Cup was all people talked about all summer; the team played before sellout crowds in the country's largest stadiums and their TV ratings shattered expectations, and anything previously accomplished by women athletes or soccer of any kind, on US television. Almost 20 million people watched Brandi Chastain rip her jersey off upon scoring the winning penalty kick against China in the final at the Rose Bowl. From then on, there were always going to be 20 million reasons why anyone who suggested there wasn't an audience for women's sports was talking nonsense.

That team of Foudy, Mia Hamm, Briana Scurry, Kristine Lilly, Chastain, and all the others accomplished so many feats. They played amazing soccer, first and foremost, but they also took it upon themselves to promote the game—those KC Current players I saw signing autographs an hour before their kickoff were following in the footsteps of these USWNT 99ers—and to become persuasive advocates for equal pay and gender equity in our society. They were also caught up in endless cultural debates over whether they had redefined what it meant to be female and athletic, posing on magazine covers, being marketed for their attractiveness, and so on.[23] The fact that many of them were clearly brighter and more eloquent than is often the norm for professional athletes raised another set of taboos for cultural critics. The country just wasn't ready for all they had to offer.

From our Great Game vantage, the greatest feat and legacy of this USWNT, and their equally remarkable successors, is that they turned soccer into a naturalized American. There was nothing foreign about the game once they were done with it. That summer of 1999 was the culmination; they'd won Olympic gold three years earlier in Atlanta, too, and the explosion of girls' soccer since the passage of Title IX meant that by the time Bill Clinton was seeking re-election in 1996, pollsters and political demographers had coined the term "soccer moms" to represent one of the most "mainstream" slices of the American electorate: suburban, upper-middle class, mostly white, fairly independent minivan-driving voters who weren't that entrenched in partisan politics but were driven by civility vibes and economic concerns. This showed how far soccer had come in my years in the United States. Fifteen years earlier, if you'd told me American political analysts were looking to define a slice of the electorate as "soccer moms," I might have guessed they were coining a term for subversive feminist voters who believed in world government.

Amusingly, late night talk show host David Letterman would appropriate the term "Soccer Moms" for a nightly segment touting the USWNT during the 1999 World Cup.

If "Americanizing" the world's game was their greatest accomplishment, the second greatest feat and legacy of this USWNT, and it's a close second, is how they inspired the rest of the world to embrace women's sports more broadly. They globalized the idea and reality of successful women's sports by how they Americanized the world's game.

This was powerfully driven home for me at an event Victoria organized on campus with Briana Scurry, the heroic goalkeeper of that '99 squad who saved a penalty kick in the World Cup final's shootout that Chastain capped off, Mexican player Ana Paola López Yrigoyen, and international students playing on our ASU team. López Yrigoyen and ASU's players talked about the influence of Title IX and of Scurry's team, and subsequent USWNT teams, in creating inspiration and concrete opportunities for them to play in their home countries. Scurry was visibly moved, saying she spends so much time supporting and thinking about women's soccer in the United States, she hardly ever gets to hear about what the rise of the game here did for women elsewhere.

"It makes me feel even more fortunate and blessed that we do have Title IX here. It really has made such an amazing impact," she said.[24]

Without the success of the USWNT in '99 and at subsequent tournaments, and the cultural phenomenon around that success, it is unlikely major clubs across Europe would be investing so heavily in the women's game. The USWNT provided the proof of concept for scaling women's sport into a commercially viable enterprise with a mass following. Instead of hanging up on Anson Dorrance, Barcelona should be sending him Thank You notes.

As they do across other Olympic sports, US colleges, home to some 14,000 Division I international student athletes, remain for now—and let's hope for the foreseeable future as it would be hard to overstate the return on this investment in terms of American prestige and soft power around the world—at the center of developing not only American talent but players from all over the world.[25] Victoria analyzed all the national team rosters going into the 2023 women's World Cup in Australia and New Zealand and found that slightly more than 20 percent of all players (151 of them) had previously played, were then playing, or had committed to play American college soccer. It's true that Spain, the eventual champions, were not interested, but twenty-two of the thirty-two teams had at least one NCAA player.[26] That same year, our ASU women's team had players from thirteen different countries, and thirty-five different nations were represented in the NCAA Division I women's soccer tournament.

I love Anson Dorrance's competitive fire and the sheer delight he took in beating the world at its own game, as he puts it, but recent years suggest that it's getting harder and harder for the US women to dominate the sport to the extent they once did. Pretty soon, the odds are the rest of the world, collectively, will overtake the United States in the title count Dorrance shared with me. And for Foudy, Dorrance, and all the remarkable women who've represented the USWNT so ably, that will be the ultimate win. They can take credit for launching the sport globally. This is a refrain you hear again and again from anyone involved in women's soccer overseas.

If 1999 and more recent high points like the 2019 World Cup win by the Alex Morgan & Megan Rapinoe generation represent the proverbial mountaintop, another anecdote Julie Foudy shared with me and my students reinforces Dorrance's underappreciated point that US women's soccer wasn't born atop it. In talking about how far the sport progressed in the 1990s and in the time the core of that '99 team represented the United States together, Foudy took us back to that first World Cup Dorrance said FIFA "hid" in China, back in 1991, when that country was less open to the outside world. Turns out, FIFA also hid the World Cup in the month of November, to further distinguish it from the men's tournaments.

This presented a problem for Foudy, then an undergrad at Stanford University, as she told us:

"So it's literally the First World Cup in China, and finals are happening too, and I had to convince my Stanford professors that I am going to this thing called the World Cup, and they're like what the hell!" She then tried to explain to them "it's like what the men do every four years," but America's relationship with the game then was tenuous enough for that not to help much. It would have been one thing if she'd told them she was off to play Berkeley, but off for a month in China for a "World Cup" sounded awfully dodgy.

"We thought that us winning would be the big game changer for the country. But I came home and my Stanford professors still didn't know that a World Cup had happened. They were like, fine you missed the last month . . . now sit down and take your final."

The ultimate game changer was still in the future, before the decade and the millennium expired.

8
But What About the Men?

When the US government orchestrated the dramatic arrest of seven senior FIFA officials suspected of corruption at a five-star hotel in Zurich in May of 2015, Russian leader Vladimir Putin was clearly upset, accusing the United States of yet another "blatant attempt to extend its jurisdiction to other states."

"It looks very strange, the arrests are carried out on the request of the USA side," Putin told reporters the next day. "They are accused of corruption—who is? International officials. I suppose that someone broke some rules, I don't know. But definitely, it's got nothing to do with the USA. Those officials are not U.S. citizens. If something happened, it was not in the U.S. and it's nothing to do with them."[1]

That US prosecutors had FIFA in their sights didn't only take Putin by surprise. People everywhere were stunned (pleasantly or unpleasantly) by the news and joined Putin in wondering what this had to do with the Americans. For the Russian dictator and FIFA's leaders, the answer was clear: this US legal assault on world football amounted to a case of sour grapes. The Americans had lost their bid to host the 2022 World Cup to Qatar and were now acting as sore losers, determined to overturn that decision, and disrupt Russia's upcoming World Cup in 2018 that had been awarded as part of the same process. No autocratic leader like Putin who embraces a state-sponsored model of sporting glory could imagine such a high-profile prosecution of FIFA officials originating anywhere other than in the White House. The case had in fact been built for years by enterprising FBI and IRS field agents in New York and California pursuing leads on money laundering and tax avoidance that implicated a powerful FIFA official based in New York, Chuck Blazer, who then acted as US law enforcement's sherpa to FIFA's crime-infested underworld.

Still, the fact that the US Attorney General Loretta Lynch and James Comey, then head of the Justice Department's Criminal Division, gave the green light to expand the original investigations and to pursue these prosecutions aggressively showed that something had indeed changed in America's relationship to the global game. At a press conference later in the year announcing a superseding indictment with new charges against even more defendants that built on the May arrests, Attorney General Lynch said that "global sports like soccer" exemplify "unifying, educational, cultural and humanitarian values" (echoing FIFA's own language) and "are one of the primary ways we teach our children about character, about fair play and about teamwork." Lynch added that the investigation "reaffirms the ideals that have always guided our society—and most importantly, our young people—toward the fair and just future they deserve."[2]

There it was. Our children. Our society. Our young people. Their future. The rationale for a case against FIFA, the governing body of the game once emphatically rejected by American society as being too foreign. It is unfathomable that any Attorney General of the United States that I came to when I was fifteen would have allocated significant effort or resources to a massive probe of FIFA. Back then, they would have likely agreed with Putin's assessment; this has nothing to do with us.

But that was before women, immigrants, and blue-chip corporations had banded together to make soccer a naturalized American pastime. The US Department of Justice may have been able to assert jurisdiction over some of FIFA's corrupt shenanigans, as a technical legal matter, because the underlying money flows engaged US financial institutions. But in a broader sense, the United States was asserting a societal jurisdiction over the case because this was now our game too.

Putin's "what's this got to do with the Americans?" query is one that has been asked often across the footballing world in recent years as people everywhere wrap their minds around two improbable developments that directly affect one of the most important things in their lives: soccer becoming part of American culture and America becoming part of global soccer culture.

I most recently heard a variant of this Putin Query, in equally annoyed tones, in Manchester, England, from a diehard Manchester United supporter assembling for a protest march against the American owners of their club: "Don't you Yanks already have enough sports and leagues of your own to stay away from ours?"

In Mexico, the US embrace of soccer, and gradual rise within the game, has been met with more of a "You've got to be kidding me, now this too" bemusement and head shake. When I was a kid growing up in that country, soccer was a US-free zone, one of the few consequential aspects of people's lives that was not dominated by the neighboring superpower. The United States hadn't even qualified for a men's World Cup since 1950, which to us kids might have been the Middle Ages. When the two nations did meet in international competition, Mexico would invariably win decisively, and to many fans it felt like payback for, you know, everything else. But now Mexico is having to make its peace with the fact that the United States is a worthy rival on the field, and a protagonist in the political economy of the game, even amid a lingering sense of denial.

In 2020, I participated in a 2-on-2 debate over whether Mexico or the United States would be the first to win a men's World Cup, and one well-known Mexican sportswriter based in Spain on the other side sought to explain to me how soccer wasn't really that popular in the United States, sounding very much like he was beaming in from 1975. His partner, the legendary coach Miguel "Piojo" Herrera, who had managed Mexico at the Brazil World Cup but was then in charge of Mexico City's Club América, was also pushing back against my thesis of the inevitable rise of the United States within soccer, but with far less conviction. He looked haunted when admitting that he had "seen things" across the border that were truly impressive.

But overall, foreign reactions to America's embrace of soccer tend to range from the ambivalent to the positive, rather than the outright hostile. At the most basic level, Americans playing, following, and caring about the world's most popular sport makes us less weird to others. Also, we are more approachable and relatable; less detached and arrogant. When you follow and play the same game as others, it creates kinship and empathy between you. It gives you something to talk about. And for as long as Americans participate fully in the sport like never before without dominating it, this presents a more relatable and humbler United States to the world than the one people overseas are accustomed to seeing in other contexts. It normalizes us.

Some of the most impassioned non-immigrant soccer fans within the United States also feel ambivalent about their country becoming a major power in the sport. They're attached to their identity as worldly, cultural contrarians, dismissive of the prevailing, insular mass sporting culture. They've loved soccer in the way some cinema aficionados embrace foreign indie films over the mainstream Hollywood fare consumed at thousands of multiplexes. To them, soccer becoming a fixture of American culture poses an identity crisis, much as it does for those foreign fans of the game whose appreciation of it was enhanced by America's absence.

Yet the extent to which international football is now our game too remains an open question, and a timely one as the 2026 World Cup to be played across North America approaches. Women, immigrants, and corporate America have all done their part, but it still isn't clear whether the world's most popular sport will become a full-fledged member, and the first imported one, of the club of most-watched and most avidly followed US professional sports, alongside the NFL, MLB, and the NBA, or whether it will remain a JV sport by comparison. Nor is it clear how much US soccer needs our men to close the gap with our women in their international competitiveness before the sport can reach its ultimate heights in this country.

There are those who claim the United States can't be a true soccer power until it's won a World Cup, and this is asserted just so, disregarding the fact that American women have already won four of them. We take for granted how far the women have brought us, which would be hard to overstate. But I do get the point that it's hard to be top-tier in the sport if you aren't competitive on the men's side. Indeed, for the world's most universal sport, international football's superpowers should thrive on both sides of the gender divide. This far into the twenty-first century, no country should be deemed a full-fledged power if it isn't competitive on the women's side either.

To reinforce this point, Victoria and I coauthored a modest proposal-style guest essay for *The Los Angeles Times* on the heels of the 2019 women's World Cup urging FIFA to scrap that tournament going forward. Instead, we argued, the men's and women's tournaments should be collapsed into one, and results should reflect performance across both teams.[3] So, for instance, if the United States were to draw Poland in the next World Cup, you'd have a doubleheader consisting of a women's and a men's US-Poland match, with the aggregate score of the two determining the outcome. Talk about an incentive for certain laggard nations to invest in their women's game! The idea was so animatedly rejected in so many disparate quarters, I suspect we might have been onto something.

Henry Kissinger used to quip that Brazil was the country of the future, and always will be, and you hear variations on that with regard to soccer as a spectator sport in America. How long can you be on the verge? But I have no doubt soccer is becoming a part of our mainstream hegemonic sports fandom culture and that the United States is becoming one of the game's superpowers on the men's side, as it already is on the women's side. Since I first arrived in the United States, back in the early days of the Reagan presidency, this country has stealthily become a formidable protagonist in the game, and we have reached a point of no return; continued ascendancy is inevitable. Naysayers and skeptics have plenty of bearish indicators to cling to: soccer's considerable deficit vs. American football as a TV and cultural product; the inability of Major League Soccer to come anywhere close to joining Major League Baseball or the NBA in occupying our sporting landscape's second tier, or to pose a competitive threat to Europe's big leagues for that matter; and, of course, the still-mediocre performance of the US men's team in international competition.

The bullish case is stronger.

For starters, it's important to separate the questions of whether soccer is anywhere near becoming the #1 sport in America from the question of whether America is anywhere near becoming the #1 power in soccer. Because as painful and insulting as this may be to people elsewhere who are entirely devoted to the world's game, it's quite possible our nation could pull off the latter feat without soccer pulling off the former. The United States has already become a protagonist in international football well before the game poses a significant threat to the popularity of our homegrown varietal of football. Indeed, within the next couple of decades, the United States could easily become the first nation to ever win a men's World Cup while caring more about other sports.

The sheer scale of the United States, and its commercial and media prowess, is the reason why this could happen. But American soccer has also attained some absolute gains, not just relative ones, that shouldn't be minimized.

Most importantly, soccer is one of the most played team sports by American kids. Millions of boys and girls at some point in their childhood go out and crowd around the ball in recreational soccer leagues, and America's physical landscape has come to resemble the rest of the world with the proliferation of soccer fields and their rectangular netted goals. As a result, according to a global census FIFA conducted in 2006, China and the United States are the two nations on earth with the largest soccer-playing populations (India may have surpassed us since or must be close, but the point is that these three countries will develop more players than smaller, far more football-mad, nations).[4]

Fine, the naysayers will tell you, but you're going to be waiting an eternity for those kids or the next generation to grow up to be avid soccer fans as adults, because that hasn't happened yet. There is something to this argument, and to the idea that we are seeing a bifurcation in America's relationship with the two footballs, with soccer increasingly the participation sport, and American football the televised spectacle and entertainment we watch, follow, fantasize about (literally, with fantasy football), and gamble on. But the point is overstated: Americans have steadily become more interested in soccer as spectators, even if the numbers and their short-term growth are less spectacular than the sport's participation rates.

Among the most eye-opening stats I like to highlight in my classes and talks on this subject are the TV ratings for the last men's FIFA World Cup final in Qatar in December 2022. The dramatic faceoff between Leo Messi's Argentina and Kylian Mbappé's France that went into overtime attracted a US TV audience of 26.73 million viewers.[5] That's a larger audience than baseball's World Series or any of the NBA's Final Championship games earlier that same year—and this for a game that featured no Americans. It's also two million more people than watched the game in France itself, where an astonishing 81 percent of all TVs were tuned in.[6] Again, scale matters; a moderately decent slice of America's attention is a lot of attention.

Even going back to the year of the spectacular arrests of FIFA officials in Zurich, the final match of the 2015 women's World Cup played in Canada between the United States and Japan amassed a nearly identical audience of 26.7 million. The previous summer, the final of the Brazil men's World Cup between Germany and Brazil pulled in 26.5 million viewers. That same tournament registered the highest rating ever for the US men's national team, when 24.7 million people watched the United States draw 2–2 with Portugal in the group stage. These numbers pale when compared to the Super Bowl, but they are highly impressive compared to anything else.

The scale and wealth of the American media market also explain why the United States is already FIFA's single most important media market to FIFA, when it comes to the organization's income from World Cup TV rights. The United States has also been among the top three countries of origin for foreign fans at the previous four men's World Cups (with the top spot among international fans attending South Africa in 2010 and Brazil in 2014). [7]

Closer to home, millions of American families organize their weekends around minivan rides to rec and travel youth soccer matches. In that sense, soccer is as ingrained in US culture as it is in the culture of any Latin American or European country, though we do lag behind those societies in the possibility of improvised, unorganized soccer breaking out at any and all times on the street, or at the local park. In too many of our suburbs, Americans treat soccer as something that requires adult supervision, well-manicured fields with proper goals, snappy uniforms, orange slices at halftime, earnest but oft-abused refs, the full works.

The United States also boasts a domestic professional league, launched in the year following the 1994 World Cup, that has its own impressive gameday convening power among impassioned local fan bases. Major League Soccer posted the second-highest attendance (a total of 12.1 million fans)[8] of any soccer league in the world over its 2024 season, second only to the English Premier League. The league has avoided the boom-and-bust cycles of previous attempts at professional soccer in this country, embracing a tightly controlled and disciplined single-entity ownership model and a strategy of consistent, gradual growth. Launched with only ten teams, MLS added San Diego as its thirtieth franchise in 2025, with its investors paying $500 million to join in.[9]

The league's greatest single accomplishment is on the ground, transforming the sporting landscape of America by building modern, soccer-specific stadiums in most major cities (although, alas, my hometown of Phoenix remains America's largest soccer desert). For all its success since then, however, MLS rarely breaks into the crowded, sprawling national zeitgeist, beyond the subculture of its own fandom, to become what Andrei Markovits described as a "hegemonic sporting culture" in our first chapter. One exception came in the aftermath of the league's bold move to sign Leo Messi, as also discussed previously, when national media were filled with stories of Messi mania—the scramble for tickets, the celebrity sightings at Miami games, and the perennial question of whether this meant soccer had finally arrived in this country. Even NPR's *Marketplace* reached out to me to discuss what was going on.

But such moments remain just that: moments. MLS, which is now corralled within the Apple paywall as we discussed in Chapter 6, has for the most part been a quiet success just under the radar of our national consciousness. In certain markets like Portland and Seattle, where the heated rivalry between them has taken hold and the clubs have significant fan bases connected to the grassroots youth game, MLS can break onto center stage of communities' sports consciousness, but that remains a sporadic occurrence.

I've always appreciated the demographics of MLS' matchday fandom; when I lived in Los Angeles and would attend LA Galaxy games in Carson, I'd see a fabulous blend of Mexican-American fans chanting in Spanish and suburban Anglo soccer families up from Orange County or down from the Valley whose universes often didn't mix, all wearing the same jerseys. MLS is a model of sustainability, if not a threat to our big three homegrown sports' pro leagues.

It's also no threat to the dominance of Europe's big leagues. Since its inception, MLS has waged a two-front struggle to gain acceptance in our national sporting ecosystem while also trying to do so in the international football one. Reflecting on the league's first three decades, Aaron Timms wrote in *The Guardian* that the league is "simultaneously too American for most international football fans and too international for the casual American sports lover."[10] To be fair, MLS has come a long way since its earliest days when it chose to express a curious American exceptionalism (and an almost apologetic embrace of its own sport) by tinkering with the rules to try making the game more "exciting" and fast-paced for an American audience. In its first seasons, there were no ties; if a game was still tied at the end of regulation it would go into a "shootout" in which players ran on goal and the opposing goalkeeper from the 35-yard line, with five seconds to get a shot off. Fortunately, such apostasy was quickly abandoned, but MLS still defies global footballing mores with its closed single-entity structure which precludes any relegation or promotion, and by scheduling its seasons in perpetual conflict with the international game's calendar, running from spring to fall, and failing to observe the almost universally observed breaks in other domestic leagues.

Then there is the all-important matter of the league's level and style of play. In my limited experience (I'll get to that in a second), MLS games are great fun—the atmosphere at the stadiums is fantastic, and matches tend to offer open, attacking play that is easy on the eye, if perhaps a notch slower and less intense than you might watch early mornings from across the Atlantic. The quality of defending is more suspect in MLS, where squads tend to be an interesting blend of young American talent, up-and-coming Latin American and African players looking to be sold on to European clubs, and some aging stars enjoying their careers' final chapters in a league offering a more forgiving pace.

One of my all-time favorite soccer-watching moments anywhere came in August 2018 at Washington's Audi Field (one of the league's impressive new grounds), in the final of six minutes of stoppage time against Orlando in a match that was all tied up 2-2. D.C. United had a corner kick that appeared to provide a last-gasp chance to win the game, so even its goalkeeper went up to try to win a header. Orlando's defense cleared the cross, and one of the team's counterattacking forwards was closing in on the ball near midfield, an entirely open field and open goal in front of him. Then out of nowhere, or at least from way behind him, as if shot out of a cannon, D.C. United's captain and former Manchester United legend Wayne Rooney, aged thirty-two and never known for his speed, caught up to the Orlando attacker as he was starting to dribble the ball with an aggressive sliding tackle after his half-field sprint. I fully expected Rooney to then take a bow for preserving the tie with his extraordinary effort, as was his due, but instead he hustled to prevent the ball from going out of the sideline, imperiously started carrying the ball back in the other direction, head held high, and then struck one of the most precise long-range crosses you'll ever see, with just the right amount of hang time and backspin to allow Luciano Acosta to score his third goal of the night with a long, looping header to defeat Orlando's keeper. To engage in a football-bridging metaphor, it was like watching a perfect Tom Brady bomb for a winning touchdown in the final seconds of a game, if Brady had first had to outsprint a young player 40 yards and then slide-tackled him to get a hold of the ball before throwing it. I think of that play when people talk about the intangibles of sporting greatness and the grit and competitive determination that isn't accessible to all of us. I also think of that play when some critics scoff at the quality of MLS offerings.

Major League Soccer has never posted blockbuster TV ratings, and since its 2023 season the size of that audience has become harder to discern and track due to the league's ten-year global deal with Apple. Absent any ratings data to the contrary, it's safe to assume that more Americans continue to tune in to Mexico's Liga MX and the English Premier League than to MLS matches. I am guilty of this, as an ardent Arsenal fan and as someone who likes to keep an eye on the Rayados de Monterrey in the Mexican league. These days, MLS is not among the three soccer leagues I follow most closely, despite having had nothing but good experiences with it.

Things might be different if Phoenix had a team, but my broader point is that in some ways MLS has become, paradoxically enough, a victim of its sport's success in America at a time when technology and globalization have so shrunk the world. To an extent unimaginable to my fifteen-year-old self who felt cut off from the rest of the sporting world upon moving to this country in the early 1980s, I can now watch practically any soccer league on earth here in the United States. So, I tune into the English Premier League (like so many people around the world) on NBC and Peacock, European Champions League matches on Paramount+, and Liga MX games on Univision. I don't have time or energy left for MLS on top of all that, but if we lived in a less connected world and it were the only soccer I could access on a regular basis—say if the government imposed a 1,000 percent tariff on watching any imported soccer to protect our national league—I would be among the league's most ardent fans. But because of the global nature of its sport, MLS is the only major professional league in the United States whose audience is cannibalized by leagues overseas.

Of course, this is a predicament faced by many domestic leagues around the world. How can Egypt, for instance, drive viewership and investment to its domestic football when Mo Salah is playing every weekend for Liverpool? In Chapter 4, we discussed why free-market liberalism makes sense for English football, but is that true everywhere?

In 2024, *The Athletic* reported that the value of the US rights to broadcast the English Premier League had increased 5.5 times since NBC Sports first acquired them for the 2013–2014 season.[11] The current deal is worth $450 million a season and runs until 2028.[12] The Comcast/NBCUniversal empire does a great job airing/streaming all 380 games each season across its network, cable, and streaming platforms (that's more games than you can watch in Britain, because of the national blackout rule there for Saturday 3:00 p.m. games) and deserves its share of the credit for helping to turn the league into another domestic league, in terms of general sports fans' awareness.

I have experienced that evolution over the past decade. Not long ago, the most frequent comment I'd get wearing an Arsenal jersey in the United States was, "Oh, do you work for Emirates Airlines?" Now, to walk down a street in downtown Washington, DC wearing an Arsenal jersey is to elicit a stream of high fives or jeers and plenty of commentary on the latest match, much as if you were wearing an NFL or NBA jersey. The nice man who checks me in at my Phoenix gym is a fellow Gunner, and the kid who masterfully serves up poke bowls down the street has the misfortune of rooting for Tottenham. On days when I am trying to observe a "news blackout" to watch a game delayed, I have learned the hard way that I can no longer wear Arsenal swag and expect to get through the day without someone reacting by giving away the score, something that never used to be a problem. When I moved within the Phoenix metro area not long ago and the movers' rep came by to give me an estimate, I had a Premier League game in the background. I was prepared to shrug it off defensively as an odd interest I had acquired growing up abroad (he wasn't one of my *paisanos*), but he lingered at the door to watch for a bit. "I'm a huge Manchester United guy," he said, "and my wife is for Chelsea, but somehow we make it work."

One study in 2020 found that 20 percent of US sports viewers are interested in the English Premier League,[13] and there is every reason to believe that percentage will continue to go up as soccer's popularity increases. MLS should grow too, but the world's best league (one increasingly owned by Americans) is as readily accessible to us, and fans of soccer anywhere will seek out the EPL in the same way that fans of basketball anywhere seek out the NBA. And so, MLS faces the same predicament that Croatia's national basketball league faces.

Keep that in mind next time you hear someone pointing to MLS' modest reach to question soccer's popularity in America. There are interesting glass "half full vs half empty" debates to be had about what Major League has accomplished, but it's a mistake to equate that with the debate over soccer's present status in America, because that is to confuse a glass with the bottle from which it, and other glasses, are being served. A healthy domestic pro league is an important measure of any nation's sporting ecosystem, but soccer in America is far greater than MLS.

The same is true when evaluating the state of American soccer's competitiveness on the field of play, because it isn't just fans that have their heads turned by Europe. Most of America's most talented players opt to play in Europe's more challenging and higher-paying leagues. At the most recent US men's national team (USMNT) World Cup match, the December 2022 3–1 loss to the Netherlands that knocked us out of the Qatar tournament in the Round of 16, the United States started only two MLS players alongside nine who play in European leagues: five in England, two in Italy, and one each in Spain and France.[14]

In the spring of 2025, Coach Mauricio Pochettino started ten American players who ply their trade in European leagues and only one MLS player in a disappointing Concacaf Nations League semifinal loss to Panama at SoFi Stadium in Los Angeles. And even that one US-based player, 37-year-old Tim Ream, might need an asterisk, because before that season he played for nine years at Fulham in the English Premier League.

The United States, much like South America's soccer powers, is an exporter of its most promising talent. In world football's food chain, MLS is a mid-level league that imports many players but not at the same level (or at the same cost) as the world's leading leagues, and it struggles to retain America's best prospects. This may or may not be good for MLS itself, but it ultimately should be beneficial for the USMNT to have more of its players competing against the world's best week in and week out (as we agreed it would be good for England's players, too, in Chapter 4, though they can do it by staying home). Mexico's richer Liga MX has an easier time retaining Mexico's top players; the bar is set higher for the point at which it makes sense for them to cross the Atlantic. Over time, the advantage the United States derives from having more players over in Europe's top leagues has helped tip the balance of power in the US-Mexico rivalry.

Much has been said about this "golden generation" of American players that have attained success in Europe. After stints in Germany and England, Christian Pulisic, arguably the country's most accomplished player of all time, has become one of the leading stars of Italy's Serie A, where he's been joined at AC Milan (a club now owned by American investors) by fellow American prodigy Yunus Musah. Pulisic had a rocky time at Chelsea after being signed from Borussia Dortmund in a splashy £58 million transfer. The manager who'd been eager to build his attack around the American was fired by the time Pulisic showed up, and the three other managers he'd play for in his four seasons in London never quite rated him in the same way. A series of injuries didn't help either. His two seasons in Milan have been more in keeping with his earlier promise, and fans have embraced him enthusiastically, their "Captain America" and leading scorer in '24-'25 from Hershey, PA.

And yet, despite Pulisic's stardom and the success of other countrymen across the Atlantic well before him (Clint Dempsey, Tim Howard, and Claudio Reyna come to mind), Americans always have to do it a bit more than anyone else to prove themselves in international football, to overcome the lingering skepticism and anti-Americanism in the game. Pulisic himself addressed this on a poignant Paramount Plus docuseries that bears his name.[15] "It pisses me off," says the normally soft-spoken player in a rare outburst near the end of the first episode, "I have seen it and felt it." His USMNT teammate Weston

McKennie, who plays for Juventus, another giant of Italian football, also speaks to the bias on the episode, talking about how every summer he feels like he has to prove himself all over again in training camp because of his Americanness: "It's like, when are you people going to see that I am good enough at this level?" He adds that this is one reason American players can be so tenacious, always playing with a "chip on our shoulders." American sports discourse has been so focused on race; it's refreshing to hear Pulisic and McKennie talk in the same way about a different prejudice they must overcome together: their nationality. Then again, it will be even more refreshing when that prejudice is also gone.

Pulisic went to Dortmund at the age of seventeen, and the documentary also covers the commitment and sacrifices required of the very top American male athletes in the world's most popular sport. Normally, it's people from elsewhere in the world who sacrifice to come to America to fulfill their potential across so many fields, but in men's international football, it's young Americans who must go elsewhere to reach for the top. Because of his age when he first arrived in Dortmund, Pulisic had to attend a local school in German, a memory he clearly doesn't relish. But because of his father's family ancestry, Pulisic was able to obtain Croatian citizenship, which hastened his move onto Dortmund's senior team (because of different rules regarding age for EU nationals).

Pulisic has no intention of ever playing for Croatia internationally, but his binational circumstances are common among US players. Many of them could opt to play for one of several countries (though once you decide on one, at the senior level, you're locked into that one, per FIFA rules).

Former president Bill Clinton pitched FIFA on the idea that with so many diasporas in the United States, every World Cup nation could fill stands with their countrymen already living in this country. At times it feels as if we could do the same for other countries' player rosters, too. US Soccer officials and the USMNT manager spend a lot of effort convincing top American players to opt for representing the Stars and Stripes instead of their other country. In recent years, they've wooed Ricardo Pepi (who could have played for Mexico), Yunus Musah (England), Sergino Dest (Netherlands), Folarin Balogun (England), Malik Tillman (Germany), and Alejandro Zendejas (Mexico), to name a few.

Milan fans have no more doubts about the caliber of American soccer, with Pulisic playing at the level he did in his first seasons with the club. Also in Italy, Timothy Weah, the son of a professional player who went on to become president of Liberia, has been at Juventus alongside Weston McKennie. There are also strong contingents of USMNT players in England (especially Antonee Robinson, aka "Jedi," and Tyler Adams), and both Dutch and German leagues have historically been the most propitious first stops for American players in Europe.

Part of the hype around this "golden generation" is a sense that some deity must have set the timer for them to peak right around the time they play the 2026 World Cup at home. Pulisic will be twenty-seven when the USMNT kicks off their first game in Los Angeles at SoFi Stadium on June 12. In Qatar, the United States routinely fielded the youngest squad in the tournament; eight of the eleven starters who were knocked out of the tournament by the Dutch were under the age of twenty-five. And so, the theory, or hope, has been that the core group will be in their prime when they get to play in the World Cup at home.

On the other hand, being known as a "golden generation" is asking for trouble for any team that doesn't win it all, and there's been plenty of grumbling already that this USMNT hasn't quite lived up to the hype, and that the whole seems to undercount the sum of its parts. The team that went to Brazil in 2014 and its predecessors this century were underdogs who punched above their weight, with players who made up in hustle and teamwork what they lacked in individual technical skill and club pedigree. Now some fans and critics are complaining the opposite is happening, that we have a team that punches below its weight, with players who might be more focused on their club careers than doing right by their national side, a complaint that used to be leveled against Leo Messi himself by Argentine fans.

The verdict on this edition of the USMNT is still out. Being knocked out of the Qatar World Cup '22 by the Dutch in Qatar was disappointing, though hardly humiliating or embarrassing, even if it did reveal a desperate need for a managerial upgrade. The federation then wasted valuable time by ignoring this takeaway, vacillating for months over whether to renew Coach Gregg Berhalter before inexplicably doing so, and then having to dismiss him in the summer of 2024 when the United States was knocked out in the group stage of the hemispheric Copa America played on our soil. Things appeared to be heading in the wrong direction, and the clock was urgently ticking toward the all-important 2026 World Cup.

That is when US Soccer, the national federation, got serious about attracting a world-class manager for the men's team (as it has for the women's team too, with Emma Hayes) and landed on Mauricio Pochettino, the Argentine who'd impressed at the helm of Southampton, Tottenham, and Chelsea in England, and Paris Saint-Germain in France. He only debuted with the team in October 2024, the same month England announced it was hiring Thomas Tuchel, another foreign manager who'd known success in the English Premier League, to lead its national team.

America has tapped an Argentine and England a German to resolve their national footballing conundrums; neither manager was hired to develop a long-term project; they are both tasked with bringing a generation's worth of effort to fruition by succeeding at the upcoming World Cup. In both cases, it's a short-term assignment, the only difference being the definition of success. Tuchel must win the World Cup for England, Pochettino has to do really well, an admittedly subjective goal that will partially depend on the luck of the draw. Being knocked out in the quarterfinals by Argentina or France in a close game might do the trick, but dropping out of the tournament at that stage would amount to disappointment if it's at the hands of one of the sport's other middling or upstart powers.

Pochettino's early days were underwhelming, though it hardly matters given the extent to which the stakes at the '26 World Cup dwarf anything else on Pochettino's to-do list, not to mention anything else US men's soccer has faced over the past generation. If the 1994 US World Cup's mission was to introduce the game as a viable sport in this country, the mission of the 2026 Cup is to propel the game into the major leagues of American sporting preoccupations, hovering somewhere alongside the NBA and MLB and below the NFL, and to permanently propel the United States into the top tier of world soccer on the men's side. In other words, no pressure.

Former USMNT players who had less storied club careers in Europe but often seemed to rise above their level when playing for their country are understandably tired of hearing the current team heralded as a golden generation. Having watched a desultory performance by the United States in the third-place consolation match against Canada in the aforementioned 2025 Concacaf Nations League after the loss to Panama, Landon Donovan, the USMNT's top scorer of all time, took to X to vent: "I'm so sick of hearing how 'talented' this group of players is and all the amazing clubs they play for," he said. "If you aren't going to show up and actually give a s!%* about playing for your national team, decline the invite. Talent is great, pride is better."[16]

That same week, Tab Ramos, who played on the US team that hosted the 1994 World Cup, vented to *The Athletic*:

> A "golden generation?" Are you kidding me? At this point I feel like I came from the golden generation. After seeing all of this? My generation was probably the golden generation. We took the U.S. to a World Cup after hopping fences to play in playgrounds and getting paid $400 a game to play for the Brooklyn Italians to prepare for the national team. If that's not golden, I don't know what is. We have just lost the essence of who we are as a soccer country.[17]

Pulisic's decision to sit out Concacaf's regional Gold Cup in the summer of 2025 to recover from a grueling season and lingering injuries led to another round of recriminations.

It's hard to overstate the pressure on these American players going into the World Cup. Any nation hosting the tournament faces high expectations and demands to outperform not just opposing teams but that nation's own historical record. The USMNT is no exception, on top of which, fairly or unfairly, they also carry on their shoulders the additional pressure of being responsible, or so they are constantly being told, for the game's prospects in America. Whether they succeed or not, it won't be for lack of caring about the national team because they are too wrapped up in their club careers. That's an accusation fans everywhere make when disappointed at their national team stumbling, but it's rarely an issue in international football. The extent to which players at all levels dream of representing their country and relish the opportunity, even when their compensation and other economic incentives are all tied to their club careers, remains one of the game's old-fashioned charms. Indeed, before his move to Italy, Christian Pulisic caught some flack in England for wearing his US Soccer sweatshirt during Chelsea's on-field post-match celebrations upon winning the European Champions League in 2021 (he became the first American to do so). Fans are jealous, and even as they celebrated, some Chelsea fans didn't appreciate that the optics on the night suggested their American star might care more about his national team than the club he'd just helped win a European title.

9

Send the Word, That the Yanks Are Coming

Back in Manchester, birthplace of the industrial revolution, on an atypically glorious Sunday in March 2025, three hours prior to kickoff against Arsenal. Outside the Tollgate Pub, less than a mile up the road from United's venerable Old Trafford Stadium, members of the club's "The 1958" supporters' group were milling about, fortifying themselves with plenty of beer for the protest march they were about to lead down to the stadium's Munich tunnel, named after the tragedy that also gave this fan group its name—the crash of the airplane bringing Manchester United's team home from European competition as it was taking off from Munich's airport on February 6, 1958. The disaster that was to become one of the club's most stirring memories and rallying cries claimed the lives of twenty-three of forty-four people on board, including eight United players and three staff members.

The air at the Tollgate was perfunctorily funereal, as the protesting supporters (an estimated 5,000 would participate in the march) wore black to mourn their club. But they also marveled at the weather and couldn't help but feel some excitement about the prospect of facing Arsenal in what was the class matchup of the Premier League in the late 1990s and early this century, when the league started attracting more of the world's attention. They also compared their placards and signs with all the familiar slogans about their loyalty being betrayed, about wanting their club back, about the ownership's greed at their expense, and most of all, about wanting the Glazers out. I was impressed that many even had "Glazers Out" football scarves, in the club's original green-and-white color scheme, which tells you something about how institutionalized such protests had become. The following month it would be a post-match sit-in.

They've been at it for two decades. It was in 2005 when Malcolm Glazer, the owner of the NFL's Tampa Bay Buccaneers, took control of Manchester United after buying his first shares in the club two years earlier. When his two sons came to take possession that summer, they were met by a throng chanting "Die, Glazers, Die!"[1] Old Trafford has remained that hospitable to the family ever since.

Across town, Manchester City fans also grumble about rising ticket prices, but for much of the past decade, City fans have defended their Abu Dhabi owners against the charges of financial doping; and you can often spot homemade signs at the Etihad thanking Sheikh Mansour, instead of asking him to die. Similarly, at Chelsea's Stamford Bridge, before Roman Abramovich was forced to sell the club when sanctions were imposed on Russian oligarchs in the aftermath of the 2022 invasion of Ukraine (and sometimes even afterward), you would often see Russian flags and placards reading "Roman's Army."

American owners aroused a particular set of suspicions and resentments across England upon first buying into the English game—and despite the Glazers' pleasant experience, many have followed in their footsteps. A map of British football nowadays resembles a map of the Isles in the spring of 1944, when American troops and materiel crammed into every village and byway awaiting their onward deployment to the continent on D-Day. That "friendly invasion" amounted to 1.5 million men; today's is a friendly invasion of investors who've acquired control of more than half of all Premier League clubs—eleven of the twenty in the 2025–6 season are American-owned—and roughly a third of clubs like Wrexham that play in the four divisions below that constitute the English Football League.

If American players, fans, and media companies have all had their heads turned by European football, it should come as no surprise that sports investors have as well, and that collectively all these transatlantic footballing bonds are further lifting soccer within America and America within the world of international football. And in the Great Game to win the upper hand to control and govern the future of sports, this massive and growing overseas commitment of American capital and business expertise to the world's most important sport, and its most important league, will prove decisive.

What distinguishes American owners from other deep-pocketed foreign owners who've bought English football clubs in recent decades is that the Americans came to do business. Many of them are already invested in sports back home, and they view English football as another product to add to their portfolio, a product with a tremendous global reach but a long history of mismanagement and financial underperformance. Other foreign owners (though not all) have bought into English football much in the same way they might buy a historic English country home or a yacht, as a prestigious trophy asset, separate from their actual businesses. Roman Abramovich was happy to lose money ("invest in the club" is how fans put it) to win trophies and acclaim. Chelsea was his passion project, hobby, and community service, not a business whose margins he was going to sweat.

Compounding the early mistrust of American owners was a visceral bias against a people who for most of their history denigrated the sport England bequeathed to the world. Whatever their motivations, Chinese, Arab, Serbian, Russian, Malaysian, Thai, Italian, Greek, and other foreign owners have snatched up English teams professing their love of the game as fans. American owners are the only ones who arrive suspected (sometimes unfairly) of not caring much for the game itself, given where they come from. Or—heresy of heresies—they arrive clearly caring more about other sports. The fact that they may already own clubs in a different sport is not especially reassuring to fans. They'd rather see owners who are rabid fellow fans of the game, regardless of whatever other strikes—human rights abuses, corruption, you name it— might lurk in their background.

Of course, not all American owners are alike, and the Glazers' tenure in Manchester has been uniquely toxic. Their acquisition of the club was heavily leveraged, and since acquiring the club they have been paying themselves handsome dividends. Hardly a scandalous thing for a private enterprise to be doing, but not very common in English football. United has spent about a billion dollars servicing its heavy debt load since the 2005 leveraged buyout.[2] The club's fading infrastructure (Old Trafford, the "Theatre of Dreams," is a leaky old venue, England's largest, with lots of red brick and character but lacking such modern amenities as a replay screen) and mediocrity since the retirement of legendary manager Alex Ferguson in 2013 have reinforced the impression of a club whose owners are underinvesting.

The truth is more complicated, and perhaps even more damning to the Glazers, because they have done an impressive job of growing the club's commercial revenue. United's level of spending on transfer fees to attract talent, and on the squad's payroll, is consistently near the league's highest. It's just that the club's spending has been far more ineffective and wasteful than that of rivals Manchester City and Liverpool, two remarkably well-run clubs in recent years with clear strategic long-range plans. Post-Ferguson United, by contrast, became football's Bermuda Triangle, a place where established stars or upcoming talents from other clubs came to fade, if not disappear. Paul Pogba, Mason Mount, Angel Di María, Donny Van de Beek, Antony, Jadon Sancho. Alexis Sánchez, Cristiano Ronaldo (the sequel, not the original). The list goes on.

Then in early 2024, the Glazers did something truly bizarre. They sold a quarter of the club to British billionaire James Ratcliffe for $1.3 billion and handed the chairman of the INEOS petrochemical giant (reportedly Britain's wealthiest individual) full control over all sporting decisions at the club.[3] Ratcliffe modestly increased his stake later that year and is widely expected to take full ownership at some point in the future, though in the meantime, he has acted very much as the man in charge, hiring a new executive team, making decisions about the team's manager, cutting costs, and announcing plans for a new stadium. Manchester United is the rare case of a club reverting from foreign to British control, and the unheard-of case where the keys have been handed over to a minority owner.

The shift hasn't yet affected the priority of United's disgruntled fans: to get the Glazers out. But over time, Ratcliffe's forceful Mancunian directness could become the focus of supporters' ire absent a turnaround in the club's fortunes. Ratcliffe could convincingly play the factory owner in a BBC period piece about the Industrial Revolution. "No one ever gave me a free lunch" he told *The Times* in explaining why he'd cut the free lunches for United's staff, after laying off 450 employees and cutting other benefits such as subsidized staff travel to watch United play at the 2024 FA Cup Final in London. Ratcliffe even cut Sir Alex Ferguson's post-retirement £2 million-a-year consulting contract (and here I had assumed he could be seen in the stands at each game out of undying love for the club).[4]

"In super simple terms, the club has been spending more money than it's been earning for the last seven years," Ratcliffe told *The Times* in the same interview published a day after the Arsenal match. The club was even paying a "body language consultant" more than $200,000, Ratcliffe complained.

United's moody captain Bruno Fernandes scored a *golazo* on a free kick to paper over another dismal performance in the first half, and by the second half, any sense of dissent or disunity in the packed stadium had evaporated. "Glazers Out" protesters and Jim Ratcliffe and his entourage in the director's box were as one, joined together in nervous excitement and a shared reflex memory triggered by playing their archrival from the glory years. Manchester United (fourteenth place in the table) were giving Arsenal (second place, vying with Liverpool for the title) a real scare. My Gunners were fortunate to head back to London with a 1–1 tie, thanks to an unbelievable double save by our Spanish keeper David Raya, despite having 68 percent possession.

I walked the two miles back to the center of Manchester, struck as I had been on the walk over by the diversity of fan clusters I saw making the trek or lingering outside pubs along the way. Chinese tourists, a few couples, broey mates still singing about Arsenal being a bunch of c-words, a family from Philadelphia, more Chinese tourists, somber pairings of season ticket-holding fathers and adult sons engaged in their multi-generational ritual and talking about the need for patience with Portuguese manager Rúben Amorim, a herd of older footballing Norwegian tourists (one helpfully wore a Viking helmet for identification purposes) in Beckham, Ronaldo, and Ole Gunnar Solskjaer jerseys (better days). Interspersed between them were some of the black-clad protesters, dragging their angry banners but relishing, most of all, the moment Fernandes hit the back of the net.

I felt for them. Who're they kidding? For most football fans across the British Isles who may be upset by the corporatization or globalization of the game (interestingly, for all the protesting on that day, no one seemed exercised about the fact that United hadn't started a single English player), or the identity of their club's dodgy overseas owner, there's no leaving. This game is just too important and too ingrained; these football clubs are what bind people to their geography, to each other, and to all their kindred—past, present, and future. As Jason Stockwood, the chairman of Grimsby Town FC, put it on *Welcome to Wrexham:* "It's a marriage you can't get out of—you're committed to your football club for life."

And to some extent, it works both ways. Toby Craig, Manchester United's Chief Communications Officer, told me back when he held a similar role at Manchester City (working with Omar Berrada, who was hired away by Ratcliffe to become United's CEO in the summer of 2024) that responsible English football club owners, far more so than their counterparts in US sports leagues, must think of themselves, first and foremost, as "custodians" of community assets. "Someone can *buy* a football club the way they might buy a company or a yacht," he explained, "but they don't *own* it in the same way, since it also belongs to its supporters and the larger community." This is a message I have heard repeatedly since, including among the newer crop of US owners buying into the English game.

Shortly after justifying the need for short-term austerity, Ratcliffe and United did a hard pivot to announce plans for a (Sir) Norman Foster-designed new stadium in the vicinity of 115-year-old Old Trafford that will seat 100,000 fans and cost an estimated £2 billion. The concept renderings looked spectacular, like SoFi in Los Angeles, but more immediately intertwined with an entertainment district.[5] A canopy would hang over the entire structure, held up and punctured by three towers, with the overall effect inspiring comparisons to an umbrella and nautical sails (or to a circus tent, among the club's more mirthful critics).

The accompanying press release splashed across the British media hit all the notes, including a blessing from the downsized Alex Ferguson, estimates of how many billions more a year the "New Trafford" will bring in economic activity to the local economy, and even a shoutout to the national government's professed desire to see more ambitious infrastructure investments in northern England (as if to say, well, feel free to chip in).

In contrast to the larger, club-recognized Manchester United Supporters Trust, which tepidly backed the plan while raising concerns about costs that could further hurt the club's competitiveness, the more militant "The 1958" group that had organized the protest march was decidedly not impressed. "Manchester United's new stadium design fails to reflect the club's deep-rooted heritage, traditions, and connection to its supporters," the group said in a statement.

Instead of embodying the gritty, historic essence of Old Trafford—a fortress built on generations of passion, emotion and belonging, the design resembles a generic, soulless corporate structure, more akin to a modern entertainment venue than a football cathedral. Its circus-like aesthetic disregards the working-class origins and the identity of a fanbase that spans generations. Rather than honoring the past and strengthening the bond with the local community, it prioritizes spectacle over substance, alienating those who have defined United's legacy for decades. It's an events stadium over a football stadium. It's a visitor experience over fan opinion and needs. Football, dignity and traditions need to be upheld and from what we can see they aren't. It should be a cathedral for fans to go and worship our team and not a circus-like tourist attraction. Once again football taking a backseat.[6]

This statement sums up so many accumulated grievances and complaints from a constituency fighting a rearguard action against the transformation—"Americanization," many might say—of the game. Corporate vs. Working-class. Tourist Attraction vs. Cathedral. Visitors vs. Supporters. These are laments you hear as you travel the length and breadth of England's footballing landscape, overrepresented in public discourse about the sport for being especially fashionable among the game's intelligentsia. Sure, almost all fans worry about the rising cost of attending games and are genuinely aghast at the ham-fisted attempt to launch the Super League in 2021. But many of them also appreciate how the league has catapulted itself into the commanding position of world football—providing them with a higher quality, more entertaining spectacle—through its modernization and globalization.

Regardless of where any of us stand on this sporting culture divide, we can all agree that the Glazers' highly leveraged buyout of United, financed by the club's future revenues, was always going to be a recipe for exacerbating suspicions about distant American owners. But the good news for Team USA in the Great Game to conquer global sport, and shape its future, is that many other US ownership groups across English football are doing a fine job as custodians of their clubs. Indeed, American-owned teams ended up sweeping the titles in each of England's top three divisions for the 2024–5 season—and claimed the runner-up spots as well.[7]

For years now I have been asking people working in the English game whether they think the American owners making up this friendly invasion would act in concert, acting upon some shared agenda or master plan. The answer has been mostly a "no, but." The "but" being that they do, to some extent, share a certain broad worldview and expectations that tend to align them in favor of measures to make the game more self-sustaining and measures that tip the balance more in favor of TV needs over the interests of fans in stadiums, including the traveling teams' "away" supporters. For all its success as a global TV offering, the Premier League still grapples with some debates that would seem quaintly anachronistic to US sports leagues. Examples include the persistence of the 3:00 p.m. Saturday blackout rules for all English games across all divisions of the football pyramid to encourage attendance at all of them; the resistance to any suggestion that a single regular season game be played outside of Britain (so, no decamping to São Paulo or Munich for a weekend, a la NFL), and opposition to rescheduling games near holidays in ways that would inconvenience traveling away supporters.

But there doesn't seem to be much merit to the concern surfaced by the Super League episode, that somehow once they have taken full control of the Premier League (especially once they control the fourteen votes needed to drive through any changes), US owners will put an end to promotion and relegation, because this is an alien concept to American sports, and one that is harmful to their investments. There might always be one or two billionaires with terrible ideas at any league's owners' meeting, but most of the American owners in the game understand that the concept of a fluid pyramid, with the jeopardy and opportunity of movement across different divisions, is one of English, and European, football's most distinctive and attractive assets. They also are sophisticated enough to know by now that the reality of promotion/relegation is baked into the game's valuations. The possibility of relegation—some might say the probability of relegation sooner or later—is the main reason Bill Foley, one of the more likable recent entrants into the Premier League owners' club, could acquire Bournemouth for less than he could acquire an MLS franchise back home in America, to become a sporting sibling to his Las Vegas Golden Knights in the National Hockey League.

Keep in mind also that the constituency of US interests in English football extends beyond Premier League owners. By the beginning of 2025, twenty-three of seventy-two clubs making up the English Football League—that includes the three divisions of the pyramid below the Premier League: the Championship, League One, and League Two—were owned by Americans, including Ryan Reynolds, Tom Brady, the San Francisco 49ers, the family of former Disney CEO Michael Eisner, and several other billionaires and powerful private equity groups.[8] Good luck trying to tell them all someday that the Premier League is becoming a "closed league" along the lines of American ones, no longer accessible through promotion.

Indeed, international football's mobility between divisions, which provides supporters with such exhilarating highs and devastating lows throughout their lifetimes, is proving to be the ultimate catnip for hyper-competitive American capitalists who spot a challenge and opportunity not available in our more socialistic leagues on this side of the Atlantic. People who have amassed a fortune in finance tend to be the type of individuals who believe they could easily buy a team in a lower division, outsmart their competitors by disrupting how things have been done, win promotions to higher divisions, and thus attain a return on their investment that would be unimaginable in US sports, as Wrexham's Hollywood owners are in the process of doing. This feature is not going away, as more and more of the transatlantic friendly invaders consider it one of the game's coolest features, not a bug.

In May of 2024, *The Guardian* published a report card for the various American owners then overseeing clubs in the league, and elsewhere in Europe. Liverpool and Aston Villa were awarded an A, Arsenal an A-, Crystal Palace a

B, Bournemouth a B-, Burnley a C-, Fulham a D, and both Manchester United and Chelsea an F.[9]

There is something obviously fickle (clickbaity!) about the exercise, but you get a sense of the range. Surely Bournemouth and Fulham would have done better a year later with their subsequent seasons. And Arsenal is an instructive caution against the rush to short-term judgments. Not long ago, fans were waving "Kroenke Out" banners, but as the club has stuck to a coherent plan built around gradual if unspectacular upticks in investment, the development of young academy players, a methodical manager, and a certain style of play that has landed them in second place in the league for three years running and in a European Champions League semifinal in spring 2025 (though Arsenal's women won Europe, as we've seen, with the aid of some Tar Heels), fans have grudgingly come to appreciate that they could have done a lot worse than these American owners, whose transatlantic sporting empire also includes the Los Angeles Rams in the NFL and the Denver Nuggets in the NBA.

It's hard to argue against the Fenway Sports Group's record of accomplishment and way of doing business up in Liverpool. Over the past decade, they have been the clear standouts among US owners, winning English and European trophies after pioneering the use of sophisticated data analytics in the game (an example of cross-sport learning within one of these conglomerates, as they transferred much of that expertise from the Red Sox). Liverpool is one of the giants of world football, so take their fans' narrative of being a scrappy David facing the two Manchester Goliaths with a grain of salt, but it's true that Liverpool has done as admirable a job as anyone at managing its squad over time. The team has also had the rare discipline of knowing when to sell big stars to keep the books balanced, and it pulled off a seamless transition from the legendary manager Jürgen Klopp to Arne Slot, who won the league in his first season on the job. Most fans understandably don't break out into songs about their billionaire owners, but maybe the reclusive John Henry deserves one or two.

When it comes to their role at these clubs, these remote foreign owners face a tough balancing act. No one wants them to be front and center all the time, making it all about them, but they need to be careful not to appear TOO distant and disinterested. I've had amusing conversations with prominent sports journalists in both Boston and Liverpool who worry that their club's owner cares more about the other. For big clubs like Liverpool and the two Manchester clubs, successful foreign owners, be they in America or Abu Dhabi, need to show that they care about their club and take their fiduciary/custodial duties seriously by installing a respected, competent management team on the ground—which City and Liverpool have excelled at for years—and holding them accountable.

Another good rule of thumb for foreign owners: it's not worth pulling a Glazer by trying to finance your acquisition, or your future living expenses, from your club's operating revenues, whether you have a right to do so or not. Better to reinvest it all in the club, with your reward being its appreciation in value during your tenure. Even better, if you do want to take out some liquidity from the club, sell a small stake to a celebrity. They can come in handy for marketing purposes, too, and it seems more and more clubs have one or two attached these days.

Chelsea's ownership group, awarded an F by *The Guardian* in 2024, arrived in the league with a big splash in May of 2022, as the British government forced Roman Abramovich to sell the club as part of the sanctions enacted against Russian oligarchs with close ties to the Putin regime. A partnership with experience owning the Los Angeles Dodgers paid £4.25 billion for the West London club and immediately started acting as an outdated parody of how American owners would behave across the Atlantic.

An executive with another club who's seen it all told me there are certain familiar cycles new owners in English football go through. First off, they show up and carry themselves as if they are the first person (or persons) with half a brain to ever run one of these clubs and know what they are doing. There's merit in thinking things could be done better, but that level of hubris doesn't tend to go well. In Chelsea's case, Todd Boehly appointed himself chairman and "interim sporting director" upon first arriving at the club, presiding over most games, freely sharing his thoughts on how the game could be modernized, and breaking with all sorts of conventions when it came to the business side of things. It was refreshing at first to see the ownership group at a major club be that proactively invested and so confident in what they were doing. Unfortunately, what they were doing so confidently ended up wreaking havoc. Contrary to expectations, the new owners didn't close off the Abramovich spigot but kept spending ambitiously on new talent, with the new wrinkle of signing young players to unprecedentedly long contracts (a trick they imported from baseball to amortize transfer fees over more years and have more latitude to spend more now without running afoul of Profit and Sustainability Rules). Chelsea's new owners spent more than anyone else in this period and quickly went through three different managers. Critics scoffed that the owners' main innovations appeared to be on the financial restructuring of things, including what might prove a smart move to spin out the women's team to the club's parent holding company to allow for the additional outside investment of Alexis Ohanian.[10] It's also been reported that the relationship between the various partners in the ownership group had frayed, especially over the fate of the club's inadequate stadium, and they were exploring the possibility of buying each other out.[11]

The cycle of stages new owners go through in English football can include learning from any initial missteps and making adjustments, so it might be too early to write off Chelsea's regime. Indeed, by the summer of 2025, a more cohesive-looking Chelsea under Enzo Maresca shocked everyone by winning the Club World Cup, and the team was obtaining decent revenue for trading its surplus talent. Who knows, in the long run this private equity crew might just get the last laugh. For now, though, the most consequential legacy of their purchase of the club from Abramovich was to underscore the fact that the balance of power between state-sponsored actors in the Great Game and US sporting interests had shifted decidedly in our favor. It's clearer than ever that Americans are increasingly the buyers of first and last resort in European football.

Bill Foley is another US investor who acquired a Premier League club off a Russian oligarch, in his case Bournemouth on the southern coast of England. His is one of the smaller clubs in the league, playing in a stadium as intimate, though nowhere near as nice, as Kansas City Current's. Although Foley is intent on changing its station in life, the club has hardly been a Premier League mainstay, having first been promoted to the division in 2015, then relegated in 2020, and bounced back the season before Foley bought the club in late 2022.

Bournemouth is clearly not Chelsea or Manchester United, and it's possible, perhaps even advisable for a remote owner in a club and community of this scale to be more visible at the helm of the club. Foley conveys one aspect of owning a sports club that often gets lost amid the talk of financial shenanigans and competitive pressure: joy. He made his billions building a title insurance empire and is now at the stage of his life where he's going to enjoy himself, and so he owns the Las Vegas National Hockey League franchise, a collection of wineries, and what looks to be cozy and sumptuous resorts and inns in places I can't afford to visit. This is a life we'd all want to have in our eighties; Foley seems to be having a blast. And a club's supporters won't hold that against an owner, so long as they perceive that his enjoyment is connected to the work and responsibility of ownership, not mere dilettantism.

And Foley, a West Point graduate who likes to say things like "If we are not advancing, we are retreating," comes across as anything but a dilettante. He talks appreciatively of the community, where he has bought a home, and the game's traditions, but also about the need to make investments that will take the club to the next level (new training facility, expanded stadium, world-class manager, better players) and secure its permanence in the Premier League. Foley, like Wrexham's Hollywood duo, manages to both treat this adventure as a great lark and a puzzle to be managed with farsighted vision and a rigorous attention to detail. The club was widely admired for its style of play under the innovative Spanish manager Andoni Iraola in the 2024–5 season, when it ended ninth in the league.

Foley experienced success with his first sporting adventure in Las Vegas, where he delivered on his promise to win the city a Stanley Cup within the team's first six years. In the more uneven playing field of English football, Foley has said his goal for Bournemouth in the next few years is to reliably finish between seventh and ninth in the league table. Audacious goals for a club of its size, amplified by Foley's claim in 2023 that within five years he'd like to see the club qualify to play in Europe.[12]

Godspeed, Bill. There are clubs such as Brighton and Brentford that manage to punch above their weight over time because they are particularly well run, and it appears that Bournemouth may join their ranks. But it never ceases to be a high-wire act given the unforgiving margins of error for smaller clubs trying to remain in the Premier League. Over the past decade, clubs like Leicester, Stoke, Burnley, and Southampton have been admired for defying the odds (Leicester most of all, by winning the league) for a time, but they have all since fallen from grace.

When Bournemouth does hit a rough patch, it will be interesting to see how local supporters feel then about their engaging American owner. So far, he's managed the club on an upward trajectory, and so he and the community are enjoying a prolonged honeymoon. And you don't need to be very likable to be accepted by local fans when you're winning; the true test of your likability comes when results sour.

In addition to Bournemouth, Foley has also acquired Lorient in France, Hibernian in the Scottish Premier League, and Auckland, a New Zealand club playing in Australia's A-League. Like so many other American investors, he is fascinated by the challenge, and potential rewards, of assembling a multi-club group, though he is careful to talk up the distinctive character of each of his clubs and his desire to preserve it.

The culture of English football is seductive to any American sports fan because it oozes nostalgia and a yearning to preserve a sense of place and connection among its people. And while Foley embraces the joy that comes with being a billionaire able to field teams to represent their communities and cheer them on, he and other foreign owners doing things right also appreciate the romance and idealism (even if they might never use those terms) baked into the quest. There is a purity to almost any English community's relationship with its football club, a sweetness even, that is alluring to any investor, and that is an often-unacknowledged inducement for the friendly invaders crossing the Atlantic. It isn't just about making money.

Jason Stockwood, the locally born-and-raised supporter turned chairman of Grimsby Town FC who appears in *Welcome to Wrexham* before facing off against his Hollywood-backed rival, sums up so much of the landscape of English football across all its divisions when he says of Grimsby:

We're a working-class town that's been down on its luck for a few years, quite frankly. Grimsby used to be the world's largest fishing port but those industries from the past have gone and we're trying to reinvent ourselves. This club has been around for 144 years. It's the one constant in people's lives, and their world is becoming more complex and ever-changing.

From there, he went on to make the comparison I cited earlier in this chapter, between supporters' relationships to their clubs and a marriage they can never escape.[13]

For these foreign invading owners, it all adds up to an opportunity to buy into something authentic, something so Old School it has overlooked its twenty-first century potential. For the Americans among them, it's akin to buying their college football team. And you can tell how irresistible they find the game's culture, as it seems to resonate with their own nostalgia for what they once thought sport was about, or for what they thought it could do in a community. It's why Tom Hanks keeps showing up at Aston Villa matches, or why when Will Ferrell invested in Leeds, he explained that it was because we Americans see in English football "a level of devotion unlike anywhere in the world, and we admire it."[14] And it's why Ryan Reynolds told Roger Bennett on *Men in Blazers* that what he's accomplished with Wrexham is the most consequential thing he's done in his career.[15]

And so, Ryan Reynolds and Bill Foley, along with all the other friendly invaders, face a complex conundrum of their own. They must walk the fine line of preserving the essence of the English game's culture while transforming its business. They have crossed the Atlantic to change the thing that seduced them over—hopefully not too much.

The week before witnessing the anti-Glazer protest march at Old Trafford in March 2025, I had been across the War of the Roses divide, an hour's train ride away in Yorkshire's proud commercial hub of Leeds. In the pyramid of English cities, London is at the pinnacle, and it's a considerable drop in terms of size, wealth, power, and cultural impact to "England's second city," a hotly contested title between Manchester and Birmingham. Hovering below those, Leeds looms largest among the next tier that includes other Northern industrial era (and footballing) powerhouses such as Newcastle, Sheffield, and Liverpool.

To arrive in Leeds is to be bombarded by claims of the city's historical significance from proud locals seeking affirmation. When people start telling me all about the nineteenth-century textile industry, my mind starts fantasizing about all the various drinks that contain caffeine, and Leeds will take credit for the fizzy carbonated ones among them as it claims to be the place where those were first served up. And cinema, too, but no word on popcorn, though the circular 1860s Corn Exchange in the city center is one of the more magnificent temples of commerce you'll ever see. The city also boasts the oldest public lending library in continuous operation.

Most significant of all, you won't go a day in Leeds without hearing that this is the country's "largest single-club city." I don't know what most of us are supposed to do with this information, other than appreciate the intensity with which all Loiners (as the locals are called, unless they were pulling my leg) support their Leeds United FC. But if you're the San Francisco 49ers and you hear this, you might decide this is where you want to make your investment in the other football, which they did.

To be precise, it was the San Francisco 49ers Enterprises, an investment vehicle attached to the NFL team that also includes outside investors, that first acquired a minority stake in Leeds in 2018. They gradually increased their investment, ultimately buying out the controlling shareholder, the Italian Andrea Radrizzani, in the summer of 2023. At that point, they assumed full control of the newly relegated club—Leeds was headed back down to the Championship after three consecutive seasons in the Premier League.

Paraag Marathe, President of 49ers Enterprises, EVP for Football Operations for the 49ers and Chairman of Leeds United, is a master practitioner of the Great Game. Three months before Leeds would secure its promotion back into the Premier League, I saw Marathe at the Spring 2025 Financial Times Football Summit in London. As I had seen him do elsewhere, he said all the right things in navigating the cultural landmines involved in the art of remote cross-sport investing.

So much of English football, and perhaps of England writ large, is about reclaiming past glories, and in the case of Leeds United, this is a Herculean task, as there actually has been quite a bit of past glory, and it's mostly quite in the past. So, Marathe made clear that the priority now is to "get back to where we deserve to be," and that in doing so, the club will push the limits of PSR. "We want to put every pound we earn back onto the field." And then some: the club's financial filings for 2023–4 showed that the owners poured $180 million into the club that year to try to sustain its drive for promotion back into the Premier League.[16]

Marathe talked about the scale of the club and how high its ceiling—and thus the 49ers' return on their investment—is given the size of Leeds' market, its history, and its global following. Even while in the Championship, Leeds has booked more commercial revenue than some smaller Premier League teams and carried a bigger payroll than them. And because the club has had several golden ages, including in the 1970s and early this century, you find colonies of hardcore Leeds fans scattered around the globe, like lost tribes in need of repatriation or assimilation into a more benign culture.

Even at a buttoned-down investors' conference at London's Peninsula Hotel, far from Leeds, Marathe also nodded to the romance of the quest: "One thing I honestly underestimated—that I didn't know—was how much I would fall in love with Leeds United," he told the audience. Initially he came to it as a business opportunity, but "I don't think anything can top this."

Leeds managed to secure its promotion none too soon. Fighting to win promotion from the Championship to the Premier League can be among the toughest and most expensive gambits in world sport, often compared to buying a very expensive lottery ticket. The payoff if you win is astonishing, starting with a roughly £75 million bump in annual TV revenue, but the ticket itself is rather expensive. Leeds itself lost £60 million in 2023–4, even with the infusion of cash from its owners and its Premier League "parachute" payment of close to £50 million. These are made, in decreasing amounts, for two or three years (depending on length of tenure in the Premier League) to relegated clubs to soften the blow and help them adjust their business more gradually. The trouble is, parachute payments give relegated clubs a massive advantage in the Championship, while not necessarily making them competitive if promoted again.[17] The growing wealth gap between the divisions is making it harder for promoted teams to have a shot at staying in the Premier League, creating the prospect of "mezzanine clubs" that hover between the two top flights of English football. The 2024–5 season was the second one in a row that all three teams that had been promoted from the Championship to the Premier League were relegated straight away.

Over a coffee in the city center the day before Leeds were to play West Brom on the first day of March 2025, Chris Harvey explained to me that Leeds fans, regardless of what division they're playing in, will always think of themselves as a "massive club." He says they will always look at teams like Bournemouth and Brighton as "Mickey Mouse clubs," even if they've had far more success of late staying up in the Premier League. For Leeds fans, their club belongs in the same discussion as Liverpool and Manchester United, which was definitely true in the late 1960s and early 1970s, when Harvey, a former Sky Sports journalist who now serves on the board of the Leeds United Supporters' Trust, started following the team as a kid. One sign of how much their paths have diverged since is that Leeds is the only one of the three clubs to have experienced life beyond the top division, not only in the Championship but even below that in League One, in the depths of a financial crisis nearly twenty years ago.

"Paraag and the 49ers have yet to score an own goal," Harvey told me, in how they have conducted themselves and managed the club. They have a strong management team in place with the experience in the game, but fans are aware and appreciate that the folks on the Pacific Coast are tuned into what's happening. And most importantly, they have the resources to invest in the club's success and have the willingness to do so, within the constraints of financial regulations.

No anti-Yankee owner protests here. No one I spoke to in a week poking about Leeds betrayed a hint of criticism about their club's American owner. And many of the fans I spoke to, including Harvey, were clear-eyed about the fact that this is a marriage of convenience, which could end whenever 49ers Enterprises gets the club to a place where they could make hundreds of millions, or perhaps even more, on their investment. "Not sure about their long-term plan, maybe we will be sold to a petrodollar state," Harvey joked. "But we know that the days when your club is owned by the local car dealer who's a big supporter of your club are long gone."

Josh Cawthorne, the chairman of the Supporters' Trust, seconded Harvey's sentiment when he told me that it's telling the club isn't owned directly by the 49ers or any one family, but by the 49ers' Enterprises, which includes investments from a number of different people (including Will Ferrell and golf stars Justin Thomas and Jordan Spieth). "These people based in Northern California think in terms of angel investors and start-ups," he explained, "so it's natural to expect that at some point they might sell, once they've pumped up the value of their investment."

It was strange to hear this all so cavalierly spelled out by leaders of the Supporters Trust. In my experience, even at clubs where things are going relatively well, such as at Arsenal, organized spokespeople for the supporters tend to skew head-in-the-clouds traditionalist, not venture-capitalist aware. But given Leeds' experience over the past thirty years, these particular California capitalists look pretty good. Leeds has had more than its share of disastrous owners, foreign and domestic.

Leeds fans have come to accept that in a world of uncertainties, their interests are aligned with any owner who wants to take Leeds from being a club they acquired for a few hundred million pounds to a club they can sell for a couple of billion. Because in order to make such a capital gain on the investment, an owner would have to upgrade the club's training and game day infrastructure significantly, establish it permanently in the Premier League, make it a club that qualifies with some regularity for European competition, and find ways of growing commercial and other revenues so Leeds can sign better players to attain these goals. Sign us up, fans are saying.

When I pressed Harvey on whether there was any suspicion of the owners on account of their nationality, he said maybe only tangentially, insofar as English fans will always be skeptical that an American can truly understand their game. But when it comes to the 49ers, the sheer ineptitude and lack of resources of some of their recent predecessors have bought them quite a bit of latitude and goodwill. And no one is confused about the competence of Marathe's team when it comes to running a world-class sports organization, from the commercial side to winning on the field and even building a new stadium. Indeed, the 49ers' Levi's Stadium in Santa Clara will be one of the 2026 World Cup venues months after hosting Super Bowl LX.

Harvey added that any lingering prejudice against Americans in football is more likely to be felt by managers, and to some extent players. "Jesse Marsch was definitely subject to a few unkind Ted Lasso comparisons when he was here," he said, referring to the American manager who had the unenviable assignment of replacing the legendary Marcelo Bielsa in 2022 and who currently coaches the Canadian men's national team. Leeds supporters were sad to see USMNT captain Tyler Adams go to Bill Foley's "Mickey Mouse club" of Bournemouth, and Brenden Aaronson remains a popular member of the squad.

Over a beer at a pub near Leeds Central Station, Stephan told me he's optimistic about the years ahead, and not just because he has moved up to 4,000th on a season ticket waitlist of 26,000 (for a stadium that only currently seats 37,000). He works in education, putting together programs for overseas students in Britain. He left Leeds for university and to work elsewhere for a few years and acquired more passion for the club when he was away; it was his connection back home. An often painful one, given so many heartbreaking seasons and organizational chaos. Depending on how you keep score of various interludes where ownership was in dispute, Leeds United has had seven different owners just this century, including a tax evader, the former chairman of a big rival who still seemed to hold a grudge against his acquisition, a Middle Eastern investment bank with murky local connections and intentions, and owners who overspent in attempts to pursue European glory at the very start of this century. By 2007, the club went into administration (that's bankruptcy in American) and descended for three seasons into League One. Radrizzani, the Italian businessman who owned the club immediately before the 49ers, did much to stabilize things and excite the fanbase with the inspired recruitment of Marcelo Bielsa as manager and of the 49ers as minority shareholders, not to mention the club's first promotion back into the Premier League in sixteen years.[18]

And what is there to say about Bielsa's three-and-a-half years as manager? "It's almost impossible to explain to an outsider," Cawthorne had told me, "the man was so incredible . . . we will never ever recreate that . . . it was a fairy tale." You hear a lot of such stammerings about Marcelo Bielsa around Leeds, as you might in a community that just witnessed the rapture. "He did speak in parables," Harvey pointed out when I put the analogy to him. "We are now 'widows of Bielsa,' which is what fans of his previous teams call themselves, and we've gone from being guided by a theologian to being in the hands of pragmatic corporate Americans." But most people seem fine with that, too. Leeds fans talk of their Bielsa passion as a once-in-a-lifetime experience, which they knew could only last for a finite period, and now they are approaching their return to the Premier League in a more sober fashion.

Argentine manager Marcelo Bielsa is one of the most brilliant and most eccentrically romantic minds of the game. This is the only reason he ended up coming to Leeds, to take charge of a struggling team in England's second division. Bielsa is picky about the projects he chooses, and when Leeds' Spanish Sporting Director Victor Orta reached out, Bielsa carefully studied not only the club and its history but the city's. Bielsa needs a cause and a narrative to inspire him, preferably a place in need of redemption, and even then, he only signs one-year contracts, as he doesn't like the idea of someone paying him not to work if a club wants to part ways. One of Bielsa's first acts as manager upon arriving at Leeds was to take his team out to pick up trash in public places for three hours, because he wanted his players to reflect on the amount of time it takes someone making average wages to earn enough to afford a ticket to watch them play. On another occasion, he famously ordered his team to let Aston Villa score against them when he felt Leeds had taken an unfair lead (because of an injury on the field that didn't stop play).[19]

He also insisted on a relentless, constantly rotating, attacking football that was a novelty in English football, and certainly in the Championship. Bielsa famously requires of his teams a level of fitness well above the norm, which is difficult to sustain over a long season, particularly at underdog clubs (his specialty) that tend not to have the deepest squad depth. Nonetheless, Bielsa got Leeds promoted back to the Premier League in his second season in 2020, after a narrow miss in his first season. One of Bielsa's superpowers is his ability to take decent but not exceptional players—Luke Ayling and Kalvin Phillips come to mind—and get them to collectively resemble Argentina or Brazil in peak World Cup form. He would coach them seated on a bucket on the sidelines, claiming that vantage provided the best sightlines. Still starting most of his Championship squad, Bielsa's Leeds stormed into the Premier League in the Covid fall of 2020, outrunning every team and often playing in the league's most entertaining match of the weekend, invariably a fast-paced shootout. By the end of the season, Leeds faded and ended in ninth place, an enviable top-half-of-the-table finish for a newly promoted side. Fans were beside themselves; even when Leeds used to be one of the giants of the game, it was known to play a turgid style of play and was often called "Dirty Leeds" by national newspaper columnists. Now they were the opposite: the embodiment of recklessly exuberant and idealistic football.

It wasn't sustainable. The 49ers were already minority partners, but Radrizzani didn't have the resources to bring in the caliber and quantity of reinforcements needed to play *Bielsabol*. That following season of 2021–2, Leeds' lack of depth was exposed by an injury crisis and things soon turned south, exacerbated by the manager's refusal to compromise on his philosophy and play more conservatively. That led to one of the most reluctant, mournful firings in football history, and the purchase of a full-page ad in an Argentine newspaper by Leeds fans, thanking him for what had ultimately proven to be a beautiful failure:

You reminded us that football can be beautiful and that a team can be greater than the sum of its parts. Side before self.

And you gave us so much more than football. You took us through a pandemic and brought us together while we were all apart.

You showed us that integrity and decency matter, in good times and bad.

You embraced our fears and turned our despair into hope and our footballers into heroes. You improved us all.

You restored our pride, gave us joy and created precious memories that will last a lifetime.

And it was beautiful, Marcelo. It will always be beautiful. Thank you.[20]

When the World Cup is played across North America in the summer of 2026, a lot of people in Yorkshire will find themselves rooting for the Uruguayan national team and its manager sitting on a bucket.

When I reached out to Phil Hay, a gifted writer at *The Athletic* who covered Leeds in the Bielsa years and wrote *And It Was Beautiful: Leeds United in the Era of Marcelo Bielsa*, he told me in his melodic Scottish accent that fans of most clubs across Britain fancy themselves uniquely victimized by their loyalty to a doomed club and the multiple emotional scars they've acquired through their years of blind devotion. "But there is something about Leeds that makes them an 'archetypal shambles,'" he added. Other clubs have had it worse objectively, never having experienced some of Leeds' success, which includes several titles (the last one being the year before the Premier League launched—which is also very Leeds). What's striking here, Hay said, was the severity of the club's rollercoaster ride and the chasm between the club's performance over time and where people, not just Leeds fans, expect it to be. There is an expression, Hay told me, for doing things like playing a European Champions League semifinal in the same decade you play three seasons in League One, two divisions below the Premier League: "It's called 'doing a Leeds.'"

Yorkshiremen like to think of themselves as hardworking, straight-talking, practical people, underappreciated and underestimated by people in London and the Southeast, and by nearer rivals in Manchester. This all adds intensity to their support for the football club that represents them all, there being no divided loyalties in this one-club city. In Manchester, Liverpool, Birmingham, or London, to identify with one football club is to identify with one of that community's factions, in opposition to the others, but in Leeds, as in Newcastle, the club's unifying and identifying power is more universal.

Supporters' confidence in the 49ers Enterprises as the club's custodians as they embark on their less frenetic, more calculated, and hopefully longer-lasting re-entry into the Premier League post-Bielsa is only rattled by one prospect. Nearly everyone I spoke to in Leeds is petrified the 49ers might sell the club to Red Bull in the not-too-distant future. The caffeinated empire acquired a minority stake in the club in May 2024, as well as the front-of-jersey sponsorship.[21]

Red Bull is one of the more enthusiastic believers in the multi-club ownership concept, operating Red Bull football teams in Austria, Germany, Brazil, and the United States. They previously had no Red Bull club in England, and so it's natural for fans to ask themselves whether this is their endgame in Leeds. The Red Bull model is for its teams to adopt one standardized, one consistent branding identity, whether it's across their fizzy drink business, Formula 1, or their football clubs. They also want their teams to all embrace the same style of play. Fans worry that Red Bull is not interested in a club's separate history or identity, or whatever angst or South American romances its supporters have experienced over the past century.

Paraag Marathe said at *The Financial Times* Football Summit that the 49ers have no intention of selling a majority stake to Red Bull, and that the Austria-based marketing powerhouse "completely understand what it means to be Leeds United; they completely understand the legacy of the club," he said. And yet club supporters can't help but think of the precedent of the 49ers themselves first arriving as passive minority investors and thus worry about their American owners picking up and leaving sometime soon.

And this is a trend across English football, in contrast to Manchester United's experience with the Glazers. Increasingly, whether it's at Bournemouth or Everton, where another American billionaire recently acquired the club and seems to be bringing that club a desperately needed period of stability, or at clubs such as West Brom or Carlisle in the lower divisions, supporters are finding, perhaps to their surprise, that they stand to benefit from America's friendly sporting invasion. American investors aren't buying clubs with the goal of stagnating in place and fatalistically accepting their station in life or in the football pyramid; they bring with them a can-do sense of optimism and competitive drive. And while there will always be reckless, incompetent US investors drawn to the game, and plenty of top-notch non-American ownership groups, Americans seem less likely to be crashing into the game on a lark. They tend to bring experience and expertise in sport and a much-needed financial discipline. The very fact that they might not be steeped in English football's history and culture and might even flub the terminology can be a sign that they have some emotional distance from the investment, which isn't always bad. Supporters only need to see some humility, appreciation, and engagement to make up for any lingering cultural suspicions.

Most supporters are savvy enough to know by now that they are participating in a spectacle that has transcended the local economy's ability to support. To turn against the concept of foreign ownership would amount to advocating for a hugely downsized football ecosystem, both in terms of its quality and ambition. And these supporters also realize that, for better or worse, there are not enough foreign investors beyond the United States to make any of this work, and that, all things considered, American investors are acquitting themselves relatively well when compared to the others. Fair game, as the Brits might say.

The English game is the most compelling of the Great Game's frontlines, but it is also illustrative of trends elsewhere. US sports interests and institutional investors are also acquiring clubs in Spain, France, Belgium, and Italy (Germany remains an outlier because it still embraces a model of majority-supporter ownership), and in some cases connecting them through multi-club consortia to English clubs. Italian soccer, especially, is benefiting from a wave of American investment, expertise, and influence at the league-wide level.

Gameday, the first Saturday of March, was unexpectedly sunny and warmish, so I walked from the center of town out to Elland Road. The stadium still being named after the road it's on is a charming nod to the game's strong localism; other stadiums in England might also have stands that go by their road name, as if the site of a friendly neighborhood scrimmage. Watching the clusters of fans converging into the flow of people headed to the stadium on my 1.5-mile walk, past a mural of Bielsa and a separate one of his overturned bucket and a heart, gave me a sense of community. Cawthorne of the Supporters Trust had told me he likes being involved with the club precisely for that community aspect, much in the same way some people become active in church. "You don't just go for the religion," he had said. "Nor do you support the club to see them win, you do because you're going to the same ground your dad took you to, and his dad took him to, and it should be all the same whether Leeds is playing Arsenal in the Premier League, or Plymouth in the Championship."

Sure, but I saw a lot of fans on the day who really did want Leeds to win and continue advancing toward promotion.

Leeds may have benefited from having its urban core renewal come a bit later than many other deindustrialized cities. Developers here, like developers everywhere, couldn't resist the mallification impulse, but instead of plopping down moated fortress-like commercial shopping centers in the middle of the city that disrupt pedestrian traffic and create a stratification between gated and street commerce, Leeds has a modern, canopied shopping area that connects seamlessly to more traditional pedestrian shopping streets and picturesque Victorian arcades. The birthplace of the Marks & Spencer retailing giant and an important financial services hub, Leeds has a youthful, dynamic feel that is enhanced by a large student population. The handsome campus of the

University of Leeds, Prime Minister Keir Starmer's alma mater, is a short uphill walk from the city center.

One of the more intriguing sights I encountered at the university was a poster in a restroom entitled "Recognising Microaggressions." Among the expressions listed that could, even unintentionally, amount to discrimination against members of a "marginalized group" was "You sound so Northern!"

As a visiting Yankee, I don't pretend to fully understand the nuances of Britain's north-south divide and the extent to which it correlates (or doesn't) with notions of class. I have noticed, though, that many people in London tend to talk about "the north" as if it were Siberia, even though to us Americans the distances between all British cities seem modest, certainly not enough to get you into another reality. Leeds is closer to London than Washington, DC, is to New York City.

I'm also aware that just about every time I visit Britain, the news seems to include stories about some promise being made or broken by some political leader to invest in northern infrastructure and transportation networks to offset the disproportionate investment and wealth flowing into London and southeast England. The political discourse is all about a hollowed-out region that has suffered from deindustrialization. A headline in the *Times of London* during my week in Leeds read like a parody: "BBC Boss: We need to hire more northerners."

I find any depiction of the north as a cultural backwater quite mystifying on account of my football tunnel vision. Because, let's face it, it's the north, not London, that is the epicenter of the world's most popular sport. There's a reason the National Football Museum, which is worth a visit, is in Manchester, and a reason why teams from the north win most of the trophies.

Still, Yorkshire, a region first defined by invading Vikings and the "ridings" (as their administrative units were called) and then hardened by William the Conqueror's "Harrying of the North" (for opposing his invasion) in the eleventh century, does seem to lean into its identity as a hardscrabble place where everyone recently crawled out of a coal mine, steel factory, or textile mill.

Rick Broadbent, a Leeds writer, explains in his book *Now Then: The Story of Yorkshire and its People*, that "Yorkshire's superiority complex even extends to championing its inferiority." He describes a 1967 TV sketch featuring

John Cleese entitled "Four Yorkshiremen," in which "four well-dressed Yorkshiremen would outdo each other with memories of their impoverished upbringings. One of the four is deemed lucky to have been brought up in one room, 'all twenty-six of us,' with half the floor missing, because at least he had a room."[22] The footballing equivalent of this is a fanbase's reveling in how hard their team has had it, the perverse—and almost competitive—pride in their intergenerational sorrows.

The city of Leeds itself has been on an upward trajectory in recent years, but it still struggles with some of the legacies of underinvestment through its postwar decades of deindustrialization. A British government policy paper on envisioning future regional prosperity, points out that for all of Leeds' vitality, it remains the biggest city in Western Europe without a light-rail or metro-style system, and that despite the city center's prosperity, nearly a quarter of its population resides in neighborhoods with the highest level of deprivation measured by the nation's Index for Multiple Deprivation.[23]

The game turned out to be a lackluster 1-1 tie against West Bromwich Albion. But never mind, Leeds fans were in a good mood as they remained in the pole position to win promotion back into the Premier League, which they would secure seven weeks later.

Elland Road (first opened in 1897) is one of those idiosyncratic English stadiums built in stages over time, lacking any symmetry. I sat in the penultimate row atop the East Stand, which was so much higher than the other three stands bordering the field that the overhang above us cut off the sightlines, blocking the screen and scoreboard across the field. All I could see over there, tempting me throughout, were ads for something intriguingly called "Flamingo Land."

The club's strong ties to Scandinavia were evident at Elland Road, as they had been even back at my hotel with all the traveling supporters in for the game. At the match, I met visiting Norwegians, Danes, Finns, and a couple from Iceland sitting next to me, who travel to Leeds several times each season to attend games. They seemed to find it perfectly normal that someone from Arizona would also want to make this pilgrimage, but I pressed the husband as to why Leeds. He explained matter-of-factly that as a kid in the 1970s on Icelandic TV they usually just showed two teams that were dominant at the moment, Leeds and Liverpool.

"And I chose the wrong one," he said. I laughed, but he didn't, which was unnerving. Was he being serious, or was this Icelandic deadpan humor?

When I asked him how he felt about the 49ers being in charge, he perked up.

"They know what they're doing, even won some Super Bowls, and built themselves an amazing stadium. We could use some of that."

Indeed, within days of securing promotion, Marathe's team had unveiled plans for Elland Road's modernization and expansion, which will take the stadium's capacity to 53,000 spectators.

But do they all know what they're doing? I wonder.

Don't get me wrong, I am sure the 49ers know exactly what they're doing with Leeds, just like Bill Foley knows what he's doing at Bournemouth, as well as Ryan and Rob in Wales and the Kroenkes in North London. I am sure that NBC knows what it is doing to maximize the value of its rights to the league, and its ownership over Sky TV, the league's main broadcaster in its home market. I am sure Apple knows what it's doing with *Ted Lasso*, and that brands like Nike and EA Sports also know what they're doing in devoting so many resources and attention to this global league across the Atlantic.

What's fascinating to ponder, though, is what this all adds up to, in terms of further dragging international football into the American mainstream and America into the heart of international football. How will all these disparate push/pull commercial and cultural footballing influences alter not only the sporting landscape over there, but the sporting landscape back home, in the American heartland?

10

The Great Game in Kansas City

The old Paseo YMCA stands on the road named after Mexico City's Paseo de la Reforma, just a block west of the intersection of 18th and Vine Street that gives Kansas City's historic African American neighborhood its name. This YMCA chapter was first organized in 1900, nine years after James Naismith invented basketball at a Massachusetts Y and two years after he was hired as a PE teacher and chaplain at the nearby University of Kansas, but the fourstory building seen today was opened in 1914. For several decades, it was the hub of social and civic life for Kansas City's African-American community, the sole venue in a heavily redlined city for dozens of clubs and community organizations to hold meetings.

The Paseo YMCA is a long way from FIFA's imposing "House of Football" headquarters in Zurich, but one small gathering held by eight gentlemen convened here by Andrew Rube Foster in February 1920 would prove an early step in Kansas City's subsequent journey toward becoming not just a Midwestern or a national sports town, but a global one—indeed, an improbable host of FIFA's 2026 World Cup. Not that the gathering more than a century ago had anything to do with soccer. The eight gentlemen represented independent Black baseball teams who'd come together to establish the first Negro National League, anchored by the Kansas City Monarchs.

There is much to be said about the history of the various Negro Leagues that would spring up around the country over the next few decades in response to Major League Baseball's persistent and pernicious color line, and many of those stories are engagingly told a couple of blocks away at the excellent Negro Leagues Baseball Museum. But for the purposes of our *Great Game* inquiry, exploring how sport has connected this city in America's heartland to the rest of the world, it's worth highlighting the pioneering international engagement of these Negro Leagues, as they sought to break loose from an American sporting isolationism and exceptionalism that, for them, in an era of racial segregation, was always going to prove suffocating.

The Negro Leagues and their players were forerunners of today's sporting globalizers. Baseball inhabited a transnational Afro-Atlantic community that covered the US mainland, Puerto Rico, Cuba, the Dominican Republic, other Caribbean islands, Venezuela, as well as Mexico's eastern coastline. There was much fluidity, with players constantly crossing borders to play a season here, a season there. The Havana Cuban Stars were one of the teams represented in that first organizational meeting at the Paseo YMCA. A poster in the museum promotes a 1938 game at Chicago's Wrigley Field between the Colored National League All-Stars and a team from Córdoba in the Mexican state of Veracruz.

In the 1930s and 1940s, many of the Negro Leagues' biggest stars played in the Mexican league, lured by bigger salaries and a reprieve from living under Jim Crow laws. Leroy "Satchel" Paige, Andrew Porter, James "Cool Papa" Bell, Roy Campanella, and Monte Irvin were among the African-American players who thrived in Mexico.

Irvin left his Newark Eagles to play for the Azules de Veracruz in the 1942 season. The baseball was great, but life off the field was even greater. Irvin, who'd eventually play for the New York Giants in the Major Leagues, would call his season in Mexico the best time of his life, which was cut shorter than he'd hoped when he was drafted to fight in the war. "For the first time in my life," he recalled later, "I felt really free. You could go anywhere, go to any theater, do anything, eat in any restaurant, just like anybody else, and it was wonderful."[1]

In 1927, a Negro Leagues all-star team toured Japan, seven years before Babe Ruth and other Major Leaguers would do so, and they were a sensation.

Bob Kendrick, the museum president, pointed out to me when I interviewed him after my visit that some of those players in the 1920s had first acquired a global consciousness going off to fight in the First World War, and then became "instrumental in making baseball a global game." Kendrick believes the popularity and success of Negro League players abroad, especially in Mexico, helped accelerate the Major League's integration, which famously started with the Los Angeles Dodgers signing Jackie Robinson away from the Kansas City Monarchs in the fall of 1945.

"These were among America's earliest ambassadors for sport, and they were fantastic at it," Kendrick said. It's one of the reasons, he added, that the museum's overall subject, though anchored in the ugliness and hatred of segregation, is also a story of triumph and resilience. These "leagues of their own" managed to connect globally even as they served their local marginalized communities. They also managed to increase baseball's overseas popularity.

Kendrick explained that the All-Stars who went to Japan in 1927, and on subsequent Asian tours, distinguished themselves by playing well without humiliating or disrespecting their hosts. "You can call it smart diplomacy," he said, "but it also came from understanding the culture and dynamic of barnstorming, as this all amounted to trans-Pacific barnstorming. These players knew that when you are barnstorming you don't ride into every town and beat up on the locals, at least not too badly; not if you're thinking about getting your paycheck and hopefully getting invited to play again."

Kendrick is proud of how the Negro Leagues pushed back against America's traditional sports insularity and views the city's selection to co-host the world's biggest sporting event in the summer of 2026 as a fitting recognition: "Our city in the middle of the country is the envy of so many cities because of what we have accomplished through sport, most recently with the Chiefs," he told me. "Sport unites us like nothing else, building community and camaraderie, and it has this wonderful clarity that comes from having rules that are apparent, unchanging, and applicable to all, which you can't always say about the business world or other aspects of our lives."

Some two miles west of the Paseo YMCA where the first Negro League was established, on the other side of downtown, you'll find another landmark in the story of how Kansas City became connected to the world through sport. On what's now Cesar Chávez Boulevard, Our Lady of Guadalupe Church was established in 1914 by two Mexican priests escaping the Mexican Revolution's anti-clericalism and eager to serve the growing *comunidad*.

Echoing the origin story of many of those fabled clubs in northern England established during the Industrial Revolution, Our Lady of Guadalupe partnered with La Union Cultural Mexicana to introduce organized soccer in the area in the early 1950s, to provide parish boys with healthy recreation. The team became known as "Los Latinos." Agustin "El Chino" Medina was its big star and providential ringer. He had played professionally in Guadalajara for Club Atlas, but his wife from Kansas City told him it was time for her to go home, and so he followed her. The team developed a rivalry with "Los Internacionales," a club made up of European immigrants, and would travel as far away as Iowa, Nebraska, and Minnesota to play other clubs.

If you think of Kansas City as an insular Midwestern city closed off from the outside world, think again. When I stepped off the plane on my first of several visits, the first two ads that greeted me in the gleaming new terminal were for the National World War I Museum and Memorial and the Harry S. Truman Library and Museum, both of which tell powerful stories of global connectivity. And the 2024 official Visit KC guide stacked up for the taking featured two KC Current stars, Hallie Mace and Lo'eau LaBonta, on its cover. Soccer Capital of America indeed!

Sitting at the confluence of the Missouri and Kansas Rivers, Kansas City has always been a connector, a hub for cultural and economic exchange, a crossroads for native nations and European powers, and often a fluid boundary between them. The place where French and Spanish designs over North America would collide; where eastern river-based development gave way to the more pioneering uncertainties that lay to the west, along the Santa Fe, California, and Oregon trails that all began here; and where north-south tensions over slavery would ignite open conflict between proslavery "border ruffians" and abolitionist "free-staters" as a prelude to the nation's Civil War. Earlier, the first European settlement here had been the French "Chez les Canses" in what is now known as the West Bottoms part of town.

Many American cities claim to be "where the West began" or the hub of westward expansion, and Kansas City's claim appears to be as strong as anyone else's.

Given its privileged geography, Kansas City was always destined to be an important river port, railroad, and aviation hub. And over time, being a logistical, commercial entrepot has a way of turning a city into a cultural entrepot too. Something about all those passing, mingling traders and influences sparking inspiration and innovation. In the same decade of the 1920s when the Negro Baseball Leagues came into being, Kansas City also became a hotbed for a new and looser style of jazz that was closer to bebop. In time, musicians like Count Basie and Charlie Parker turned Kansas City into a jazz destination, alongside New Orleans, St. Louis, New York, and Chicago.

Living in what I often refer to as "MexUs," the vast swath of the Sun Belt that has been a part of both Mexico and the United States and is the cultural synthesis of the two (if we were a third country, we'd be the world's third largest economy and have a population of more than 80 million people), I tend to be acutely aware of the Mexican and Spanish influence that helped shape and define modern-day San Francisco, Los Angeles, and Phoenix, and all the great cities across Texas. But I am always surprised, though I really shouldn't be, when I find the imprint of these same cultural influences elsewhere in the United States, outside of historical MexUs, such as in Kansas City.

I've already mentioned that the early twentieth-century boulevard here, designed to become the city's showcase of municipal pride and beauty, was inspired and named after Mexico City's Paseo de la Reforma. Then there's Country Club Plaza, considered the nation's first planned outdoor shopping center (opened in 1922), which took its architectural inspiration from Sevilla. This is one of the most confusing places in Kansas City, incidentally, as it is neither a country club nor a plaza; it isn't really a shopping center either, in the enclosed sense of the term. It's more of a district covering about a dozen blocks that share an aesthetic of terracotta roofs, bell towers, intricate tilework, and fountains (of which KC supposedly has more than any other city). The whole place feels like the fevered, kitschy creation of someone who REALLY enjoyed their junior year abroad in Spain. But it's also a successful concept that was well ahead of its time; a century later, staged urban spaces that blend retail, restaurants with residential and office towers have become all the rage across affluent suburbs.

At the Museum of Kansas City, which occupies the gorgeous 72-room mansion built in the first years of the twentieth century by lumber tycoon Robert A. Long atop the limestone bluffs that rise from the riverside train tracks and factories, I also learn that the "place to see and be seen" for the city's elite in the late 1920s and early 1930s was the El Torreon ballroom, though there is no explanation why they'd name such a place after the unglamorous city in Coahuila we used to go play soccer tournaments in when I was in middle school.

Gene Chavez, the museum's historian in residence (who obtained his doctorate at the Arizona State University!), told me it was quite common to see Spanish names and influences across a community that "has been connected to the Latino world for several centuries," dating back to the expedition of Francisco Vasquez de Coronado in 1541. "Missouri," he added, " became a state the same year Mexico acquired its independence [1821], and ever since then both have been connected by increasing social, cultural, and economic exchanges." By the time the Mexican Revolution detonated the year the Longs moved into the home that now houses the museum [1910], Kansas City had supplanted St. Louis as the key rail hub in north-south trade with Mexico and as a safe haven for wealthier, conservative Mexicans fleeing the revolution as well as poorer Mexican laborers. At one point, an estimated 90 percent of the area's railroad workers were Mexican, and today's CPKC railroad—resulting from the 2023 merger of Canadian Pacific and Kansas City Southern—is the main freight carrier between the three North American nations, in addition to being the first corporate sponsor of a women's professional football stadium.

Chavez took me to Carniceria San Antonio on Independence Avenue for *carne asada* and *al pastor* tacos. The crammed grocer is a treasure trove of every imaginable Mexican foodstuff from my childhood—the Knorr's packets of instant *sopa de fideos*, Pulparindo spicy tamarind candy, a range of Gamesa cookies and Conchas Bimbo—displayed beneath hovering piñatas and alongside religious candles tailored for any life exigency. We were there the week after the Chiefs had won their third consecutive AFC title and were packing their bags to head to New Orleans to play in Super Bowl LIX, and nearly everyone in the store wore Chiefs swag, though one of the proprietors from Monterrey, Mexico, was teasing a customer for wearing a Chivas de Guadalajara jersey.

There are roughly 200,000 people residing in the Kansas City metro area of Mexican descent, according to Mexico's Consul General Soileh Padilla Mayer, a thoughtful diplomat with a deep appreciation for her posting. "This really is the heart of the United States in a geographic sense, of looking at a map seeing what's in the middle and then analyzing the arteries—rivers, rail routes, highways—that flow through here and bind regions together," she told me when I dropped by the consulate (a neighbor of the architect Tom Proebstle's Generator Studio) for a coffee. "But sometimes I wonder if there isn't even more to the heart metaphor, when you look at what Kansas City represents in terms of a place, an incredibly diverse place, where people have a deep sense of belonging."

"That's why your subject of sport is so interesting here," she said, playing to the crowd, "because part of belonging is turning into an impassioned fan for all the sports teams representing your community."

The confluence of rivers, rail lines, and cultural influences made Kansas City by the early twentieth-century an overgrown cow town. Where the original French settlement once stood became the nation's second-busiest stockyards, in the shadows of downtown, until their closing in 1991. KC burst with earnest energy and innovation, as expressed in the "Kansas City" number in the Rodgers & Hammerstein *Oklahoma!* musical ("Everything is up to date in Kansas City"), its Chamber of Commerce's slogan in 1928 ("Not just a city but an empire"), and Norman Rockwell's mid-century painting *The Kansas City Spirit*. Today's Crosstown arts district includes "film row," twenty buildings in a four-block area in which all major movie studios once stocked their films (highly flammable in the early days of cinema) for distribution across the country.

The same year the first Negro League was born, the Dubinsky brothers opened a movie theater in town that would become AMC Theatres, inventors of two of America's greatest cultural innovations: the multiplex movie theater and the cup holder at your seat. Also in that same year of 1920, Laugh-O-

Grams was established in a red brick building at 1127 East 31st Street. The company's animated cartoons for local theaters were better than its business model, and three years later its founder Walt Disney would close shop and leave the city he'd grown up in, on a train headed west for Hollywood. His next venture would strike important deals with a company that did thrive back in Kansas City thanks to illustrators like him who would flock to the Midwestern city to share their talent with the world.

Fresh out of high school in Nebraska, J.C. Hall had arrived in Kansas City in 1910 carrying an inventory of two shoeboxes of picture postcards. He set up a shop to sell postcards and what had come to be known as "greeting" cards. Within a decade, he had acquired an engraving business to print his own cards and expanded into other products for "when you care to send the very best," such as gift wrap. Hallmark's licensing deal with Disney proved an early boost and model for how the company and IP owners could mutually benefit from people's emotional investment in certain characters, be they Mickey Mouse or Snoopy. More recently, Hallmark also came to curate Christmas for millions of Americans, not only through its cards and decorations but through its cable TV channel's holiday movies.

As a kid growing up in Mexico, the most American thing imaginable was your classic indoor shopping mall, and when we'd drive up to El Paso, Texas in the late 1970s and early 1980s, what struck me as the most quintessentially American institution within that quintessentially American institution of the mall was the Hallmark Store. And so, one of the highlights of my Kansas City reporting trips was the Hallmark Visitors Center in the company's Lumonesque Crown Center HQ complex, which triumphantly tells its corporate history as a tale of Horatio Alger-like gumption and American ingenuity. Also, while there, I learned that the company now owns Crayola. How did I not know that?

Although greeting cards may now seem a quaint throwback to simpler times, all I could think about as I watched the stirring propaganda film and made my way through the exhibits was that this was one of our nation's earliest social media companies. And that it must say something about Kansas City that this all came into being here. And yet, despite being a connector of river traffic with Manifest Destiny trails and rail lines, and a distribution center for livestock, crops, Hollywood films, and curated emotional greetings, what would end up connecting more twentieth-century Kansas Citians to the world beyond America's shores were the two tragic world wars.

A couple of blocks away from Hallmark and across from Union Station, you'll find Kansas City's most impressive public space: the National World War I Museum and Memorial. Within a year of the end of the First World War, the people of Kansas City had come together to raise $2.5 million to build a 217-foot-tall Liberty Memorial Tower and a Memory Hall containing the massive *Panthéon de la Guerre* mural and bronze tablets listing the 441 Kansas Citians who died in the conflict. The memorial sits on 47 acres of city-owned parkland and includes a state-of-the-art underground museum added in 2006. The Memorial Tower was dedicated in a 1921 ceremony that brought together the five supreme Allied commanders for the first time in the same place. Captain Harry S. Truman, a local veteran who'd led the 129th Field Artillery unit with distinction in France and acquired a global perspective that would come in handy a quarter-century later for both him and his country, was chosen for the honor of presenting flags to the Allied commanders. He was one of 60,000 American Legion men to march on the day, before 100,000 spectators.[2]

Matt Naylor, the museum's Australian president and CEO, told me when I stopped by for a visit that the lawn sweeping down from the Memorial Tower toward Union Station plays an important civic role as the city's "front porch," where people gather for July 4th or to celebrate sports titles (a tragic shooting spree on the street in front of Union Station that left one onlooker dead and two dozen others injured marred the 2024 Chiefs' Super Bowl win celebrations).

When the NFL draft came to Kansas City in the spring of 2023, the entire memorial's grounds were taken over by the league, and its epic 148-foot-long frieze depicting mankind's progression from war to peace served as a perfect improvised screen on which to project the helmets of teams in the club, and their picks. Naylor used the opportunity to prepare and distribute materials on the involvement of First World War veterans in the NFL's founding days.

The museum has also hosted watch parties for European soccer matches, even setting up a traditional pub for the occasion. The game was already a cherished pastime for the war's combatants. The museum has on exhibit a soccer ball that Captain Frank Edwards of the 1st Battalion of the London Irish Rifles kicked and dribbled with his men as they stormed German positions at the Battle of Loos in 1915. The museum also recounts the well-known story of the 1914 Christmas truce, when German and French troops emerged from their opposing trenches to play a friendly football match, in what Naylor described as "an example of people's humanity shining through the horror of war."

The World War I Museum and Memorial is slated to be Kansas City's officially designated Fan Zone during the World Cup, where visiting and local fans can come together to watch games on big screens, mingle, and try some of the local BBQ. "Sport is a lubricant for cultural exchange," Naylor said, "and this is a game that continues to unite people across all sorts of trenches. So, we will want to be here providing a gathering space and celebrating the enduring impact of sport and the enduring impact of World War I and those who sacrificed in the conflict to secure our democracy."

As a native of Australia, Naylor has an outsider's perspective on how Kansas City is perceived in the world, but he has also lived here long enough to feel like he has seen an "adolescent metropolis grow into adulthood, become less of a 'flyover city,' and continue to grow in confidence." Sport has a lot to do with that, he added, providing Kansas Citians with a "shared language" and "purpose." When traveling abroad, Naylor no longer gets as many confused looks or questions when he says where he is from, and that he also attributes to the growing awareness of KC sporting feats. He believes the World Cup will take this to new levels.

Kathy Nelson is certainly banking on that. She heads up the Kansas City Sports Commission and Foundation, which she explained to me was initially established in 1966 to sell Chiefs tickets to convince the team to stay in town, to help bring a professional baseball team back to the city, and to rally support for private and public investment in new stadiums. Nelson describes her mission as "making a better Kansas City through sports," and one of the ways she advances that mission is by attracting big sporting events to the city.

There is no sporting event bigger than the FIFA World Cup, and Nelson spent years working hard on ensuring that Kansas City pulled off the upset of becoming what *The Guardian* called "the World Cup's most unlikely host city."[3] Nelson found out the city had succeeded in its bid with the rest of a crowd crammed into a live watch party in the Power & Light District for the host cities' unveiling on June 16, 2022, but the process was a long and arduous one.

First, the United States, Canada, and Mexico jointly pursued the 2026 tournament for North America, which they were awarded by FIFA at its Congress in Moscow on the eve of the 2018 World Cup. From there, the contest was on to be chosen as one of the host cities. Ultimately, forty-four cities across North America submitted bids for sixteen slots (eleven in the United States, three in Mexico, and two in Canada). Kansas City, the thirty-first largest metro area in the United States, is the smallest of the sixteen cities chosen. *The Guardian* was not alone in considering it the most surprising place on the list of hosts, especially considering that neither Chicago nor Washington, DC will host this time around. Kansas City also beat out Denver, Nashville, and Orlando, among others.

Nelson told me over a Zoom interview in early 2025 that she and the rest of the Kansas City bid team had faced an uphill battle: "I remember we had to spend time with FIFA in Zurich just explaining who we were. People often don't understand where we're located, we don't have a mountain or an ocean." Nelson recalled that some of the FIFA staffers would drop the "City" in early meetings, thinking the delegation had only added it on as a helpful descriptor, so she'd scramble to make sure theirs didn't come to be known only as the "Kansas" bid. She added that both the states of Kansas and Missouri supported the bid, and that both would participate in hosting fans and teams during the tournament, as befits a metro area that straddles the border between the states. Nelson credited the bid's ultimate success to a highly motivated team effort.

> Our superpower was the unity of purpose and collaboration across our city, country, and state governments, and our business community, including all our sports teams. Everyone put on the boxing gloves to go get this, and Salvador Perez and Patrick Mahomes were outstanding as our bid co-chairs and athlete ambassadors. Everyone understood there is no more impactful event we could pursue as a region than a World Cup. Being a World Cup city, like being an Olympic city, puts you in an entirely different league.

Nelson said Kansas City's growing reputation as a successful sports town and Lamar Hunt's legacy of bridging the two football worlds and growing soccer in America helped advance the city's case. "I remember feeling fortified in our efforts when we stopped by Adidas global headquarters in the small German town of Herzogenaurach, and I saw these huge banners of Patrick Mahomes, one of their favorite sponsored athletes."

In a separate interview, Joe Reardon, the CEO of the Greater Kansas City Chamber of Commerce, told me about being with a colleague at the Qatar 2022 World Cup on a crowded bus with fans from all over the world. They asked a family where they were from, and they answered "Iran." When the boy asked back where Reardon and his colleague were from, they replied they were from America. But the kid persisted, asking where in America, to which they sheepishly replied something along the lines of "oh, you probably don't know of it, but it's called Kansas City," to which, of course, the boy perked up excitedly and started talking about the Chiefs and Mahomes. Sport fandom can be a wonderful geography instructor.

Nelson and Reardon are excited for the World Cup to put their city on the map for even more visitors and investors around the world. Kansas City will be the only Midwestern World Cup city this time around (in addition to Chicago, Detroit also hosted matches in 1994) and will host six games over a three-and-a-half-week period. Nelson said when the site evaluation team came to town, they appreciated that this was a place with "a genuine Americana feel," and far more amenities and points of interest for outside visitors than they might have expected. Still, Kansas City had to counter the evaluators' concerns about the lack of public transportation. "That is when we introduced our visitors to the concept of tailgating and our local BBQ," she said mischievously.

Chicago was initially expected to be among the selected cities, but it withdrew from consideration because it didn't like FIFA's terms, and it's always going to be the case that different cities will have different levels of appetite for investing in these types of events.[4] In Dallas, where Clark Hunt's brother Dan co-chairs the city's World Cup organizing committee, Cowboys owner Jerry Jones said this of being able to host a World Cup in his community and stadium [as compared to a Super Bowl]: "Candidly, I think it's of broader interest from the perspective of Dallas. The longer I'm in sport, the more I realize how important soccer is to this world. To be able to participate in such an event is . . . really awesome and inspiring."[5] That's something my fifteen-year-old self never would have imagined hearing from the Dallas Cowboys.

Ann Gaffigan, the chief operating officer of the United Way of Greater Kansas City, told me that it isn't just political spin to say that the community has a way of coming together around shared objectives. "I was neither born nor raised here, and when you first move to KC from elsewhere, you quickly realize this place is different," she said,

> when it comes to the level of pride and enjoyment its people take in their community. At first it took some getting used to, it was almost too much, but now I appreciate it. And it's especially strong when it comes to rallying around our sports teams as the face and representation of the community. That's one reason the city has been such fertile ground for women's soccer, and our NWSL team [which has a partnership agreement with the United Way], because people will turn out to root for KC in any sport, no matter what.

She added something I would then notice on my subsequent visits to the city: Kansas Citians wear an awful lot of KC swag. It would be like going to New York and seeing many locals (as opposed to tourists) wearing "I [heart] NY" t-shirts. You see a lot of its teams' swag, sure—especially Chiefs' gear during football season—and that is not unique to Kansas City, but you also see a lot of people wearing clothing that celebrates their city more generically. There's a popular Charlie Hustle brand of clothing that sprang out of Covid times that markets endless "KC" within a heart logo design you see all over town.

It's emblematic of the community, Gaffigan added, to have a megastar like Patrick Mahomes not just collecting his paycheck for delighting fans in his sport but also going out and investing as a part-owner of the Royals, Current, and Sporting KC, and plugging the city's World Cup bid.

All of this reminded me of my days living in Pittsburgh back in the 1990s. That is another city whose significant historical bequests to the nation aren't always sufficiently appreciated by people elsewhere, or so locals worry. There may have been some of this in Leeds, too, come to think of it. This concern creates an earnest and at times fevered collective boosterism, and an extreme devotion to local sports teams as a manifestation of the community's broader quest for vindication and national recognition. It's an intense force for social cohesion and unity that won't be as strong in cities that are more secure about their place in the world. If you live in Los Angeles or New York and express zero interest in any one of the local sports teams, even one involved in a close title race, that's your prerogative. And you won't be alone. Proclaiming zero interest in the Chiefs or the Steelers around December or January in Kansas City or Pittsburgh is an altogether different matter, a form of troubling antisocial behavior.

Michael McGough, my mentor at the *Pittsburgh Post-Gazette* (and thereafter), is as proud a Pittsburgher as you will ever meet, if not the most avid sports fan, and he used to joke that the community's (and our newspaper's) all-encompassing Steeler fever amounted to a form of "sports fascism." But he doesn't underestimate the positives of sports' unifying power in a community, especially when people are so polarized culturally and politically. Across sprawling metro areas like Kansas City and Pittsburgh, a shared love for the Chiefs and Steelers, or the Royals and Pirates, is about the last thing binding people together across radically differing backgrounds, interests, and beliefs.

Kansas City hosting a World Cup is not something Peter Vermes would have imagined when he played the game, but he now believes it is a great recognition of how KC has become one of America's leading soccer communities. He retired as a player with Lamar Hunt's Kansas City Wizards in 2002 and returned as technical director and then coach of the MLS club after it was sold and rebranded Sporting KC. Vermes was the longest-serving coach in league history, managing the team from 2009 until the spring of 2025. I spoke to him during what would be his final weeks on the job, and he reminisced about how far soccer has come in the United States, and how much closer we are to the outside world as a result.

Vermes and I are roughly the same age, so he remembers the days when the United States was cut off from the world's game. "I used to get excited to watch an hour a week of German soccer highlights on PBS, that was our only fix back then," he said. "Oh, and I had this VHS Spain '82 highlights show narrated by Sean Connery that I must have watched a thousand times."

The game certainly wasn't foreign to the Vermes household. Peter's father had been a professional soccer player for the Hungarian powerhouse Honved (the club that played under the lights against Wolverhampton in the 1954 game that helped spur the establishment of a European Cup) but fled the country in the aftermath of the 1956 uprising and ensuing Soviet crackdown.

Peter thus grew up in a soccer-mad household in New Jersey, mostly oblivious to any question of whether it was or wasn't as American a sport as any other. "I do remember though watching an Olympics with my dad," he told me, "and asking him 'Why don't they have soccer in the Olympics?' and him answering 'They do, but the TV network assumes that isn't what people in America want to watch, so they don't put it on.' I remember that did make an impression on me."

Vermes was a transatlantic ambassador and bridge builder for the game in the critical years when the United States was seeking to be readmitted to the global football community. After playing at Rutgers, Vermes played professionally in Hungary, the Netherlands, and Spain. In Hungary, he was feted as the return of a prodigal son, and the narratives around him were understandably all about his Hungarian roots and family history. But in the Netherlands and Spain, he got a taste of what it was like to play as a representative of American soccer and have every move and all his performances judged through that lens.

Then came the 1990 World Cup in Italy, America's first appearance in the tournament since 1950. Unlike today's USMNT that includes stars from some of Europe's biggest clubs, that 1990 squad was a bunch of unknowns. Vermes' limited experience in Europe made him one of the worldlier members of a team that included several players straight out of college.

Vermes has many memories from that summer, but one that still moves him as "one of those moments when you realize something different is happening here," is the bus ride to the Stadio Olimpico in Rome, to face none other than Italy itself. "We all had this feeling of being taken to the Coliseum to be fed to the lions," Vermes remembered,

> but then we turn a corner and go down a street approaching the stadium where there are crowds amassed wearing red, white, and blue and chanting "U-S-A," and we got so excited. We were so used to being treated like the

away team in so many of our matches back home, and so to see we had fans who'd shown up for us in Rome in a match against Italy, that was something.

Jacob Wagner, co-founder of the University of Missouri-Kansas City's Center for Neighborhoods and an associate professor of urban planning and design (who also fondly remembers the old "Soccer Made in Germany" PBS program), is eager to channel the upcoming World Cup's energy and passion for the benefit of the entire community, not only wealthier residents who can afford to attend pricey matches, including those upcoming World Cup ones.

Wagner worked in New Orleans to bring neighborhoods back to life in the aftermath of Hurricane Katrina, then eventually realized that certain neighborhoods in his hometown of Kansas City could use a similar approach and effort, not to recover from a natural disaster but from decades of deindustrialization and underinvestment.

Wagner and his colleagues offer trainings and a collaborative network for neighborhood leaders across the metro area. He is also a kindred spirit, I discovered in our first conversation, in how he thinks about his community's global connectivity through culture—though in Wagner's case, he is primarily focused on music. He led an effort to make Kansas City a member of UNESCO's Creative Cities Network, its only recognized "City of Music" in the United States. Wagner believes such recognition is overdue given that Kansas City's importance as a crossroads in jazz history can easily be overshadowed by the musical, tourism-attracting claims to fame of cities like New Orleans, New York, and Nashville. Wagner's father, incidentally, worked at Hallmark for decades and was the creator of the crotchety Maxine character for the Shoebox line of cards.

In Kansas City, Wagner said, "sports are in the driver's seat now in connecting our community to the outside world. But once you get international visitors here, they're blown away by all the other things this city has to offer, including its live music scene."

The power of big-time sport makes its behaviors around major events especially significant, not just because of the resources involved, but because of its power to set an example and influence attitudes. That is why Wagner was heartened that when the NFL held its draft in Kansas City in 2023, community representatives were able to collaborate with the league on a tree-planting project and a recycling plan for the materials used by the league.

In that same vein, Wagner and his students have been presenting to the local World Cup organizing committee research and ideas on how to create a more inclusive citywide tournament celebration and ensure a positive lasting legacy once it's over. Wagner said these big-time sports leagues and international federations are often more open to talking about issues like inequality and climate change than some political leaders closer to home. He realizes that some of it might just be for optics or PR, but whatever their organizers' motives, he is eager to explore how these high-profile sporting events and the resources they command might make a lasting difference, even if a modest one, in the communities that host them, as opposed to merely being fleeting circuses that come and go.

To the east of the 18th and Vine district, Wagner noted there are dozens of nationalities represented in the school district's student population, and that, "You don't have to tell people in these neighborhoods how to celebrate a World Cup, they've been doing it all their lives."

When rebuilding neighborhoods one block, often one house, at a time, Wagner described parks and playgrounds as the canary in the gold mine: "When neighbors reclaim their parks, that is often the turning point." And one of the cultural battles Wagner and others have engaged in is getting overgrown baseball diamonds converted to soccer fields, reflecting the area's changing demographics and interests, though the Royals did open an impressive Urban Youth Academy for baseball in the area, perhaps feeling the competitive heat.

Wagner was excited to show me the soccer complex on 9th and Van Brunt in the historic Lykins neighborhood, which has been renovated by the City's Parks and Recreation Department at the behest of neighborhood groups. Along Van Brunt Avenue, across the street from the fields, a long succession of flags painted on a concrete wall represents the nationalities encompassed by the neighborhood. Across 9th Street I spotted a *fruteria* and an auto repair shop called "La Chispa." Wagner walked me over to an outdoor amphitheater at a corner of the complex, facing a colorful mural named *The Sun and the*

Moon Dream of Each Other that I interpreted as conveying that bountiful fields will harvest children holding soccer balls.

"This is the place where we should celebrate Kansas City's World Cup," Wagner said. "Watch parties, concerts, other cultural activities . . . FIFA, local organizers, the city, everyone needs to figure out how these neighborhoods are included in the world's biggest sporting celebration. The tens of thousands of people who will experience the matches live at the stadium and might make it to the central fan festival at the World War I Memorial are a small percentage of the metro area's 2.4 million population, and many of them will be visitors," Wagner said.

Wagner generously spent an entire morning driving me around his city, tracing its physical, social, and economic topographies: the bend in the river, the industrial legacy and mindset of being a port city (even if an inland one), as well as the legacies of racial redlining and immigration across various neighborhoods. He took me by the river to demonstrate how, like in so many other ports, Kansas City mostly turned its back on its riverfront, an area associated with industrial residue and entertainment venues that need to be socially distanced from well-to-do neighbors. Some of the city's best live-music venues, such as Knuckleheads Saloon, which stands where Kansas City's "Electric Park" amusement park stood over a century ago, remain in this area, reveling in the historic grit.

A bit further to the west, we bump into CPKC Stadium and its adjacent park and residential developments, discussed in Chapter 7, which is the most ambitious modern effort to alter the city's relationship with its river.

KC being the undisputed global hub of sports architecture, as Tom Proebstle had pointed out to me when we discussed his design of CPKC, is one of the more unexpected ways in which sport connects Kansas City to the rest of the world.[6] If sport is a twenty-first-century religion for millions of us fans around the world, KC firms are the modern world's cathedral builders. Ten of the 2026 World Cup's sixteen stadiums were designed or redesigned by Kansas City firms.

It's a fascinating case study of how specialized expertise tends to cluster in one place, in this case thanks to the Truman Sports Complex containing the Chiefs' Arrowhead and the Royals' Kauffman Stadiums.

Ron Labinski, the lead architect on the much-lauded project, wanted his team at Kivett & Myers to parlay their triumph into a new type of specialized sport and entertainment practice that would build venues elsewhere. Labinski made a survey of all the outdated multi-purpose stadiums and their lease expiration dates and pursued their tenants' business.[7] In addition to Arrowhead, his team also designed two other World Cup venues, Giants Stadium and the Hard Rock in Miami (which pioneered the concept of club seating when it opened in the late 1980s as the Dolphins' Joe Robbie Stadium). Labinski's baseball business exploded after the acclaim that greeted the opening of Baltimore's Camden Yards in 1992, his stadium credited with blending the nostalgia associated with the game with the distinctiveness of its surrounding neighborhood.

Today there are about a half-dozen such firms based in Kansas City, some of them with offices all over the world, that have shared origins and overlapping histories resulting from spinoffs and mergers. And even when other major firms decide to get into, or grow their sport and entertainment practices, they can feel compelled, as Gensler did in 2024, to open an office and locate that practice in Kansas City, given that this is where the talent resides.[8]

Populous is one of the global firms headquartered in Kansas City specializing in designing the "places where people love to be together," and it is the one that traces its lineage back to Labinski's team. The Sphere in Las Vegas and Tottenham's stadium in London have been among the firm's more high-profile projects in recent years, but it also does more prosaic ones such as Vanderbilt University's new basketball training facility. And, given the political economy of sport these days, quite a few of its works in progress are in Saudi Arabia.

Bego Benjumeda, a Spanish interior designer at Populous who first came to study in the United States on a tennis scholarship at the prestigious Savannah College of Art and Design, is one of the thousands of young professionals who have flocked to Kansas City to work on what she calls the "environmental design" of our sport and entertainment venues. She told me that when people hear "interior design," they tend to think of aesthetics, but what she focuses on is as much the challenge of "how people move through spaces" and what our hospitality experience is like when we go to a ballpark or a music hall. "What do you walk by when you go from your seat to get a refreshment, what do you see, and how can we improve that experience?" she asked, conveying that these are no small questions.

I asked Benjumeda what she would have known about Kansas City a decade ago, as a teenager back in Cádiz, Spain. She gave me a bit of a blank stare, then blurted out "corn fields" and "Wizard of Oz." She has been surprised by the wealth of professional opportunities the city offers, but also appreciates that it is a place where athletes and others can excel because there aren't *too* many distractions. She should know—in addition to her design work at Populous, Benjumeda plays padel professionally, and recently her team came in third at the Miami Open, which was played alongside the tennis tournament at the Populous-designed Hard Rock complex. There are two courts of this predominantly European and Latin American racquet sport in KC, but more on the way.

Benjumeda had been in town for less than a year when we spoke, but she said it was hard not to feel at home in a place where people are both friendly and sincere, and where the "super walkable" Country Club Plaza neighborhood, where she lives and where Populous has its office, was inspired by Sevilla (this last part was said tongue-in-cheek). She's also been amazed by the universal urge in town to participate in civic life, including the sports scene. "In Atlanta," where she lived before, she said, "I felt like hardly anyone talked about the sports teams, but here it's constant, people going to watch Royals or Chiefs or KC Current or Sporting KC matches, or organizing watch parties somewhere, and it's all contagious."

Benjumeda has been pleasantly surprised to run into plenty of other Spaniards in KC; she's in a WhatsApp group with ninety of them, who constantly organize bonding activities, as if an alumni club. Next up when we talked was a Feria de Andalucia in Lawrence, Kansas.

Kansas City has experienced many magical sporting moments in recent years, many of them provided by "you've gotta be kidding me, how did he do that?!" Chiefs quarterback and Current co-owner Patrick Mahomes. But in my book, the greatest sporting achievement ever in KC took place on Sunday, February 2, 2025.

The Great Game in Kansas City

Arsenal was hosting archnemesis and defending champions Manchester City in the English Premier League. I was on one of my KC trips and, not wanting to watch the game alone in my sad hotel room, I walked a few blocks to Johnny's Tavern on Grand Boulevard in the Power & Light District. I had read online that this was the Arsenal fans' ("KC Gooners") place to congregate, but I was skeptical as I walked over that a sports bar would be open for a Sunday 8:30 a.m. kickoff on Peacock.

Boy, were they ever. The place was crammed with folks in Arsenal jerseys, standing room-only in the front room, with many others filling tables in the larger downstairs area, audio from the live feed from London resounding over the place. There were young couples, groups of friends, a few families, some older folks, all wearing a collage of Arsenal swag from its Adidas present and recent Puma and Nike pasts.

I have watched Manchester City destroy Arsenal live a few times, both in London and Manchester, and it wasn't fun. I have also watched Arsenal capitulate miserably to City too many times on my TV screen, or have fluky things go against them when they have managed to keep games close (and by fluky, I mostly mean bad refereeing). But the balance of power between the two clubs seemed to be shifting. Arsenal were six points ahead of City going into the game, behind only Liverpool. The first game between the two teams that season, in September in Manchester, had ended in a 2–2 tie, after Arsenal desperately failed to preserve a 2–1 lead when they were down a player due to a (fluky) red card.

Now in the London/KC edition of the game, Martin Odegaard put Arsenal ahead within the first two minutes. Johnny's Tavern went wild—beers toasted, scarves lifted, chants sung, high-fives, a little disbelief. A lot for 8:32 a.m. on a Sunday. Arsenal was dominant the rest of the first half, but in a bit of a trend for the season, the Gunners didn't capitalize on their opportunities, allowing City to remain within a one-goal striking distance as the game went into halftime. We were then all invited to march out to the outside courtyard for a big group picture. There were about seventy to eighty of us in it, lined up in four rows.

I asked the guy standing next to me if "it is always like this," and he said pretty much, though this obviously felt like a bigger game than most. "Is this your first time?" he asked in return, as a volunteer usher might at a church.

Small world, it turns out. Matt Waggoner is originally from the Phoenix area. What's more, he is a graduate of none other than our fine Walter Cronkite School of Journalism and Mass Communication, where I teach. He couldn't believe it, and I couldn't believe it. What are the odds? And more importantly, what did it mean for the second half?

Matt had worked in television in several markets, including Kansas City, but had moved to finance, working at a wealth management firm. He told me about growing up in Mesa as "the weird kid who was into soccer." Well before the days of streaming England's top export on Peacock or tuning in on USA or NBC, Matt's family had one of those big satellite dishes in the backyard that would beam in his beloved Parma from Italy, starring legendary goalkeeper Gigi Buffon, and that North London club managed by the philosophical Frenchman who seemed more intent on playing with flair than necessarily winning.

Before long, Matt had checked out all the library's books on European football and had a "Victoria Concordia Crescit" (Arsenal's "Victory grows through harmony" motto) poster in his bedroom, along with one of Kasey Keller (Matt was an aspiring keeper). "I was definitely aware that this was a counterculture," Matt told me, "that there was something almost un-American about being that into soccer, when other people were always talking about baseball or NFL football."

But Matt doesn't regret that his niche passion has become more mainstream. Quite the contrary: "The explosion of the sport's popularity since the 1990s when I was that lonely soccer fan among my friends has brought me more joy in life than almost anything else," he said. It's been a step-by-step journey. Matt can recall the days when many of his friends started to play the FIFA video game, and through it began to appreciate the beauty of the game and its culture. "Suddenly all these other kids were telling me some variation of 'So this is what you've been obsessing over all this time. It's pretty cool.'"

Arsenal has provided Matt with a community and an international family. "You find our people wherever you go," he said, such as when he first moved to Kansas City from Oregon and started coming to Johnny's. He said his wife and their young children sometimes come with him, though he acknowledged he can be a lot to be around on a tough day for the Gunners. "I can get very nervous, and emotional, around these games," he said, very calmly. He has taught his kids all the Arsenal songs and chants, "which is funny when you think about how they were written, and are sung, so many thousands of miles away."

Erling Haaland, Manchester City's 14-foot-tall Viking striker, tied things up early in the second half, and the mood at Johnny's tensed up. You could hear more of the TV announcers as if someone had turned down the animated conversation in the bar and people started receding into their own thoughts. We had been there too many times, on the cusp of surpassing City, only to fade. Arsenal has a reputation for being brittle and for "bottling it," as the Brits say, when the pressure is on. Also, this was Manchester Inevitable City, league title winners in six of the past seven seasons. Steamrolling Manchester City.

But then, a minute later . . . Thomas Partey! Our Ghanaian midfielder pulled us back from our dark ruminations with a decisive shot to the bottom right corner. And from there, Arsenal out-Cityed Manchester City. We moved the ball around with swagger, won every duel, and took advantage of our opportunities. Our eighteen-year-old Academy star Myles Lewis-Skelly scored the crucial third goal, and even better, celebrated it by mimicking Haaland's trademark meditation pose—payback for Haaland sneering at our youngster and dismissively barking at him, "Who the f#*k are you?!" during last fall's encounter. Then Kai Havertz scored a fourth and our seventeen-year-old wunderkid Ethan Nwaneri a fifth! Each goal seemed more emphatic than the last. Both Lewis-Skelly and Nwaneri joined Arsenal at the age of eight, so their involvement in our historic 5–1 crushing of our archnemesis made the occasion extra significant.

As for me, at that moment, surrounded by the good cheer of my fellow Kansas Citian Gooners and now knowing my encounter with Cronkite Matt was a sign from God that this was all meant to be, the future seemed clear. "Oh dear," Victoria texted me from Arizona, as if reading my thoughts across two time zones, "you're now going to want to watch every Arsenal game in Kansas City." It isn't about wanting, though Johnny's is a fantastic venue; it's about one's duty. Any responsible sports fan knows that our habits and behaviors when watching our team on TV can make a material difference to their performance, and that if you do anything out of the ordinary that results in your team overcoming its generational boogeyman and accomplishing a previously unimaginable feat, that needs to become your new gameday routine.

"We can still see each other over the summers," I replied.

Spoiler alert: I did not watch any more Arsenal games at Johnny's that season, and because of that the Gunners were unable to leverage the historic day into a title-winning run. Instead, they bottled the league, losing and tying a series of games they had no business losing and tying (including the one against Manchester United I would attend at Old Trafford), finishing the season 10 points behind Liverpool. I failed them.

Walking back toward my hotel, I passed the Phillips Hotel on 12th and Baltimore Streets. A different hotel, the Glennon, stood here before 1930, and one of its street-level retailers from late 1919 to the fall of 1922 was a clubby men's clothing store, remembered for its immaculately shined tile floor, gleaming glass displays, and overhead wire that ran the length of the store displaying hundreds of colorful ties. The store went out of business due to an economic downturn that collapsed farm prices and severely dampened demand for $16 silk shirts.[9]

It's hard to know what path history would have taken had Truman & Jacobson flourished instead of failed, keeping Harry S. Truman away from his next career in politics (under the patronage of KC's notorious Pendergast machine). What's pretty clear is that far less of that history would have flowed through, and emanated from, this region.

Truman would become the accidental president twenty-three years after his store failed, after being hastily added to the fourth Franklin Roosevelt presidential ticket in 1944 because party bosses were nervous about keeping FDR's third term vice president, Henry Wallace, a (fading) heartbeat away from the presidency. Roosevelt himself, like so many powerful leaders, dared not dwell on his own mortality or succession, so he only met with his new vice president a couple of times and made no effort to keep him in the loop on sensitive wartime diplomatic and military matters. When Truman was sworn in as president the day Roosevelt died in April 1945, he famously did not know about the atomic bomb being readied for testing in New Mexico. Following the patrician, cosmopolitan FDR, the plainspoken Missourian was mocked in some quarters as an unworldly rube. He was our last president to not have attended college, and even when he was sworn in, he was the first president with that distinction in six decades.

But Harry Truman, an avid student of history, had decidedly strong views on the foundational American conundrum discussed in Chapter 1, on whether to stand apart from the rest of the world or be a global player, and he acted on these views with a stunning clarity of purpose and conviction at one of the most important junctures in US history.

Truman embodied this region's values and swirling interests, and he was informed by them in designing the postwar world. He'd been a farmer, businessman, county officeholder, member of Congress, and, crucially, as mentioned earlier, an artillery officer whose first trip to Europe was to fight the German Kaiser's army and make the world safe for democracy. His second trip to Europe would be as president to confer on the contours of the postwar order with Winston Churchill and Joseph Stalin on the outskirts of Adolf Hitler's destroyed Nazi capital. Woodrow Wilson's postwar plans a generation earlier had been thwarted by a Republican Congress with little appetite for seeing America become a permanent global player, and in Truman's mind that was why the world hadn't been made safe for democracy after all, despite what he and his 129th Field Artillery, and millions of other US soldiers, had accomplished. Truman was determined not to similarly negate the triumph and sacrifice of the millions of GIs who'd served in the Second World War by once again disengaging from the world.

The legacy of Truman's determination is staggering: the Truman Doctrine's aid to Greece and Turkey, the Berlin airlift, the Marshall Plan to rebuild a devastated Europe, the Bretton Woods web of economic multilateral institutions, the launch of the United Nations, the recognition of a new Jewish state of Israel, and the strategy of containment that led to the Korean War. All of this set the course for what we variously refer to as the postwar era, the American Century, or the Pax Americana that would endure for decades, warts and all, a period of American global leadership and engagement. Sport was one aspect of life, as discussed earlier, where American society was able to cling to its historic isolationism for a bit longer, though something tells me Harry Truman would get a kick out of the fact that his hometown will be hosting a World Cup on the nation's 250th birthday.

The Truman Presidential Library and Museum, some 15 miles from downtown Kansas City in the nearby town of Independence, is one of several outstanding sites foreign fans coming to Kansas City will be able to visit. They can pay their respects to the former president, who is buried in an inner courtyard, and walk through interactive exhibits depicting his origins and legacy, and the choices he faced in navigating the country's foundational conundrum in the atomic age. Some of that legacy may feel less permanent than it once did. I reflected on my visit in spring 2025 as I read over the educational interactive questions that schoolteachers guiding field trips must relish. Related to the Marshall Plan, one screen poll asked visitors: "Do you think foreign aid is necessary to promote U.S. interests?" I don't know if this was intended as a hypothetical or as a settled historical question, but it was brimming with urgency on the weekend of my visit, coming shortly after a subsequent US president had moved to shut down the United States Agency for International Development.

Kansas City's Latino godfather, "El Padrino" Raúl Villegas, went to the 2022 World Cup in Qatar, where he rocked a Chiefs jersey at an Argentina game, so it's understandable that he's more than a little excited about the World Cup coming to town. Villegas is an entrepreneur and community leader who moved to Kansas City more than twenty years ago from Los Angeles, where his family had migrated from Puebla, in Southern Mexico. His El Padrino stores—the most recent one is a piñata emporium—offer soccer gear and party supplies, "the two things our community cares about most."

Villegas also runs a thriving indoor soccer venue called Soccer Nation, in an industrial patch in the Kansas City that is actually in the state of Kansas and whose population is 35 percent Latino. From the outside, Soccer Nation looks like a hermetically sealed warehouse, but walk through the door on a wintry Saturday afternoon, and you'll find a buzzy, festive atmosphere with teams playing on two turf fields, teams waiting anxiously to go on next, and other teams in full post-match taco mode, courtesy of the in-house Señor Avocado stand.

Villegas told me he played "at the state level" when he was young in Puebla but then had to give it up when he worked in Los Angeles. He is acutely aware of the struggle immigrant families face to balance what can often be two jobs with the need for recreation and play. "We don't appreciate the sacrifice of parents who work those types of hours and still get their kids signed up for a league and get them to their games." Or the lengths to which some of these parents themselves want to stay connected to the game: Soccer Nation has 180 adult teams playing in its leagues, and on weeknights there are games going until almost midnight.

The United States has a highly developed, massive system of youth soccer, though at its most competitive level, across the top academies and travel leagues, it is most often a pricey "pay to play" model, costing families a few thousand dollars a year. As a result, the country's elite youth teams representing US Soccer don't always draw from the broadest range of talent available to them.

Although Soccer Nation is a business and Villegas is a savvy entrepreneur, he said his mission is to provide affordable access to the game to immigrant families and a healthy social space around sport where they can also be acclimated to life in the United States. This is a national trend, with scrappy Latino leagues (often called "pirate leagues" by the sport's Anglo establishment) operating in the shadows of the US Soccer and MLS academies.

In addition to worries about cost, many immigrant families often shy away from the non-Latino clubs and leagues for cultural reasons. One family I spoke to while they watched their kid play goalie said some of the clubs had unreasonable expectations around practice times and were too serious about everything. "It felt like a second school," the father told me, and they want too much paperwork. "As if applying for a job," mom said. Immigrant families often fear that signing up their kid in a big "mainstream" soccer club can expose some of their relatives to deportation, even if the kid playing is a US citizen. Even in this space, which I visited less than ten days after President Trump was sworn into office, Villegas worried some families might stay away. "It does no one any good for kids not to be out playing with others, getting exercise," he said.

A few years ago, a Soccer Nation Academy team won the state championship, and the cost of taking the team to play at regionals was going to be an additional $60,000. Other team coaches from affluent suburbs at the state championship "helpfully" offered to take Soccer Nation's place if "for some reason" they couldn't go. Villegas and other Latino community leaders raised funds to cover the cost, including a sizable donation from Sprint, the phone company that was based in KC until it was acquired in 2020 by T-Mobile. But that funding model is hardly as sustainable as the one prevalent on most elite travel teams, where families are each expected to write a check to cover their player's expenses. Soccer Nation hasn't fielded an elite Academy team since the pandemic. Instead, Villegas considers it one of his roles to scout the most talented players from the community and connect them to Sporting KC's Academy, or college coaches. "When sport is a catalyst for education, that's something especially beautiful," he said.

"There is a gulf separating the two soccer cultures here," Villegas said. For many American families, he explained, this is a hobby; the kids might be doing soccer now after doing taekwondo and before trying baseball. For the Mexican families, by contrast, this isn't a hobby; it's their culture, their shared multi-generational passion. And it's *fútbol de barrio*, from the street.

"The American game is more disciplined," Villegas said, "more systematic, more we-paid-our-fee-and-obtained-our-permit to use this field for the next 90 minutes; the Mexican and immigrant game is more based on self-expression, instinct and guile (*picardía*)."

Villegas said he is always looking for ways to help educate families on how to navigate "the environment here" and find ways of minimizing the gaps that exist across communities in accessing sports. Villegas said having the World Cup come to Kansas City will reinforce the message that soccer belongs to the entire community. A KC World Cup will help on that front.

"It's going to be totally crazy," he said, shaking his head as if still not quite believing this latest twist in the Great Game. "Six games in KC ... I cannot wait."

Neither can I.

Notes

Prologue

1. Michael MacCambridge, *Lamar Hunt: A Life in Sports* (Kansas City: Andrews McMeel Publishing, 2012), 172.

Chapter 1

1. Mike Katz and Lawrie Mifflin, "Scouting," *New York Times*, June 18, 1982, 20.
2. I should disclose my Mexican father had earlier worked for The Coca-Cola Company and would subsequently work for one of its larger bottling partners. Both my familial insight into the company's workings and my schoolmates' relationship with the beverage reinforced in my mind the full "Mexicaness" of the brand.
3. Mark Pendergrast, *For God, Country & Coca-Cola* (New York: Basic Books, 2000), 8–9.
4. Simon Parkin, "FIFA: The Video Game that Changed Football," *The Guardian*, December 21, 2016.
5. Parkin, "FIFA."
6. Parkin, "FIFA."
7. https://news.ea.com/press-releases/press-releases-details/2018/EA-SPORTS-FIFA-is-the-Worlds-Game and https://news.ea.com/press-releases/press-releases-details/2018/Fans-Are-Going-Mad-for-Madden-EA-SPORTS-Madden-NFL-Franchise-Passes-130-Million-Copies-Sold
8. "Electronic Arts Reports Q3 FY 25 Results," February 4, 2025, https://www.ea.com/news/electronic-arts-reports-q3-fy25-results.
9. Parkin, "FIFA."
10. Lorne Michaels, producer, *Saturday Night Live*, Season 49, Episode 3, hosted by Nate Bargatze. Aired on NBC on October 28, 2023.

11 Michaels, *Saturday Night Live*, Season 49, Episode 3.

12 David Wangerin, *Soccer in a Football World: The Story of America's Forgotten Game* (Philadelphia: Temple University Press, 2006), 23–6.

13 Ryan Swanson, *The Strenuous Life: Theodore Roosevelt and the Making of the American Athlete* (New York: Diversion Books, 2019), 64.

14 Swanson, *The Strenuous Life*, 205–10.

15 Elliott J. Gorn and Warren Goldstein, *A Brief History of American Sports* (Chicago: University of Illinois Press, 1993), 172–7.

16 Swanson, *The Strenuous Life*, 124, 168–9.

17 Robert Edelman and Christopher Young, eds. *The Whole World Was Watching* (Stanford: Stanford University Press, 2020), 3.

18 NPR, "'Red Army' Explores How the Cold War Played out on Ice," January 22, 2015, https://www.npr.org/2015/01/22/378916505/red-army-explores-how-the-cold-war-played-out-on-ice.

19 Matthew P. Llewellyn and John Gleaves, *The Rise and Fall of Olympic Amateurism* (Urbana: University of Illinois Press, 2016), 51.

20 David Goldblatt, *The Games: A Global History of the Olympics* (New York: W. W. Norton & Company, 2016), 80–3.

21 Jim Riordan, "Sport and Soviet Foreign Policy," *International Journal* 43, no. 4, Sport in World Politics (Autumn 1988): 586.

22 John F. Kennedy, "The Soft American," *Sports Illustrated*, December 26, 1960, 15–16.

23 https://www.jfklibrary.org/learn/about-jfk/jfk-in-history/physical-fitness

24 Rule 6 of the Olympic charter spells it out: "The Olympic Games are competitions between athletes in in dividual or team events and not between countries." International Olympic Committee, *Olympic Charter* (Lausanne, Switzerland, 2024), 19.

25 Goldblatt, *The Games,* 101.

26 Llewellyn and Gleaves, *The Rise and Fall of Olympic Amateurism*, 107–17.

27 Llewellyn and Gleaves, *The Rise and Fall of Olympic Amateurism,* 171–2.

28 Llewellyn and Gleaves, *The Rise and Fall of Olympic Amateurism,* 172.

29 Gerald R. Ford, "In Defense of the Competitive Urge," *Sports Illustrated*, July 8, 1974.

30 Jack McCallum, *Dream Team* (New York: Ballantine Books, 2013), 48.

31 Scott Cacciola, "The '72 Basketball Team Still Wants Gold Medals," *New York Times*, September 9, 2022, 9 (B).

32 David Filipov, "A New Russian Film Takes Us Back to the U.S.S.R. to Celebrate a Soviet Olympic Miracle," *The Washington Post*, December 31, 1917.

33 McCallum, *Dream Team*, 293.

34 McCallum, *Dream Team*, 248–49.

35 Harvey Araton, "Theme Comes True: The Dream Team Captures the Gold," *New York Times*, August 9, 1992, Section 8, 1.

36 Araton, "Theme Comes True."

37 *The New York Times*, President Obama's State of the Union Address, January 25, 2012.

38 Andrei S. Markovits and Steven L. Hellerman, *Offside: Soccer & American Exceptionalism* (Princeton: Princeton University Press, 2001), 270.

39 David A. F. Sweet, *Lamar Hunt: The Gentle Giant Who Revolutionized Professional Sports* (Chicago: Triumph Books), 137.

Chapter 2

1 Isaac Deutscher, *Stalin: A Political Biography* (London: Oxford University Press, 1967), 281–7.

2 New York Times Editorial Board, "Socialism Triumphs on the Gridiron," *New York Times*, December 30, 2000, A14.

3 Andrés Martinez, "Along with a Super Bowl, the N.F.L. Needs a Farewell Bowl," *New York Times*, January 19, 2003, 12; Andrés Martinez, "Nowadays, Owning a Ball Club Means Always Having to Say You're Sorry," New York Times, December 14, 2003, 10.

4 Some representative examples: "How Socialism Boosts American Sport," *The Economist*, February 24, 2023; Jesse Berett, "The NFL: America's Socialist Utopia," *Washington Post*, February 2, 2018; David Berri, "America's Socialist Sports League: The NFL," *The Atlantic*, March 26, 2015.

5 Michael MacCambridge, *America's Game: The Epic Story of How Pro Football Captured a Nation* (New York: Anchor Books, 2005), 130.

6 Andy McCullough, "As the $476 million Dodgers face the $69 million Marlins, MLB's Payroll Gap has Never Been Wider," *The Athletic*, April 28, 2025.

7 MacCambridge, *America's Game*, 131.

8 MacCambridge, *America's Game*, 40.

9 MacCambridge, *America's Game*, 44.

10 MacCambridge, *America's Game*, 44.

11 Michael MacCambridge, *Lamar Hunt: A Life in Sports* (Kansas City: Andrews McMeel Publishing, 2012), 165–70.

12 Mike Florio, "Ted Cruz has been 'Tiptoeing Up to the Rule' Protecting College and High School Football," *NBCSports.com*, May 6, 2025, https://www.nbcsports.com/nfl/profootballtalk/rumor-mill/news/ted-cruz-nfl-has-been-tiptoeing-up-to-the-rule-protecting-college-and-high-school-football.

13 MacCambridge, *America's Game*, 453.

14 Kurt Badenhausen, "How NFL Teams and Owners Make their Money," *Sportico*, August 29, 2024, https://www.sportico.com/leagues/football/2024/how-nfl-teams-owners-make-money-1234795113/.

15 Kevin Baxter, "Galaxy and LAFC are Paying a Price for their Success. Are They Still MLS Cup Contenders?" *The Los Angeles Times*, February 21, 2025, https://www.latimes.com/sports/soccer/story/2025-02-21/galaxy-lafc-2025-mls-season-parity-rules; Sam Stejskal, "MLS' Parity Compared to Top European Soccer Leagues is Proving to be a Weakness," *The Athletic*, August 17, 2022, https://www.nytimes.com/athletic/3514232/2022/08/17/mls-parity-competitiveness-european-leagues/; Jeff Kasouf, "NWSL v. UWCL, WSL: Will Parity Keep the U.S. League on Top?," *ESPN.com*, May 1, 2025, https://www.espn.com/soccer/story/_/id/44926493/nwsl-vs-uwcl-wsl-parity-keep-us-league-top.

16 ESPN Staff, "USL to Adopt Promotion-Relegation in Historic 1sr for U.S. Soccer," ESPN, March 19, 2025, https://www.espn.com/soccer/story/_/id/44315033/usl-votes-adopt-pro-rel-2027-division-one-launches.

17 Andrés Martinez, "Brutality of Relegation one of Great Dramas of Premier League," *Global Sport Matters*, May 11, 2018.

18 Matt Philipps, "What Tanking Did for the Mavericks and Their Draft Lottery Odds," *SBNation*, April 26, 2023.

19 Mike Vorkunov, "Can the NBA Fix Its Big Tanking Problem?" *The Athletic*, March 31, 2025, https://www.nytimes.com/athletic/6235572/2025/03/31/nba-tanking-problem-fix-draft/.

20 Dermot Corrigan, "Barcelona's La Liga Salary Has Been More than Doubled," *The Athletic*, September 12, 2024.

21 Peter Rutzler and Matt Slater, "Premier League Clubs Agree to Push Ahead with Spending Cap Plans," *The Athletic*, April 29, 2024.

22 Deloitte Sports Group, *Annual Review of Football Finance 2024*, June 15, 2024, https://www.deloitte.com/uk/en/services/financial-advisory/research/annual-review-of-football-finance-europe.html.

23 Deloitte Sports Group, *Deloitte Football Money League 2025*, January 23, 2025, https://www.deloitte.com/uk/en/services/consulting-financial/analysis/deloitte-football-money-league.html.

24 Simon Kuper and Stefan Szymanski, *Soccernomics: Why England Loses: Why Germany, Spain, and France Win; and Why One Day Japan, Iraq, and the United States will Become Kings of the World's Most Popular Sport* (New York: Hachette Book Group, 2018), 291.

25 Kuper and Szymanski, *Soccernomics*, 292–3.

26 Kuper and Szymanski, *Soccernomics*, 299.

27 Kuper and Szymanski, *Soccernomics*, 299.

28 Katie Campione, "25 Most-Watched TV Programs of all Time," *Deadline*, February 9, 2024.

29 Anthony Crupi, "NFL Owns 72 of TV's Top 100 as Politics Loosens Sports' Grip," *Sportico*, January 3, 2025, https://www.sportico.com/business/media/2025/nfl-owns-73-of-top-100-broadcasts-election-undermine-sports-tv-dominance-1234822548/.

30 Joe Flint, "Super Bowl Viewership Hits New Record with Big Boost from Free Streaming," *Wall Street Journal*, February 10, 2025.

31 Ken Belson and Kevin Draper, "N.F.L. Signs Media Deals Worth Over $100 Billion," *New York Times*, March 18, 2021.

32 Michael Ozanian, "CNBC's Official NFL Team Valuations 2024: Here's How the 32 Franchises Stack Up," *CNBC*, September 5, 2024, https://www.cnbc.com/2024/09/05/official-nfl-team-valuations-2024.html.

33 ASU Great Game Lab Set Piece recorded with David Dein, April 16, 2024, https://greatgamelab.asu.edu and subsequent interview in London on September 25, 2024. The NFL's influence on the thinking of Premier League founders, including Dein and Manchester United's Martin Edwards and Tottenham's Irving Scholar, is also a theme throughout Joshua Robinson and Jonathan Clegg's excellent *The Club: How The English Premier League Became the Wildest, Richest, Most Disruptive Force in Sports* (Boston: Houghton Mifflin Harcourt, 2018). See, for instance, 47–51, on how Manchester United was inspired by the NFL to reconsider its approach to commercial marketing.

34 Lori Ewing, "English Football Governance Bill to be Introduced to Parliament," *Reuters*, October 23, 2024, https://www.reuters.com/sports/soccer/english-football-governance-bill-be-introduced-parliament-2024-10-23/.

Chapter 3

1 Steve Wulf, "How the NFL's First Foray Into Mexico Went South, and Back North," *espn.com*, November 17, 2017, https://www.espn.com/nfl/story/_/id/21426010/how-nfl-first-attempt-play-mexico-city-went-south-back-north.

2 Gordon Forbes, "Snead Breaks Leg as Lions Jolt Eagles," *Philadelphia Inquirer*, August 12, 1968, 21.

3 Ron Jaworski, "Mexico City a Bad Trip for Us," *Philadelphia Daily News*, August 7, 1978, 62.

4 "Fernando Von Rossum Selected to Receive Ralph Hay Pioneer Award from Hall of Fame," *profootballhof.com*, June 18, 2024.

5 Michael MacCambridge, *America's Game: The Epic Story of How Pro Football Captured a Nation* (New York: Anchor Books, 2005), 324.

6 Abraham Nudelstejer, "How the Dallas Cowboys Became Mexico's Favorite NFL Team," *Dallas Morning News*, January 11, 2024, https://www.dallasnews.com/sports/cowboys/2024/01/11/how-the-dallas-cowboys-became-mexicos-favorite-nfl-team.

7 Part of my conversation with Jason Garrett was recorded as a "Set Piece" for Arizona State University's Great Game Lab, August 29, 2024, https://greatgamelab.asu.edu/set-pieces.

8 Kamol, "The Biggest Crowds in NFL History Were Preseason Games," *NFLPreseasonStats.com*, August 10, 2024.

9 Roger Bennett, *(Re)Born in the USA: An Englishman's Love Letter to His Chosen Home* (New York: Dey Street, 2021), 13.

10 Bennett, *(Re)Born in the USA*, 113.

11 NFL, "2024 NFL Season Global Markets Program," August 22, 2024, https://www.nfl.com/international/global-markets-program.

12 Associated Press, "Roger Goodell Says NFL Could Have an International Super Bowl if League Expands Outside the US," February 3, 2025.

13 Joshua Robinson and Jonathan Clegg, *The Club: How the English Premier League Became the Wildest, Richest, Most Disruptive Force in Sports* (New York: Houghton Mifflin Harcourt, 2018), 292.

14 15 USC Ch 32: Telecasting of Professional Sports Contests.

15 Terrence McCoy, "How Soccer-Mad Brazil Fell for the NFL—and the Green Bay Packers," *The Washington Post*, September 5, 2024.

16 Richard Ryman, "Green Bay Packers Fans in Brazil Thrilled to Have Game in São Paulo, Saying 'We Will Be Wild,'" *Green Bay Press-Gazette*, April 11, 2024.

17 David Maraniss, *When Pride Still Mattered: A Life of Vince Lombardi* (New York: Simon & Schuster, 1999), 192.

18 "Set Piece with Mark Murphy" in conversation with Victoria Jackson, recorded for *Arizona State University's Great Game Lab*, July 18, 2024, https://greatgamelab.asu.edu/set-pieces/mark-murphy.

19 Robert Zizzo, "Packers Score Big Points by Hosting the Other Football, and Would Be Wise to Make Soccer a Regular Gig," *Milwaukee Journal Sentinel*, July 24, 2024.

20 Jack Nicas and Sara Ruberg, "Eagles Players Feared Crime in Brazil. Have they Considered Philadelphia?" *The New York Times*, September 6, 2024, https://www.nytimes.com/2024/09/06/world/americas/eagles-packers-nfl-game-brazil-crime.html.

21 While in Brazil, I wrote a short commentary for *Time* magazine that included some of these quotes and observations: Andrés Martinez, "The NFL's Brazil Game is Still Just the Beginning of Football's Global Push," *Time*, September 6, 2024, https://time.com/7021106/nfl-brazil-global-expansion/.

22 R. J. Kraft, "Eagles' Saquon Barkley Sets Combined Rushing Yards Record for Single Season," *The Athletic*, February 9, 2025, https://www.nytimes.com/athletic/6089695/2025/02/09/saquon-barkley-rushing-yards-single-season-mark-eagles/).

Chapter 4

1 https://www.theifab.com.

2 Nick Hornby, *Fever Pitch* (New York: Riverhead Books, 1992), 29–30.

3 David Edgerton, *The Rise and Fall of the British Nation: A Twentieth-Century History* (London: Penguin Books, 2018), xxiv.

4 Tim Spiers, "How Raul Jimenez Came Back From a Life-Threatening Fractured Skull to Play for Wolves Again," *The Athletic*, August 6, 2021, https://www.nytimes.com/athletic/2752803/2021/08/07/how-raul-jimenez-came-back-from-a-life-threatening-fractured-skull-to-play-for-wolves-again/.

5 Joshua Robinson and Jonathan Clegg, *The Club: How the English Premier League Became the Wildest, Richest, Most Disruptive Force in Sports* (New York: Houghton Mifflin Harcourt, 2018), 23–7, 39–43.

6 Leonard Shapiro and Tom Shales, "Fox Lands Contract to Televise the NFL," *The Washington Post*, December 17, 1993, https://www.washingtonpost.com/archive/politics/1993/12/18/fox-lands-contract-to-televise-the-nfl/7c20a84e-aa1b-4226-a0b4-fe724031cc17/.

7 Graham Satchell and Jessica Rawnsley, "More than 400 People Come Forward Over Al Fayed Sexual Abuse Allegations," *BBC*, October 31, 2024, https://www.bbc.com/news/articles/cy7dgrkp2vzo.

8 James Olley, "Todd Boehly Completes Chelsea Takeover in Deal Worth up to £4.25 Billion," *ESPN*, May 28, 2022, https://www.espn.com/soccer/story/_/id/37628834/todd-boehly-completes-chelsea-takeover-deal-worth-425bn.

9 Dominic Sandbrook, *The Great British Dream Factory* (London: Penguin Random House, 2015), xxvi–xxxi, 251–65.

10 Deloitte Sports Group, *Annual Review of Football Finance 2024*, June 2024, https://www.deloitte.com/uk/en/services/financial-advisory/research/annual-review-of-football-finance-europe.html.

11 https://www.premierleague.com/about/what-we-do.

12 Deloitte Sports Group, *Deloitte Football Money League 2025*, January 23, 2025, https://www.deloitte.com/uk/en/services/consulting-financial/analysis/deloitte-football-money-league.html.

13 Robinson and Clegg, *The Club*, 233–5.

14 https://www.cityfootballgroup.com/company.

15 Robinson and Clegg, *The Club*, 143–52.

16 Raffaele Poli, Loïc Ravenel, and Roger Besson, "Global Economic Analysis of the Transfer Market (2015–2024)," CIES Football Observatory, September 2024, https://football-observatory.com/MonthlyReport97.

17 Minhea V. Cuibus, "Migrants in the UK: An Overview," *The Migration Observatory at the University of Oxford*, August 9, 2024, https://migrationobservatory.ox.ac.uk/resources/briefings/migrants-in-the-uk-an-overview/; and US Census Bureau, "New Report on the Nation's Foreign-Born Population, April 9, 2024, https://www.census.gov/newsroom/press-releases/2024/foreign-born-population.html.

18 Yasmine Alsayyad, "Liverpool F.C.'s Mohamed Salah, an Arab Muslim Sports Star Subtly Confronting Racism and Islamophobia," *The New Yorker*, May 25, 2018, https://www.newyorker.com/sports/sporting-scene/liverpool-fcs-mohamed-salah-an-arab-muslim-sports-star-subtly-confronting-racism-and-islamophobia.

Chapter 5

1 Tariq Panja and Rory Smith, "The World Cup that Changed Everything," *New York Times*, November 19, 2022.

2 Sam Borden, "FIFA Confirms Winter World Cup for 2022," *New York Times*, March 19, 2015.

3 Ken Bensinger, *Red Card: How the U.S. Blew the Whistle on the World's Biggest Sports Scandal* (New York: Simon & Schuster, 2018), 48–51; David Conn, *The Fall of the House of FIFA: The Multimillion-Dollar Corruption at the Heart of Global Soccer* (New York: Nation Books, 2017), 73, 89–92; Associated Press, "FIFA's Former Leader Says Making Qatar a World Cup Host Was a Mistake," November 8, 2022,

https://www.npr.org/2022/11/08/1135102137/sepp-blatter-qatar-world-cup-mistake-fifa-sarkozy.

4   The US Delegation's Presentation is Available on YouTube: https://www.youtube.com/watch?v=Oe6yMPeU0DE.

5   Conn, *The Fall of the House of FIFA*, 99–104.

    Bensinger, *Red Card*, 65–74.

6   Bensinger, *Red Card*, 28–34.

7   Bensinger, *Red Card*, 136.

8   Rebecca R. Ruiz and Tariq Panja, "FIFA Convictions Are Imperiled by Questions of U.S. Overreach," *New York Times*, January 27, 2024.

9   Associated Press, "FIFA's Former Leader Says Making Qatar a World Cup Host Was a Mistake," November 8, 2022.

    Tariq Panja, "France to Investigate How Qatar Got the World Cup," *New York Times*, December 11, 2021, https://www.nytimes.com/2019/12/11/sports/soccer/qatar-world-cup-michel-platini.html.

10 Conn, *The Fall of the House of FIFA*, 88.

11 Conn, *The Fall of the Hose of FIFA*, 89.

12 Ken Belson, "Trump and the NFL: A Fraught Relationship Stretching Back Decades," *New York Times*, February 9, 2025.

13 Alexander Abnos, "'They'll Have to Go Home': Trump's World Cup Task Force Touts Welcome, Warns Visitors," *The Guardian*, May 6, 2025.

14 Adam Crafton, "UEFA Delegates Exit FIFA Congress After Gianni Infantino Arrives Late from Donald Trump Tour," *The Athletic*, May 15, 2025, https://www.nytimes.com/athletic/6359867/2025/05/15/uefa-fifa-walk-out-infantino-trump/.

15 Thom Poole and Patrick Jackson, "Who is Alina Kabaeva, Putin's Alleged Girlfriend?" *BBC News*, May 13, 2022, https://www.bbc.com/news/world-europe-61353020.

16 Tim Daniels, "Poland Refuse to Play Russia in 2022 WC Qualifier over Russian Invasion of Ukraine," February 26, 2022.

17 Joe Lynskey, "Ten Years on, Can China Still Meet Grand Football Plans?" *BBC Sport*, March 20, 2025, https://www.bbc.com/sport/football/articles/cgq9pl21y79o.

18 The Economist, "Winging It; China and the Beautiful Game," August 27, 2016, https://www.economist.com/business/2016/08/27/winging-it.

19 Amy Hawkins, "Chinese Football Stars and Officials Held in Xi's Corruption Crackdown," *The Guardian*, March 18, 2023, https://www.theguardian.com/world/2023/mar/18/chinese-stars-officials-held-xi-jinping-football-corruption-crackdown.

20 Jiang Yang and Lingling Wei, "China's President Xi Jinping Personally Scuttled Jack Ma's Ant IPO," *The Wall Street Journal*, November 12, 2020, https://www.wsj.com/world/china/china-president-xi-jinping-halted-jack-ma-ant-ipo-11605203556.

21 Mariko Oi, "China Former Football Chief Sentenced to Life for Bribery," *BBC*, March 25, 2024, https://www.bbc.com/news/business-68662441.

22 Hannah Beech, "The Chinese Sports Machine's Single Goal: The Most Golds. At Any Cost," *New York Times*, July 29, 2021, https://www.nytimes.com/2021/07/29/world/asia/china-olympics.html.

23 Sopan Deb and Marc Stein, "N.B.A. Executive's Hong Kong Tweet Starts Firestorm in China," *New York Times*, October 6, 2019, https://www.nytimes.com/2019/10/06/sports/daryl-morey-rockets-china.html.

Ravi Ubha, "Mesut Ozil vs. China: Arsenal Star Makes Human Rights Stand," *CNN*, December 16, 2019, https://www.cnn.com/2019/12/16/football/ozil-arsenal-china-football-intl-spt.

24 James Horncastle, "Oaktree Capital Management Assume Control of Inter Milan as Suning Default on Debt," *The Athletic*, May 22, 2024, https://www.nytimes.com/athletic/5509404/2024/05/22/inter-oaktree-capital-management/.

25 Michael Ratney, "This is Not the Saudi Arabia Trump Visited Before," *New York Times*, May 13, 2025, https://www.nytimes.com/2025/05/13/opinion/saudi-arabia-trump-visit.html.

Matt Slater, "Might Saudi Arabia Actually Be a Good Choice for a Men's World Cup?" *The Athletic*, December 11, 2024, https://www.nytimes.com/athletic/5981357/2024/12/11/saudi-arabia-world-cup-fifa-choice/.

26 Dan DeLuce, Ken Dilanian, and Robert Windren, "How a Saudi Royal Crushed His Rivals in a 'Shakedown' at the Ritz-Carlton," *NBC News*, November 3, 2018, https://www.nbcnews.com/news/mideast/how-saudi-royal-crushed-his-rivals-shakedown-ritz-carlton-n930396.

27 Riyadhair.com (as of May 2025).

28 BBC, "Newcastle United Takeover: LGBTQ+ Fans Hope Saudi Deal a "Sign For Change," *NNC*, October 8, 2021, https://www.bbc.com/news/uk-england-tyne-58826839.

29 Some of my reporting from Newcastle, Including the Fans' Quotes, Appeared in a Blog of our Arizona State University blog Global Sport Matters: Andrés Martinez, "English Soccer Wrestles with Saudi Takeover of Newcastle," *Global Sport Matters*, November 24, 2021, https://globalsportmatters.com/culture/2021/11/24/english-premier-leagues-wrestles-newcastle-united-fc-saudi-arabia-public-investment-fund/.

30 Mark Ogden and Beth Lindrop, "The Wait is Over: Newcastle Beat Liverpool, End Trophy Drought," *ESPN*, March 16, 2025, https://www.espn.com/soccer/story/_/

id/44250965/the-wait-newcastle-united-beat-liverpool-carabao-cup-end-trophy-drought.

31 Reuters, "US Justice to Investigate PGA Tour-LIV Golf Pact, Wall Street Journal Reports," *Reuters*, June 15, 2025, https://www.reuters.com/sports/us-doj-investigate-pga-tour-liv-golf-pact-wsj-2023-06-15/.

32 Jacob Whitehead, "Jamal Khashoggi's Widow Says FIFA Should Commemorate Him at Saudi Arabia World Cup," *The Athletic*, January 25, 2025, https://www.nytimes.com/athletic/6063594/2025/01/26/jamal-khashoggi-saudi-arabia-world-cup/. A year and a half earlier, Hanan Khashoggi had expressed similar sentiments regarding the proposed LIV-PGA deal, when she told NBC News in an interview that aired on June 16, 2023, that she didn't want Saudi Arabia to become a sporting pariah: https://www.youtube.com/watch?v=pWa7BJAmzYY.

33 FairSquare, "Substitute: The Case for the External Reform of FIFA," October 2024, https://fairsq.org/wp-content/uploads/2024/12/FIFA_Substitute_Report_v5_Pages.pdf.

Chapter 6

1 Alex Weprin, "At the Upfronts, Sports Sideline Scripted TV as Studios Lean in to Live Sports," *The Hollywood Reporter*, May 15, 2025, https://www.hollywoodreporter.com/business/business-news/2025-upfronts-sports-nfl-dominate-1236217928/.

2 Matthew Belloni, "The Unofficial '25 TV Upfront Awards," *Puck*, May 16, 2025, https://puck.news/tv-upfronts-report-plus-unofficial-awards/.

3 Stephen Battaglio, "Super Bowl LIX Scores a Record 127.7 Million Viewers Despite Blowout," *The Los Angeles Times*, February 10, 2025, https://www.latimes.com/entertainment-arts/business/story/2025-02-10/super-bowl-lix-scores-126-million-viewers-despite-blowout.

4 Harry Enten, "Trendlines: Everything about the NFL is Trending Up," *CNN*, April 25, 2025, https://www.cnn.com/2025/04/25/sport/trendlines-nfl-draft-spt.

5 Michael McCarthy, "From Jordan to Brady and ESPN Pivot, Sports Took Over Upfronts," *Front Office Sports*, May 13, 2025, https://frontofficesports.com/from-jordan-to-brady-and-espn-pivot-sports-took-over-upfronts/.

6 *Charlotte Observer*, October 12, 1995, 49.

7 Anthony Crupi, "NFL Owns 72 of TV's top 100 as Politics Loosens Sport's Grip," *Sportico*, January 3, 2025, https://www.sportico.com/business/media/2025/nfl-owns-73-of-top-100-broadcasts-election-undermine-sports-tv-dominance-1234822548/.

8   Anthony Crupi, "NFL Swallows TV Whole, with 93 of Year's Top 100 Broadcasts," *Sportico*, January 5 2024, https://www.sportico.com/business/media/2024/nfl-posts-93-of-top-100-tv-broadcasts-2023-1234761753/.

9   Anthony Crupi, "2022 TV: It's the NFL's World; The Rest of Us Just Live In It," *Sportico*, January 6 2023, https://www.sportico.com/business/media/2023/nfl-games-account-for-82-of-100-top-tv-broadcasts-1234700381/.

10 Marc Gunther and Bill Carter, *Monday Night Mayhem: The Inside Story of ABC's Monday Night Football* (New York: Beech Tree Books, 1988), 303.

11 Benjamin G. Rader, *In Its Own Image: How Television Has Transformed Sports* (New York: The Free Press, 1984), 113.

12 Alex Sherman, "David Zaslav's Top Priority at Warner Bros. Discovery: Get the Cash Flowing Again," *CNBC*, December 6, 2022, https://www.cnbc.com/2022/12/06/david-zaslav-warner-bros-discovery-cash-flow-debt.html.

13 Rader, *In Its Own Image*, 24–5.

14 Rader, *In Its Own Image*, 52.

15 Rader, *In Its Own Image*, 86.

16 Ben Fischer and David Broughton, "NFL Attendance Ticks Up Again in 2024, but Caveats Emerge," *Sports Business Journal*, January 9, 2025, https://www.sportsbusinessjournal.com/Articles/2025/01/09/Football/nfl-attendance-figure-2024/.

17 Rader, *In Its Own Image*, 5–6.

18 Todd Spangler, "Netflix Is 'Not Anti-Sports, We're Just Pro-Proft,' Ted Sarandos Says," *Variety*, December 6, 2022.

19 Anthony Crupi, "Cable's Not Dead Yet, But it Sure Does Smell Funny," *Sportico*, January 10, 2025, https://www.sportico.com/business/media/2025/cable-bundle-sports-decline-1234823339/.

20 Ben Strauss, "Amazon is Building a Sports Media Empire. What's Next?" *The Washington Post*, July 25, 2024, https://www.washingtonpost.com/sports/2024/07/25/amazon-prime-video-nba-nfl-sports-rights/.

21 Bill Gates, "*The Road Ahead* after 25 Years," *Gates Notes*, November 23, 2020, https://www.gatesnotes.com/the-road-ahead-after-25-years.

22 Graham Ruthven, "Sky Transformed English Soccer. Will Apple's $2.5 billion Deal do the Same for the MLS?" *The Guardian*, June 16, 2022, https://www.theguardian.com/football/2022/jun/16/mls-broadcasting-deal-apple-tv-soccer.

23 Chrstiaan Hetzner, "Apple is Reportedly Willing to Lose $1 Billion Every Year Just to Fuel its Streaming Ambitions," *Fortune*, March 22, 2025, https://fortune.com/2025/03/22/apple-tv-plus-losing-1-billion-annually-streaming-ambitions/.

24 Harshita Mary Varghese, "Netflix Shares Hit Record as Subscriber Growth Defies Odds Once Again," *Reuters*, January 22, 2025, https://www.reuters.com/technology/netflix-shares-soar-record-subscriber-gains-planned-price-hikes-2025-01-22/; Katie Campione, "Netflix Boasts Impressive Audiences For Christmas Day NFL Games; 27M Viewers Tune in For Beyoncé," *Deadline*, December 31, 2024.

25 Julia Alexander, "The Sports Streaming Battle Royale," *The Varsity* podcast with John Ourand, Puck News, March 26, 2025, https://podcasts.apple.com/us/podcast/the-sports-streaming-battle-royale/id1762692129?i=1000700876528.

26 Puck News, "Jimmy Pitaro's New ESPN," *The Grill Room* from Puck News, May 20, 2025, https://open.spotify.com/episode/5sHoe6qXWU4rHqxZEqywha.

27 Mark Mwachiro, "Nielsen's The Gauge Streaming Ratings for April 2025," *Adweek*, May 21, 2025, https://www.adweek.com/convergent-tv/nielsen-streaming-ratings-april-2025/.

28 Andrés Martinez, "Why Ted Lasso is a Match Made in Globalizer Heaven," *The Los Angeles Times*, September 23, 2021, https://www.latimes.com/opinion/story/2021-09-23/ted-lasso-soccer-premiere-league-apple-globalization.

29 Richard Sutcliffe, "Wrexham Season Review: Historic Promotion, Premier League in Sight, Scenes at the 'Circus,'" *The Athletic*, May 3, 2025, https://www.nytimes.com/athletic/6318063/2025/05/03/wrexham-promotion-reynolds-mcelhenney-parkinson/.

30 Steve Douglas, "In Wrexham, the 'Rob and Ryan Effect' Goes Beyond the Soccer Club as Tourism and Investments Grow," *Associated Press*, October 10, 2024, https://apnews.com/article/wrexham-reynolds-mcelhenney-soccer-fe2203a29b36cc3e6b161f91cb9edd56.

31 NPR, "*Always Sunny* Creator Rob McElhenney on His Pandemic Purchase: A Welsh Soccer Team," *Fresh Air*, June 12, 2024.

32 Spotify, "Rob McElhenney on Merging Soccer, Celebrity, and a TV Empire," *The Town with Matthew Belloni*, December 7, 2022.

33 Douglas, "In Wrexham the 'Rob and Ryan' Effect Goes Beyond the Soccer Club as Tourism and Investment Grows."

Chapter 7

1 *For The Win: NWSL*, Season 1, Episode 4, directed by Marie Margolius, Amazon Prime, March 6, 2025, https://www.amazon.com/gp/video/detail/B0D9PCTQ6X/.

2 CBS Mornings, "A First Look at Kansas City's CPKC Stadium Before the NWSL Championship," *CBS News*, November 22, 2024, https://www.cbsnews.com/video/a-first-look-at-kansas-citys-cpkc-stadium-before-the-nwsl-championship/.

3 *For the Win: NWSL*, Season 1, Episode 2.

4 Suzanne Wrack, *A Woman's Game: The Rise, Fall, and Rise Again of Women's Football* (London: Guardian Faber, 2022), 56–7.

5 Jennifer Haskel, Pete Giorgio, Zoe Burton, and Lizzie Tantam, "Beyond the Billion-Dollar Barrier: Charting the Next Phase of Growth," *Deloitte Perspective*, March 17, 2025, https://www.deloitte.com/global/en/Industries/tmt/perspectives/charting-the-next-phase-of-growth.html.

6 FIFA Women's World Cup Australia & New Zealand 2023 Global Engagement & Audience Report, https://inside.fifa.com/tournament-organisation/audience-reports/australia-new-zealand-2023.

7 M. A. Voepel, "Nebraska Volleyball Sets World Record for Women's Sports Attendance," *ESPN*, August 30, 2023, https://www.espn.com/college-sports/story/_/id/38294591/nebraska-volleyball-sets-world-record-attendance-women-sporting-event.

8 Richard Deitsch, "Women's Basketball is Hot as Ever, but Will March Madness Still Soar Without Caitlin Clark?" *The Athletic*, March 20, 2025, https://www.nytimes.com/athletic/6206920/2025/03/18/womens-college-basketball-viewership-post-caitlin-clark/.

9 Emma Bowman, "Paris Games are Being Hailed as the Gender-Equal' Olympics. Let's take a Closer Look," *NPR*, July 31, 2024, https://www.npr.org/2024/07/31/g-s1-14470/paris-games-is-gender-equal-olympics.

10 Alex Brodie, "Serena Williams' Husband, Reddit Co-founder Alexis Ohanian, Buys Stake in Chelsea Women," *The Athletic*, May 14, 2025, https://www.npr.org/2024/07/31/g-s1-14470/paris-games-is-gender-equal-olympics.

11 Jeff Kassouf, "NWSL vs. UWCL, WSL: Will Parity Keep the U.S. League on Top?" *ESPN*, May 1, 2025, https://www.espn.com/soccer/story/_/id/44926493/nwsl-vs-uwcl-wsl-parity-keep-us-league-top.

12 Cesar Hernandez, "How NWSL, Its Players Plan to Thrive Without College Drafts," *ESPN*, March 7, 2025, https://www.espn.com/soccer/story/_/id/44045194/how-nwsl-players-plan-thrive-college-drafts.

13 Brenda Elsey and Joshua Nadel, *Futbolera: A History of Women and Sports in Latin America* (Austin: University of Texas Press, 2019), 233–42.

14 Wrack, *A Woman's Game*, 66.

15 *Copa 71*, directed by Rachel Ramsey and James Erskine, Greenwich Entertainment, 2023, https://www.imdb.com/title/tt18163414/.

16 Garrett M. Graff, *Watergate: A New History* (New York: Avid Reader Press, 2022), 209–10, 633–6.

17 Sherry Boschert, *37 Words: Title IX and Fifty Years of Fighting Sex Discrimination* (New York: The New Press, 2022), 47–71.

18 Alexandra Petri, "Once an 'Easy Way Out' for Equality, Women's Soccer is Now a U.S. Force," *New York Times*, June 27, 2022, https://www.nytimes.com/2022/06/27/sports/soccer/title-ix-soccer.html.

19 Wrack, *A Woman's Game*, 105.

20 Wrack, A Woman's Game, 103.

21 Wayne Coffey, "How an Influx of Elite Youth Players to NWSL is Impacting the College Landscape," *The Athletic*, March 13, 2025, https://www.nytimes.com/athletic/6199487/2025/03/13/nwsl-college-soccer-youth-movement/.

22 "Set Piece with Julie Foudy," in Conversation with Andrés Martinez, recorded for Arizona State University's Great Game Lab, February 13, 2025, https://greatgamelab.asu.edu/set-pieces.

23 Jere Longman, "Pride in Their Play, and in Their Bodies," *New York Times*, July 8, 1999, D1.

Caitlin Murray, *The National Team: The Inside Story of the Women Who Changed Soccer* (New York: Abrams Press, 2019), 50–3.

24 Scott Bordow, "Former Olympic Soccer Goalie Briana Scurry Shares Her Story at ASU Event," *ASU News*, October 6, 2022, https://news.asu.edu/20221006-global-engagement-former-us-goalie-briana-scurry-featured-speaker-title-ix-and-global.

25 https://www.ncaa.org/sports/2018/3/21/international-student-athlete-participation.aspx.

26 Victoria Jackson, "The U.S. Law That Made the Rest of the Globe So Strong at the Women's World Cup," *Slate*, July 29, 2023, https://slate.com/culture/2023/07/world-cup-college-soccer-players-title-ix.html.

Chapter 8

1 Guardian Sport, "Russia's Vladimir Putin Accuses United States of 'Meddling' Over FIFA Arrests," *The Guardian*, May 28, 2015, https://www.theguardian.com/football/2015/may/28/vladimir-putin-fifa-united-states-meddling.

2 U.S. Department of Justice, "Attorney General Loretta E. Lynch Delivers Remarks at Press Conference Announcing Law Enforcement Action Related to FIFA," Archives U.S. Department of Justice, December 3, 2015, https://www.justice.gov/archives/opa/speech/attorney-general-loretta-e-lynch-delivers-remarks-press-conference-announcing-law.

3 Victoria Jackson and Andrés Martinez, "Great World Cup, FIFA. Now Scratch the Whole Thing and Start Over," *The Los Angeles Times*, July 11, 2019, https://www

.latimes.com/opinion/op-ed/la-oe-jackson-martinez-fifa-world-cup-women-reform-20190711-story.html.

4 "FIFA Big Count 2006: 270 Million People Active in Football," FIFA, May 31, 2007, https://digitalhub.fifa.com/m/55621f9fdc8ea7b4/original/mzid0qmguixkcmruvema-pdf.pdf.

5 Rodney Reeves, "The Most Watched Soccer Games in U.S. Television History," *Front Office Sports*, August 4, 2024, https://frontofficesports.com/most-watched-soccer-games/.

6 https://publications.fifa.com/en/annual-report-2022/tournaments-and-events/fifa-world-cup-quatar-2022/fifa-world-cup-qatar-2022-in-numbers/wq.

7 BBC News, "World Cup: Does US Really Have the Most Fans in Brazil?" *BBC*, June 25, 2014, https://www.bbc.com/news/blogs-magazine-monitor-27978699.

8 https://www.mlssoccer.com/news/mls-second-highest-attended-league-in-the-world.

9 Cesar Hernandez, "San Diego Awarded 30th MLS Team, Will Debut in 2025," *ESPN*, May 18, 2023, https://www.espn.com/soccer/story/_/id/37676377/mls-names-san-diego-30th-team-debut-2025.

10 Aaron Timms, "MLS Year 30: A League at a Philosophical Crossroads as World Cups Loom," *The Guardian*, February 21, 2025, https://www.theguardian.com/sport/2025/feb/21/mls-30-years-apple-tv-season-preview.

11 Dan Sheldon, "How the Premier League Grew Into the Biggest Soccer League in the United States," *The Athletic*, January 22, 2024, https://www.nytimes.com/athletic/5218686/2024/01/23/premier-league-united-states/#.

12 Adam Crafton, "NBC to Continue Push for Premier League Games in U.S., Says Leading Exec," *The Athletic*, April 30, 2024, https://www.nytimes.com/athletic/5460003/2024/04/30/premier-league-games-united-states-nbc/.

13 Altman Solon, "U.S. Sports Struggle to Find Fans in Europe, European Soccer Draws Fans in U.S.," October 2020, https://www.altmansolon.com/insights/us-euro-sports-survey-spotlight.

14 "FIFA World Cup 2022: USA vs. Netherlands—Lineup, Schedule & TV Channels," US Soccer, December 3, 2022, https://www.ussoccer.com/stories/2022/12/fifa-world-cup-2022-usmnt-vs-netherlands-starting-xi-lineup-notes-tv-channels-start-time.

15 CBS Sports, *Pulisic*, December 8, 2024, https://www.paramountplus.com/shows/pulisic/.

16 Paul Tenorio, "USMNT Frustrations Boiling Over as World Cup Clock Keeps on Ticking," *The Athletic*, March 24, 2025, https://www.nytimes.com/athletic/6226004/2025/03/24/usmnt-nations-league-disappointment-world-cup-pochettino/.

17 Pablo Maurer, "Worry, Anger, Frustration: What Past USMNT Greats Think of Struggling Side," *The Athletic*, March 26, 2025, https://www.nytimes.com/athletic/6231309/2025/03/26/usmnt-players-dempsey-donovan-ramos-world-cup/.

Chapter 9

1 Joshua Robinson and Jonathan Clegg, *The Club: How the English Premier League Became the Wildest, Richest, Most Disruptive Force in Sports* (New York: Houghton Mifflin Harcourt, 2018), 104.

2 https://swissramble.substack.com/p/why-are-manchester-united-cutting.

3 Adan Crafton, "How Sir Jim Ratcliffe's INEOS Took Charge of Manchester United's Football and Business," *The Athletic*, April 30, 2024, https://www.nytimes.com/athletic/5462234/2024/05/01/ineos-manchester-united-economic-control/.

4 Matt Lawton, "Jim Ratcliffe: Ruben Amorim is Not Perfect but He's Doing a Great Job," *The Times*, March 10, 2025, https://www.thetimes.com/sport/football/article/jim-ratcliffe-manchester-united-old-trafford-amorim-ten-hag-mistake-mfclgpckk.

5 https://www.nytimes.com/athletic/6184205/2025/03/11/manchester-united-stadium-new-old-trafford/#.

6 BBC, "'Spectacle over Substance'—Protest Group on Stadium Design," March 11, 2025, https://www.bbc.com/sport/football/articles/cwydgnen2xxo.

7 Joshua Robinson, "American Owners Got Chewed Up by English Soccer. Now They Can't Stop Winning," *The Wall Street Journal*, April 27, 2025, https://www.wsj.com/sports/soccer/english-soccer-liverpool-wrexham-tom-brady-66990058.

8 Greg O'Keefe, "Why Almost One-Third of English Football Clubs Are Now American-Owned," *The Athletic*, January 4, 2025, https://www.nytimes.com/athletic/6004266/2025/01/05/american-owner-investment-efl/.

9 Gratham Ruthven, "An A for Villa to an F for Man Utd: How US owners Have Fared in European Football," *The Guardian*, May 23, 2024, https://www.theguardian.com/football/article/2024/may/23/an-a-for-villa-to-an-f-for-man-utd-how-us-owners-have-fared-in-european-football.

10 Greg Barringer-Grimes, "Chelsea's Sale of Their Women's Team to Themselves—What Does It Mean?" *BBC News*, May 23, 2025, https://www.bbc.com/sport/football/articles/cdd2egjrp31o.

11 Liam Twomey and Simon Johnson, "Chelsea's Ownership Structure: Who Owns What at Stamford Bridge?" *The Athletic*, September 10, 2024, https://www.nytimes.com/athletic/5758157/2024/09/11/chelsea-ownership-boehly-clearlake-walter-wyss/.

12 Ben Fisher, "'In Europe Within Five Years': Bournemouth Owner Foley Sets Target," *The Guardian,* December 14, 2023, https://www.theguardian.com/football/2023/dec/14/bournemouth-owner-bill-foley-europe-five-years-iraola-new-stadium.

13 *Welcome to Wrexham,* season 1, episode 18, "Do or Die," with Ryan Reynolds and Rob McElhenney, aired on FX, October 12, 2022.

14 Nathan Edwards, "'We're Finally Catching Up'—Will Ferrell Explains the Rise of American Investment in English Football," *Goal,* September 14, 2024, https://www.goal.com/en-us/lists/will-ferrell-explains-american-investment-english-football-leeds-investor-wrexham-ryan-reynolds-rob-mcelhenney/blt7378c82782fb6812#.

15 Roger Bennett, "Ryan Reynolds Special," *Men in Blazers,* Season 11, Episode 10, January 22, 2025, https://www.youtube.com/watch?v=Q9S5v5muYfg.

16 Beren Cross and Chris Weatherspoon, "Leeds United's Accounts Explained: £60M Loss, £140M 49ers Support and PSR Situation," *The Athletic,* April 2, 2025, https://www.nytimes.com/athletic/6249399/2025/04/02/leeds-united-accounts-explained-loss-psr/.

17 Kevin Day, Kieran Maguire, and Guy Kilty, *Unfit & Improper Persons: An Idiot's Guide to Owning a Football Club* (London: Bloomsbury, 2023), 96–100.

18 Phil Hay, *And It Was Beautiful: Leeds United in the Era of Marcelo Bielsa* (London: Seven Dials, 2021), 85–103.

19 Hay, *And It Was Beautiful,* 69.

Jonathan Wilson, "How Marcelo Bielsa Gave Leeds Fans Something to be Proud Again," *The Guardian,* April 29, 2019, https://www.theguardian.com/football/2019/apr/29/marcelo-bielsa-aston-villa-goal-leeds-proud.

20 Hay, *And It Was Beautiful,* 280–1.

21 BBC Sport, "Red Bull Takes Minority Ownership Stake in Leeds," May 30, 2024, https://www.bbc.com/sport/football/articles/cx88w2nneego.

22 Rick Broadbent, *Now Then: The Story of Yorkshire and its People* (London: Allen & Unwin, 2023), 210.

23 https://www.gov.uk/government/publications/a-vision-for-leeds-a-decade-of-city-centre-growth-and-wider-prosperity.

Chapter 10

1 https://sabr.org/bioproj/person/Monte-Irvin/.

2 David McCollough, *Truman* (New York: Simon & Schuster, 1992), 150.

3   Dave Caldwell, "How Kansas City Became the 2026 World Cup's Most Unlikely City," *The Guardian*, June 30, 2022, https://www.theguardian.com/football/2022/jun/30/how-kansas-city-became-the-2026-world-cups-most-unlikely-host-city.

4   ESPN Staff, "Chicago Withdraws From 2026 World Cup Bid Over Lack of Assurances," *ESPN*, March 15, 2018, https://www.espn.com/soccer/story/_/id/37548142/chicago-withdraws-2026-world-cup-bid-lack-assurances.

5   Cesar Hernandez, "World Cup 2026 Host Cities Revealed, With 11 Venues in U.S., 3 in Mexico and 2 in Canada," *ESPN*, June 16, 2022, https://www.espn.com/soccer/story/_/id/37629375/world-cup-2026-host-cities-revealed-11-venues-us-3-mexico-2-canada.

6   Tim Newcomb, "Kansas City: The Story of the Sports Architecture of the World," *Forbes*, October 29, 2019, https://www.forbes.com/sites/timnewcomb/2019/10/29/kansas-city-the-story-of-the-sports-architecture-capital-of-the-world/.

7   Richard Sandomir, "Ron Labinski, Who Designed a Cozier Future for Stadiums, Dies at 85," *New York Times*, February 9, 2023, https://www.nytimes.com/2023/02/09/sports/ron-labinski-dead.html.

8   https://www.gensler.com/blog/next-chapter-sports-entertainment-kansas-city.

9   McCollough, *Truman*, 147.

Index

Aaronson, Brenden 222
ABC/ESPN 138, 146
Abello, Kerry 161
Abramovich, Roman 92, 101, 103, 117, 127, 204–5
AC Milan 120, 122, 197
Acosta, Luciano 194
Adams, Tyler 199, 222
AFL 41
Alberto, Carlos 72
Alexander, Julia 150
Alexander-Arnold, Trent 105
Al Jazeera 153
All or Nothing (Amazon Prime show) 155
Allen, Marvin 176
Amazon Prime 138, 144, 146, 148, 151, 152, 154, 161, 164
American Century 20, 23, 93, 255
American exceptionalism 18–19, 33–4, 162, 193
American soft power 2, 173
America's Game: The Epic Story of How Pro Football Captured a Nation (MacCambridge) 39, 42
"America's team," Dallas Cowboys 62, 64
Amorim, Rúben 207
And It Was Beautiful: Leeds United in the Era of Marcelo Bielsa (Hay) 224
Andonovski, Vlatko 170
Andrade, Rebeca 79
Ant Group 120
Antony 206

"Any Given Sunday" mantra 43–4, 48, 51, 58
Apple TV+ 55–6, 144, 146–51, 155, 194, 230
    acquisition of MLS rights 155
    intentions and strategy in live sports 147–8
Arsenal (football club) 45, 50, 83, 95, 102, 104, 122, 145, 159, 169, 203, 207, 251, 253
Ashley, Mike 126
Asian Football Confederation 109
Aston Villa (football club) 94, 120, 153, 211, 217, 223
Athletic, The 39, 47–8, 195, 201, 224
Atlético Español (football team) 3, 17, 47, 120, 124, 173
Ayling, Luke 223

Bach, Thomas 118–19
Bagley, Elizabeth 79
Balogun, Folarin 198
Bank of America 129
Bargatze, Nate 18
Barkley, Charles 29–30
Barkley, Saquon 70, 79, 137
Basie, Count 235
Bay, Willow 168
Bayern Munich (football club) 53–4
beach tennis 73
Beatles 93
Beckenbauer, Franz 81
Beijing Winter Olympics 117, 119

beIN Sports   111–12, 153
Belichick, Bill   53, 68, 175–6
Bell, Bert   39–41, 57
Bell, James "Cool Papa"   232
Belloni, Matt   138, 158
Benjumeda, Bego   249–50
Bennett, Roger   65, 217
Benzema, Karim   124
Berhalter, Gregg   199–200
Berman, Jessica   169
Bielsa, Marcelo   222–3
Bielsabol   224
Biles, Simone   168
Bird, Larry   29, 31
Birmingham, England   120
Bitcoin   167
Black Panther   123
Blair, Tony   91
Blatter, Sepp   109, 111
Blazer, Chuck   110, 186
Boehly, Todd   213
Boeing   129
Bolsheviks   37, 39
Bonas, Marilia   73
Bond, James   83, 93
Bowser, Muriel   139
Bradshaw, Terry   2, 17, 60–1
Brady, Tom   18, 53, 57, 68, 194, 211
Breaking Bad   142
British footballing culture   157
Broadbent, Rick   228
Brooks, Herb   24
Brunt, Van   247
Buck, Jack   61
Budweiser   15
"Bud" Wilkinson, Charles   25
Burn, Dan   130
Burns, Jim   126–7, 129
Bush, George W.   20–1
Byers, Dylan   151

Cameron, David   119
Campanella, Roy   232
"Carioca residents"   71
Carpentier, Georges   143

Castro, Fidel   21
Cawthorne, Josh   220, 222, 227
CBS   41, 59, 91, 141, 146, 154, 164
Cesar Chávez Boulevard   233–4
Champions League   49, 92, 97–8, 102,
   117, 145–6, 170, 194, 202, 212, 225
   Women's   179
Charles Miller Square   72
Chastain, Brandi   172, 174, 181–2
Chavez, Gene   236
Chávez, Hugo   21
Chelsea (football club)   45, 50, 92, 101,
   103, 117–18, 125, 129, 142, 213–14
Chicago Bulls   53
China, investment in European football
   and sport strategy   119–29
Churchill, Winston   107, 255
Cincinnati Bengals   46
Cinderella   45, 152
Citigroup   129
City Football Group (CFG)   100
"city upon a hill" sermon (Winthrop)   21
Cleese, John   229
Clegg, Jonathan   91
Cleveland Browns (football team)   38,
   45–6, 51
Cleveland Bulldogs (football team)   37–8
Clinton, Bill   108–9, 114, 182, 198
*The Club: How the English Premier League
   Became the Wildest, Richest,
   Most Disruptive Force in Sports*
   (Robinson and Clegg)   91
Cobey, Bill   176, 179
Coca-Cola   13–15, 19, 114, 154
Coimbra, Herlander   30
Cold War Olympics   26
Cold War rivalry   24
Cole, Andy   126
collegiate-backed "amateurism"   26
Colts of Johnny Unitas   61
Comcast Corporation   145
Comcast/NBCUniversal empire   195
Comey, James   186
CONCACAF (league)   109–10
CONMEBOL   134

Cooke, Jack Kent   87
"Cool Britannia" branding campaign   91
Cooper, Michelle   163
Copa '71 documentary   171-2
cord-cutting   145
Corinthians   73-4, 77, 80
Cosby Show, The   141
Cosell, Howard   141
Country Club Plaza, Kansas City   235, 250
CPKC Stadium   161, 163, 165, 248
Craig, Toby   208
Cruz, Ted   42

Dallas Cowboys (American football team)   17, 42, 51, 60, 62-3, 138
Dallas Mavericks (basketball team)   46-7
Dallas Texans (football team)   41
Dassler, Horst   110
de Beek, Donny Van   206
de Coronado, Francisco Vasquez   236
de Coubertin, Pierre   25-6
Dein, David   56, 89, 91
Delgado, Alexia   173
Deloitte's Annual Football Money League   48
Dempsey, Jack   143
Denver Broncos (American football team)   64, 138
Dest, Sergino   198
Dijk, Virgil van   94
Di María, Angel   206
DirecTV   144
"Dirty Leeds"   224
Disney Corporation   29-30, 114, 129, 137-8, 145, 168, 238
Ditka, Mike   65
Donovan, Landon   108, 201
Dorrance, Anson   176-9, 183-4
"Dream Team"   28-31, 108
Drive to Survive, Netflix docuseries   149-50
Dunn, Crystal   179

EA Sports   15-16, 19, 32, 114, 154, 230
Edelman, Robert   24

Edgerton, David   84
Eisenhower, Dwight   25
Eisner, Michael   211
English Premier League (EPL)   45, 49-50, 55, 57, 67, 93, 96-7, 154, 164, 191
Espanyol (football club)   120
ESPN   16, 65, 68, 138, 151-2
Everton football club)   45, 65, 85-6, 226
Ewing, Patrick   29

Fayed, Mohamed Al   92
Federer, Roger   53
Fenway Sports Group   212
Ferdinand, Les   126
Ferguson, Alex   98, 206-8
Fernandes, Bruno   94, 207
Ferreira, Fernando   74
Ferrell, Will   153, 217, 221
Fever Pitch (Hornby)   83
FIFA   3-4, 14-16, 82, 107, 109, 115-16, 134, 162, 185, 191, 198
"Financial Fair Play" regulations   102-3
Financial Times, The   93, 218, 226
Fitzgerald, Larry   75
flag football   73-5, 173
Flores, Diana   74
"Fly Eagles Fly" anthem   59, 74
Fodden, Phil   105
Foley, Bill   211, 214-15, 217, 222, 230
Football Association   23, 57-8, 82, 165
Football Supporters' Federation   67
Ford, Gerald   27
49ers' Levi's Stadium in Santa Clara   221
Foster, Andrew Rube   231
Fosun Group   121
Foudy, Julie   162, 172, 180-1, 183-4
"Four Yorkshiremen"   229
Fox TV   55, 91, 138, 146-7
Freeman, Morgan   108, 112-14, 122

Gaffigan, Ann   243
Garrett, Jason   63-4, 78
Gates, Bill   146
Gifford, Frank   141

Ginola, David   126
Glazer, Malcolm   204
Gleaves, John   24
Global Markets Program, NFL   66
"glocalization"   96
Going Vertical (Russian movie)   29
Goodell, Roger   57–8, 66–7, 70, 76, 80, 138–9, 150, 153
Goodman, Glen   71
Great British Dream Factory: The Strange History of Our National Imagination, The (Sandbrook)   93
Green Bay Packers   40, 68–9, 71, 77–80
Greene, Mean Joe   13–14, 18, 60–1
Grill Room, The (podcast)   151–2
Guardian, The   15, 192, 211, 213, 240–1
Guardiola, Pep   99
Guevara, Che   21
Guimarães, Bruno   130
Gulati, Sunil   108–9

Haaland, Erling   94, 253
Haldeman, Bob   174
Hall, J. C.   238
Hamad bin Jassim, al Thani   111
Hammam, Mohamed bin   109–10
Hamm, Mia   162, 179
Hanks, Tom   153, 217
Harris, Franco   17, 60–1
Harvey, Chris   220–2
Havana Cuban Stars   232
Havelange, João   15, 110
Havertz, Kai   253
Hawkins, Trip   15
Hay, Phil   224–5
Heath, Tobin   179
Hee-chan, Hwang   88
"hegemonic sports culture"   33–4, 192
Heidenheim (football club)   54
Heinrich, April   177, 179
Herrera, Miguel "Piojo"   187
Hillsborough tragedy   89–90
Hitler, Adolf   132, 255
Holder, Eric   108
Holstein Kiel (football club)   54

Home Improvement   140
Hornby, Nick   83, 105
"House of Football"   231
Hunt, Clark   10–11, 242
Hunt, Lamar   35, 41, 62, 87, 90, 138, 140, 149, 241
Hurts, Jalen   70

"Ice Bowl" championship game (1967)   80
IFAF   74
Iger, Bob   137, 168
In Its Own Image: How Television Has Transformed Sports (Rader)   144
Infantino, Gianni   74, 115–16, 134, 153
Inter Milan   95, 120–1
International Football Association Board (IFAB)   82
International Olympic Committee   26, 168
"International Sport and Leisure" firm   110
"invincibles," Arsenal   56
Iraola, Andoni   215
Irvin, Monte   232
It's Always Sunny in Philadelphia   155

Jackson, Riley   179
Jacksonville Jaguars (American football team)   42, 51
Jairzinho   72
Jaworski, Ron   60
Jets, New York Football Club   46, 51
Jiménez, Raúl   86, 88
Jinping, Xi   119–21
Johnson, Magic   29
Jones, David   127
Jones, Jerry   242
Jones, Russell   86–8, 121
Jones, Sarah   128
Jordan, Michael   29, 176
Juventus (football club)   94–5, 115, 198–9

Kajiwara, Cris   73, 77
Kansas City Chiefs (football club)   9, 50–1, 63, 79, 169

Kansas City Sports Commission and Foundation   240
Kardashian, Kim   153
Kelly, Jack   27
Kendrick, Bob   232–3
Kennedy, John F.   21, 25
Kennedy, Ted   24
Ker, Humphrey   155
Khashoggi, Jamal   124, 131
Kimmel, Jimmy   137
Kissinger, Henry   189
Klopp, Jürgen   212
"Kroenke Out" banners   212
Kuper, Simon   50–1

Labinski, Ron   249
LaBonta, Lo'eau   234
La Liga   47, 49, 57, 93, 124, 146
Lake Placid   24
Lambert, Jack   60–1
Leal, Ubiratan   65, 78
Ledecky, Katie   168
Leeds United (football club)   218–20, 222, 226
Lenin, Vladimir   37
Letterman, David   182
Lewis, Mark   15–16
Lewis-Skelly, Myles   253
Liga MX   194, 197
Lilly, Kristine   179
LIV Golf   131
Liverpool (football club)   45, 67, 85, 89, 104, 211–13, 220
Llewellyn, Matthew   24
Lockwood, Chris   172
Lombardi, Vince   68
Long, Angie   164, 169
Long, Chris   164
Los Angeles Dodgers (baseball team)   39, 92, 233
Los Angeles Times, The   189
Los Internacionales, Kansas City football club   234
Los Latinos, Kansas City football club   234
Louis, Joe   143

Love, Jordan   79
Lynch, Loretta   186

Ma, Jack   120
MacCambridge, Michael   39, 42
McCann-Erickson (ad agency)   13
McCutcheon, Haley   161, 169
McDonald's   15
Mace, Hallie   234
McElhenney, Rob   155–7
McGough, Michael   244
McKee, Tanner   70
McKennie, Weston   197–9
McLaughlin-Levrone, Sydney   168
Madden NFL video game franchise   15
Madison Avenue firms   137
Mahomes, Brittany   164
Mahomes, Patrick   18, 57, 137, 242–3
Major League Baseball   54, 65, 141, 143, 189, 232
Major League Soccer (MLS)   44, 100, 146–8, 192–5
Manchester City   48–9, 69, 95, 97–8, 101, 126, 129, 208
Manchester United   35, 45, 104, 206–7, 209, 220
Mansour, Sheikh   204
Mara, Tim   40
Maradona, Diego   14
Maraniss, David   68
Marathe, Paraag   218–19, 226
Maresca, Enzo   214
Markovits, Andrei   33–5, 140, 192
Marks & Spencer   227
Márquez, Gabriel García   145
Márquez, Rafa   86
Marsch, Jesse   221–2
Marshall Plan   20, 255–6
Martinez, Emiliano   94
Masters, Richard   93
Mayer, Soileh Padilla   237
Mbappé, Kylian   111, 190
Mean Joe Greene commercial   17
"Mean Joe Maradona" commercials   14, 16
"Mean Joe Zico" commercials   14

Medina, Agustin "El Chino"   234
Men in Blazers   65, 217
Mendes, Jorge   86
Meredith, "Dandy Don"   141
Messi, Lionel   111, 129, 148, 190, 192
Mexican Revolution   234, 236
Miami Dolphins (American football team)   46, 75
Miller, Charles   72, 79
Mills, A. G.   23
Ming, Yao   121
"Miracle on Ice" (movie)   24, 27–9
Monahan, Jay   131
Monday Night Football   56, 85, 140–1, 153
Moreira, Marcio   13–14
Morey, Daryl   121
Morgan, Alex   162, 183
Mount, Mason   206
Mubarak, Khaldoon Al   99
Muftah, Ghanim Al   113
Müller, Gerd   81
Murdoch, Rupert   56, 89, 91, 144
Murphy, Mark   69
Musah, Yunus   197–8
"Muscular Christianity" movement   23
Museu do Futebol, São Paulo
"Must See TV" NBC primetime lineups   139
Mythic Quest   155

National Collegiate Athletic Association   23, 26
National Football Museum, Manchester   4, 228
National Women's Soccer League   44, 73, 161, 168, 175, 178, 179, 182, 183, 243
National World War I Museum and Memorial, Kansas City   234, 239–40
Naylor, Matt   239–40
NBC   41, 61, 138–9, 146, 154, 252
Negro Leagues Baseball Museum   231–2, 235

Nelson, Kathy   240–2
Neo Química Arena   75, 77
Netflix   55, 138, 144, 147, 149, 152
Newcastle   101, 103, 126–8, 130, 217
"New Coke"   95
New England Patriots   51, 75
"New Trafford"   208
New York Giants   40
New York Jets   46
Neymar   75, 111, 124
NFL   38–9, 62, 71, 91, 139, 146, 150, 212
   first-ever game in Brazil   78, 80
   Global Markets Program   66
   Madden, video game franchise   15
   Mexican TV   3
   Premier League   56
   Sports Broadcasting Act   42
Nike   30, 114, 230
Nixon, Richard   27, 174, 177
Now Then: The Story of Yorkshire and its People (Broadbent)   228
NVIDIA   167

Oaktree Capital Management   121
Obama, Barack   33, 113–14
Obrador, Andrés Manuel López   21–2
Odegaard, Martin   94, 251
Offside: Soccer and American Exceptionalism (Markovits)   33, 35
Ohanian, Alexis   168, 214
Old Trafford Stadium   104, 203, 209, 217
Olympics   7–8, 23–4, 31, 33, 59, 114, 117–18, 132, 179
O'Malley, Walter   39
Orta, Victor   223
Ottawa Rough Riders   63
Overbeck, Carla   179
Özil, Mesut   121

Page, Michael   132–3
Paige, Leroy "Satchel"   232
Panini albums   75
Paramount Plus   146
Paris Saint-Germain (football club)   94, 111–12, 115, 122, 200

Parker, Charlie   235
Partey, Thomas   253
Paseo YMCA, Kansas City   231, 233
Paul, Jake   150
Pax Americana   20
Payton, Walter   65
Pearlman, Chris   45
Pelé   6, 72, 83, 171
Pepi, Ricardo   198
Permanent revolution   37–8
Perry, William   65
Petri, Alexandra   175
Philadelphia Daily News   60
Philadelphia Eagles   40, 59, 68–9, 73, 147, 157
Philadelphia Inquirer   59
Phillips, Kalvin   223
Pickford, Jordan   86, 105
Pitaro, Jimmy   151
Pittsburgh Post-Gazette   244
Pittsburgh Steelers   13, 17, 49, 60
Platini, Michel   111
Pochettino, Mauricio   196, 200
Pogba, Paul   206
Populous   249
Porter, Andrew   232
Porter, Jim   61
Portman, Natalie   168
Potter, Harry   93
Premier League   45, 47–8, 56, 88–9, 158, 195, 214, 229
Presidential Council on Physical Fitness   25
Proebstle, Tom   165–7
profit and sustainability rules (PSR)   48, 103, 130
Public Investment Fund   124–5, 129
Puck News   150
Pulisic, Christian   197–9, 202
Putin, Vladimir   113, 117, 119, 185–7

Qatar   123–125, 134, 196
   FIFA World Cup   101, 107, 108, 117, 122, 133, 140, 185, 190, 199, 242, 256

Qatari bid   107, 111, 112
   and Russia   109, 111, 113, 115, 116

Rader, Benjamin   144
Radrizzani, Andrea   218, 222, 224
Raine Group   142
Ralph Hay Pioneer Award   61
Ramos, Tab   201
Rapinoe, Megan   162, 183
Rashford, Marcus   105
Ratcliffe, James   206–8
Raúl Villegas, El Padrino   256–8
Ravitch, Joe   142
Raya, David   207
Rayados, de Monterrey (football club)   194
Reagan, Ronald   21
Real Madrid   47–8, 62, 67, 73, 94–5, 122, 170
Reardon, Joe   242
(Re) Born in the USA (Bennett)   65
Red Bull model   100, 225
Reddit   160
Reebok   30–1
Reynolds, Ryan   155, 157, 211, 217
Richardson, Sha'Carri   168
Richmond FC club   46
Rise and Fall of Olympic Amateurism, The (Llewellyn and Gleaves)   24
Rise and Fall of the British Nation: A Twentieth-century History, The (Edgerton)   84
Riyadh Air   123–4
Roberts, Julia   153
Robinson, Jackie   233
Robinson, Joshua   91
Rockwell, Norman   237
Rodman, Trinity   162, 179
Romanelli, Victor   75
Ronaldo, Cristiano   124, 206
Rooney, Wayne   193–4
Roosevelt, Franklin   254
Roosevelt, Teddy   23, 25, 117
Roosevelt, Theodore   24
Rozelle, Pete   39–42

"Russian Olympic Committee" 118
Russo, Alessia 179
Ruth, Babe 232
Ryan, Bob 62

Saka, Bukayo 105
Salah, Mohamed 94, 104
Salman, Mohammed bin 123
San Francisco 49ers 211, 218
Sánchez, Alexis 206
Sánchez, Hugo 86
Sancho, Jadon 206
Sandbrook, Dominic 93
São Paulo 65, 67, 71–3, 77, 83
Sargent, Dudley 22–3
Sarkozy, Nicolas 111
Saturday Night Live 18, 154
Schmeling, Max 143
Scudamore, Richard 67
Scurry, Briana 182
"shamateurs" 26
Shearer, Alan 126
Shula, Don 56
Sin Cara 88
Sirianni, Nick 70
Slay, Darius 70
Slot, Arne 212
soccer moms 182
Soccernomics (Kuper and Szymanski) 50–1
Sochi Winter Games (2014) 117
"Socialism in One Country" doctrine 37–8, 169
SoFi Stadium 196, 199, 208
"Soft American," (Kennedy) 25
Spalding, Albert 23
Sportico 140
"sportification" of media 137
sporting-industrial complexes 26
Sports Broadcasting Act 42
Sports Illustrated 25, 27
sportswashing 101
St. Petersburg 117
Stalin, Joseph 37–8, 255
Star Wars 176, 180

Starmer, Keir 228
"Steel curtain" 17
Steeler-Cowboys rivalry 61
Stockwood, Jason 208, 216
Sudeikis, Jason 46, 154
Sunday Night Football 64
Sunderland 'Til I Die docuseries (Netflix) 155–6, 158
Super Bowl 13, 55, 66, 74, 115, 140
Super League 95
Swann, Lynn 17, 60
Swanson, Mallory Pugh 179
Szymanski, Stefan 50–1, 53

Tamim bin Hamad, Al Thani 111
Taylor, David 128–9
Ted Lasso 46, 82, 154, 221–2, 230
Televisa 62
"The 1958" supporters' group 203
Thewarapperuma, Neil 15
TikTok 153
Tillman, Malik 198
Timms, Aaron 192
Title IX 163, 169–70, 174–5, 178–9, 182–3
Tottenham (football team) 45, 50, 95, 102, 154, 195, 200, 249
Trippier, Kieran 130
Trochet, Pierre 74
Truman, Harry S. 239, 254–5
Truman Sports Complex 164–5
Trump, Donald 21, 115–16, 131, 139
Tuchel, Thomas 200
Tyson, Mike 150

Uber 129
UEFA 111, 134
United Soccer Association 87
United Soccer League 44
US Department of Justice 110, 131, 186
US men's national team (USMNT) 196–7, 199, 201

Vance, J.D. 116
Vermeil, Dick 60

Vermes, Peter   244–5
VISA   15
"Vision 2030" Saudi masterplan   123–4
Von Rossum, Fernando   60–3, 147

Waggoner, Matt   252
Wagner, Jacob   246–8
Wallace, Henry   254
Wallschleager, David   80
Warner, Jack   109–10
Washington Post, The   124
Watt, Ally   161
Weah, Timothy   199
Welcome to Wrexham   155-157, 204, 208, 216
West Bromwich Albion (football club)   120
When Pride Still Mattered (Lombardi)   68–9
Whole World Was Watching: Sport in the Cold War, The (Edelman and Young)   24

Williams, Serena   168
Wilson, Andrew   16
Wilson, Woodrow   20, 255
Winthrop, John   19
Wolverhampton Wolves (football club)   86–8, 120
Woman's Game, A (Wrack)   178
Woods, Tiger   53
World Cups   3, 7, 72, 109–10, 115, 179, 191
World Wildlife Fund   88
Wrack, Suzy   178
Wubben-Moy, Lotte   179

Young, Christopher   24
YouTube   55, 138, 152–4
Yrigoyen, Ana Paola López   182

Zaragoza, Silvia   171–2
Zaslav, David   141
Zendejas, Alejandro   198

About the Author

Andrés Martinez, a native of Mexico, is the co-director of The Great Game Lab at Arizona State University, where he also teaches at the Cronkite School of Journalism and Mass Communication, serves as a special advisor to the university president, and directs the Future Tense collaboration with the independent New America think tank in Washington, DC.

Martinez was previously Vice President and National Fellows Program Director at New America, Editorial Page Editor at *The Los Angeles Times* and Assistant Editorial Page Editor at *The New York Times*, where he was a Pulitzer Prize finalist for a series of editorials on the impact of US farm subsidies on the developing world. Martinez also worked at *The Wall Street Journal* and *The Pittsburgh Post-Gazette,* and he has written about sports and globalization for *Slate, Time, Reuters, The Washington Post, Reforma, The Los Angeles Times*, and *Zócalo Public Square.*

Martinez is the co-editor of *Future Tense Fiction: Stories of Tomorrow* and the author of *24/7: Living It Up and Doubling Down in the New Las Vegas.* Martinez earned a Bachelor of Arts degree in history at Yale, a Master of Arts degree in Russian history at Stanford University, and a Juris Doctor degree at Columbia University Law School, where he was a member of the Columbia Law Review.

He roots for Arsenal, the Pittsburgh Steelers, Rayados de Monterrey, Iga Swiatek, and the Sun Devils. Growing up, he'd typically root for Germany in World Cups once Mexico was knocked out.